Exploring
EXODUS

Exploring
EXODUS

Literary, theological and
contemporary approaches

Edited by Brian S. Rosner and Paul R. Williamson

APOLLOS

APOLLOS (an imprint of Inter-Varsity Press)
Norton Street, Nottingham NG7 3HR, England
Email: ivp@ivpbooks.com
Website: www.ivpbooks.com

First published 2008

British Library Cataloguing in Publication Data
A catalogue record for this book is available from the British Library.

UK ISBN: 97 8-1-84474-313-1

Set in Monotype Garamond 11/13pt
Typeset in Great Britain by Servis Filmsetting Ltd, Stockport, Cheshire
Printed and bound in Great Britain by Ashford Colour Press Ltd, Gosport, Hampshire

Inter-Varsity Press publishes Christian books that are true to the Bible and that communicate the gospel, develop discipleship and strengthen the church for its mission in the world.

Inter-Varsity Press is closely linked with the Universities and Colleges Christian Fellowship, a student movement connecting Christian Unions in universities and colleges throughout Great Britain, and a member movement of the International Fellowship of Evangelical Students. Website: www.uccf.org.uk.

CONTENTS

CONTRIBUTORS

George Athas teaches Old Testament, Hebrew and Church History at Moore College. He has taught biblical languages and biblical studies at the University of Sydney and Southern Cross College, and is the author of *The Tel Dan Inscription: A Reappraisal and a New Interpretation* (Sheffield Academic Press, 2003).

Andrew Cameron teaches Ethics and Philosophy at Moore College, and also makes a significant contribution to Australian Christian life and thought in his role as chairman of the Sydney Diocesan Social Issues Executive.

Constantine R. Campbell teaches Greek, Hebrew and New Testament at Moore College. He is the author of a monograph on *Verbal Aspect, the Indicative Mood and Narrative* (Peter Lang, 2007).

Greg Clarke is Director of both the Centre for Public Christianity and the Macquarie Christian Studies Institute in Sydney. His books include *666 and All That: The Truth about the Future* (with John Dickson) (Aquila, 2007) and *Is it Worth Believing? The Spiritual Challenge of the Da Vinci Code* (Matthias Media, 2005).

Richard Gibson teaches Greek, New Testament and Early Church History at Moore College. He has edited several volumes in the college's 'Explorations' series (Openbook and Paternoster), and has completed doctoral research on divine and human emotion in early Christian thought.

Michael Raiter is the Principal of the Bible College of Victoria. Formerly Head of the Department of Mission at Moore College, Michael has also worked for many years as a missionary in Pakistan. His popular monograph *Stirrings of the Soul* (Matthias Media, 2003) was awarded Best Christian Book by the Australian Christian Literature Society in 2004.

Brian S. Rosner teaches Ethics and New Testament at Moore College and also oversees Faculty Research. His numerous published works include *Beyond Greed* (Matthias Media, 2004), *Greed As Idolatry* (Eerdmans, 2007) and *The Consolations of Theology* (ed., Eerdmans, 2008). He also co-edited (with T. D. Alexander) the award-winning *New Dictionary of Biblical Theology* (IVP, 2001).

Barry G. Webb is a senior research fellow at Moore College, having served for many years within and subsequently as Head of the Old Testament Department. His published works include best-selling commentaries on the books of Isaiah and Zechariah in IVP's Bible Speaks Today series, and *Five Festal Garments* (Apollos, 2000).

Paul R. Williamson teaches Hebrew and Old Testament at Moore College, and formerly taught at the Irish Baptist College in Belfast. He is the author of *Abraham, Israel and the Nations* (Sheffield Academic Press, 2001) and *Sealed with an Oath* (Apollos, 2007).

INTRODUCTION

Brian S. Rosner and Paul R. Williamson

If the Bible is history, literature and theology, historical concerns
have dominated since the Enlightenment, while the literary dimensions of the text have received significant attention only in the last
few decades. Both approaches are legitimate. Without exception,
the biblical documents are historically rooted and have aesthetic
value. But both the historical and literary approaches keep the
books of the Bible at arm's length, treating them merely as either
intriguing ancient artefacts or engaging texts. In recent years, a
theological reading of the books of the Bible has been revived.
Put simply, theological interpretation reads the Old and New
Testaments as they want to be read, not at a critical distance, but as
Christian Scripture, as communicating a message to be heard, felt
and embraced. *Exploring Exodus* seeks to contribute to such a
reading of the book of Exodus.

When it comes to Exodus, 'written for us' is hardly the conclusion most readers come to. Its stories and instruction seem more at
home in a museum than in our postmodern world. Yet, if Paul can
be believed, reading Exodus as direct address is the appropriate
Christian stance. He says as much with reference to the OT in

Romans 4:24 and 1 Corinthians 9:10. This book acknowledges that reading Exodus for all its worth, as a witness to the gospel and as wisdom for Christian living is an enormous challenge. But as Greg Clarke writes in chapter 1, the book's appeal for today is unmistakable, in terms of its epic scope and moral complexity. With reference to the appropriation of Exodus in everything from cartoons to high culture, to blockbuster films and ambitious social projects, Clarke challenges readers to feel the book's raw power, by facing squarely its moral challenges and being shaped by its sometimes bewildering theology.

In order to equip readers to answer this challenge, the seven chapters that follow Clarke's provocative foray into the 'uses, reuses and misuses' of Exodus explore the big blocks of the text of Exodus and the main theological and ethical issues they raise. In chapter 2, George Athas examines the exodus event itself as it is presented in Exodus 1 – 18. He argues that when read in its ancient Near Eastern context, the exodus is more than simply a story of the liberation of the Israelites from Egypt. Rather, the exodus is the revelation of a personal God who desires to be in relationship with his chosen people. More surprisingly, according to Athas, the exodus is portrayed as nothing less than an act of creation that brings the nation into being so that they can serve God as a son serves his father. Thus the chapter underlines the cosmic proportions of the exodus event.

In chapter 3, Michael Raiter assesses the significance of the exodus event in contemporary theologies of liberation. Raiter reminds us that, disturbingly, the good news of giving slaves their freedom still resonates in many parts of the world today. Looking at the widespread use of the exodus in a variety of theologies of liberation, Raiter also traces the use of the exodus motif and divine liberation in the Bible. The appeal to William Wilberforce is a sober reminder of the importance of not losing sight of 'the peculiar doctrines of Christianity'.

In chapter 4, Paul Williamson examines the second major unit in the book of Exodus, chapters 19–24. Acknowledging the literary artistry and complexity of the Sinai pericope, which largely comprises 'promises with strings attached', Williamson offers a close reading of the material that illustrates both the structural

coherence and theological significance of its canonical arrangement. Rather than recourse to source-critical theories of multiple
redaction or literary devices such as 'resumptive repetition',
Williamson maintains that the Sinai pericope – incorporating multiple treks up and down Mount Sinai – is best understood in terms
of Moses' mediatorial role in the covenant established on Sinai
between Yahweh and the people he had delivered from servitude
in Egypt.

In chapter 5, Andrew Cameron looks at the 'logic of law in
Exodus'. Without exaggeration, the status of the law in the Bible
and in much theology could be said to be ambivalent. Paul could
say both that we are not under the law and that the law is good and
Christians fulfil it. Set within the context of Reformed thinking
about the law, Cameron's solution is to argue that law in Exodus is
a very pointed response to two elemental aspects of human life:
desire and sociality. This results in an insightful proposal for
reading the law as Christian wisdom.

In chapter 6, Barry Webb looks at the last major section of the
book of Exodus, namely the tabernacle instructions. Commonly
regarded as among the most tedious units in the Bible, Webb asks
honestly, 'What does it all mean? And how can we pursue that
question without going insane?' For Webb, the tabernacle material
teaches that the worship of God is both the goal and foundation
of the redeemed life. In terms of its symbolism, the tabernacle is
'Heaven on Earth'. Considered theologically, the tabernacle has
much to teach concerning the holiness, transcendence and immanence of God, as well as contributing to the doctrines of sin,
atonement and last things.

In chapter 7, Constantine Campbell takes up where Webb leaves
off, looking at the tabernacle in the NT. In a model biblical-
theological study, Campbell answers two fundamental questions:
'What is the relationship between the tabernacle and the temple in
the New Testament?' and 'Who or what *is* the tabernacle in the
New Testament?' Central to the many uses of tabernacle imagery
is the concept of the dwelling of God. Strikingly, in the NT the
tabernacle gets replaced by one Man, to whom others are added by
faith. Far from arcane or speculative, this teaching carries profound pastoral implications for the holiness of God's people.

In the final chapter, Richard Gibson steps back from detailed
exegetical and theological discussions to ask the big-picture question, not how we should preach *from* Exodus, but how to preach
Exodus. In other words, what is the essence of Exodus? Gibson
surveys the various alternatives on offer, including the one that
informs many of the contributions to this volume, the narrative
movement *from slavery to service*, and finds each of them deficient.
Instead, he focuses on that which drives God's redemption of the
Israelites. Preaching Exodus is essentially about naming God. In
his view, the name that takes us to the heart of God is 'Jealous'
(Exod. 34:14). Consequently, to pastor and preach to God's people
we need to feel God's jealousy burning within us. Exodus testifies
to how much God wants his people.

1. EXODUS IN CULTURE:
USES, REUSES AND MISUSES

Greg Clarke

Exodus past?

I was not at all pleased when I was asked to open the 2007 Moore College school of theology with a paper on Exodus in the arts. My negativity had nothing at all to do with the occasion or the inviters, but simply the sense that I was being asked to dwell on the past. Surely, an examination of the uses and abuses of this magnificent series of stories, images, scenes and startling divine commands would be a nostalgic exercise in cultural archiving – a survey of seventeenth-century painting, early biblical epic films and great choral music. Great, but passé. With Rembrandt, Handel and Cecil B. DeMille crowding my mind, I assented to the request, reluctantly.

Aided by Google, I began to dig up instances of representation or cultural appropriation of the book of Exodus. My initial discoveries were indeed around 400 years old. I stared long at the famous Rembrandt Moses, ready to dash the first two stone tablets to the ground in despair at the idolatrous Israelites. The prophet's tired face was illuminating, but hardly seemed

significant to our theological consideration of Exodus here in
the twenty-first century. Likewise, Poussin's Bacchanalian romp
around the Golden Calf and scenes on Flemish tapestries
seemed remote and irrelevant to understanding Exodus today, a
museum of images that would be invisible to the public eye were
it not for the power of the Internet to make everything that is
past present. Was an exploration of Exodus in the arts going
to offer anything to today's preachers, exegetes and Christian
believers?

And then I discovered *The Margate Exodus.*

The week before our school of theology, a film premiered at the
Venice Film Festival: *Exodus,* directed by prominent UK film
director Penny Woolcock. This *Exodus* tells the story of a politi-
cian, Pharaoh Mann, who has found the Promised Land – at least,
the political solution to all of his social problems. He has located a
place to put all of his outcasts, refugees, asylum-seekers and crim-
inals – they will be forced to live in Dreamland, a rundown hovel
built on the site of a disused funfair. This film (which at the time
of writing I have been unable to see) is part of a two-year project
in the seaside community of Margate, near Dover in England. *The
Margate Exodus* is a community art venture that culminated in what
was called 'Exodus Day' on 30 September 2006. As the project's
website describes it, 'On Saturday 30 September lice, locusts, frogs
and flies, a 25-metre high sacrificial sculpture and a cast of thou-
sands dramatically transformed the south coast town of Margate
into a contemporary setting for an epic film inspired by the Old
Testament Book of Exodus.'[1]

As well as recording for the film just released, the day involved
performances of an album's worth of songs about the biblical
plagues, commissioned from prominent (albeit alternative) UK
contemporary artists, such as Rufus Wainwright and Brian Eno.
There was also a photographic exhibition on the migrant experience, and the burning of 'The Waste Man', a 30-foot high wooden
junk-giant built by Margate residents, who glowed like a pillar in

---

1. See <http://www.themargateexodus.co.uk/home.html>, accessed
   29 Feb. 2008.

the night after some prophetic ranting to onlookers. Without pre-empting my argument regarding Exodus in today's culture, it is safe to say that a rudimentary understanding of the biblical book of Exodus is essential for the Margate activities to have any conceptual or moral coherence.

The rationale of the Margate project (as found on their website) is given as this:

> The story of Exodus is thousands of years old and cuts across many faiths and cultures. Immigration has never been more meaningful than it is today. Exodus begins with the Egyptians complaining about the immigrant Hebrews – there are too many of them, they're having too many children. They are 'the undesirables' and a problem to get rid of.
>
> Margate is a seaside resort in Kent, on the South Coast of England. An historic place of natural beauty, and a town with a diverse population. Nearby Dover is one of the main entry points for asylum seekers and illegal immigrants, making the area a perfect place to explore issues of identity, tolerance and social equality.

To gain an understanding of and to depict and explore today's ethical, racial and social realities in 'post-Christian' Britain, a contemporary film maker turned to the biblical book. In an interview, Penny Woolcock said, 'The emotional truths of the Old Testament, where the oppressed are brutalised and become brutal, where terrible injustice leads to horrific acts of terrorism, are all as vital today as they were in Biblical times.'[2]

I cannot comment on what the *Exodus* film is like; the early reviews I read were mixed. I do not know what Margate residents and visitors, let alone the many YouTube clip-hunters, made of the instalment and performance art of Margate. But *The Margate Exodus* project suddenly and with flair returns Exodus to the centre of any contemporary Bible teacher's concerns. Here is a secular, government-supported project drawing upon the biblical

---

2. See <http://entertainment.timesonline.co.uk/tol/arts_and_entertainment/film/article2357885.ece>, accessed 29 Feb. 2008.

account in order to tell its story.[3] Immediately, according to the twenty-first-century measures of relevance (publicity, visuality, emotional impact), Exodus matters again.

Twentieth-century Exodus

Primed by the discovery of *The Margate Exodus* project, I began to notice other instances of the importance of Exodus in the arts in between Baroque painting and the 2007 Venice Film Festival! There seemed to have been a 'return' of Exodus to cultural importance in the twentieth century, partially due to the Hollywood epics, and partially due to what might be called a thematic appropriation of Exodus for purposes beyond historical record and nation-making for Israel.

The most famous of Exodus explorations is the 1956 *The Ten Commandments*, directed by the great film maker, Cecil B. DeMille, who was responsible for some of the most lavish and expensive films of all time. This was not the first version of the film – that was made in 1923, and it was a silent film (there were in fact at least six films about Moses in the silent-film era).[4] The 1923 film is stunning – stunning in its depiction of the cruelty of the Egyptians, and stunning in its philosophical and political heaviness. In the aftermath of the First World War, it was presented as a story that would lead nations out of the wilderness of horror and destruction, and into the peace and order of civilization. After the biblical story has been conveyed, the second half of the film explores the lives of six people set in modern San Francisco, examining the difference following the Ten Commandments makes in their lives.

---

3. The project is a collaborative venture, commissioned by Artangel, an arts body supported by the UK government's national arts development agency, Arts Council England. See <http://www.creative-partnerships.com>, accessed 29 Feb. 2008.

4. Codex: The Old Testament/Hebrew Bible on film website, <http://biblical-studies.ca/pop/OT_on_film1.html>, accessed 29 Feb. 2008.

The film was an incredible success, although whether it was a lesson in morality or titillation (with its scenes of sex, dance and spectacle) is something critics discuss at length (Solomon 2001: 145).

The 1956 remake shows the influence of Hollywood's historical romances, with expansive explorations of the young Moses and extra-biblical plotlines about his life among the Egyptian rulers (the 'prince of Egypt' story). While the screenplay follows the biblical account, Philo, Josephus and Eusebius are sources, too, as is the book by Dorothy Clarke Wilson, *The Prince of Egypt*. DeMille had established a large research department with global resources, and the historical and theological research informed every part of the film, from choreography to make-up to the awe-inspiring set design. The intention was to depict the seriousness of the biblical moral vision, in particular its importance for a defence of human freedom from tyranny. Famously, the first screen in the 1923 film declares that 'The 10 Commandments are not laws – they are THE LAW,' establishing a moral philosophy in reaction to post-war scepticism. Cecil B. DeMille himself appears on screen to introduce the 1956 version, giving a forthright speech not only about the ancient historical reliability of his story, but also about its contemporary significance in a time when human freedom and moral stability were perceived to be in need of fortification.[5]

The success of DeMille's *The Ten Commandments* seems to have returned the book of Exodus to a significant place within popular art and culture. Perhaps due to political forces (discussions of nation-building, of recovering a sense of humanity after the two world wars, of exploring the idols of modernity) the stories of Exodus found expression in a growing range of art forms and a breadth of metaphorical or symbolic modes. Burt Lancaster, in his first television appearance, took up the role of Moses in the 1974 mini-series *Moses the Lawgiver*. Despite the role, Burt's biography says, 'The Ten Commandments were fine, but not for him' (Buford

---

5. His speech can be heard and seen online at YouTube, <http://www.youtube.com/watch?v=R-XGcNzVsNs>, accessed 12 Mar. 2008.

2000: 277).[6] Thomas Keneally wrote a historical novel to accompany the television mini-series, in his usual simple, documentary style. The Exodus story was once again mainstream. In another Australian appropriation (Keneally is Australian), the painter Arthur Boyd developed a wonderful interpretation of Moses leading the Israelites through an Australian wilderness, one of a series of Exodus-related Boyd paintings in the post-Second World War period.

Whether it was informing Harrison Ford's quest in *Raiders of the Lost Ark* (1981), providing material for parody in Dudley Moore and Richard Pryor's very silly *Wholly Moses!* (1981; a kind of Monty Python's *Life of Brian* where a man called Herschel wants to be Moses but can't quite pull it off), or the lavish animation that is Disney's *The Prince of Egypt* (1998), parts of the Exodus narrative became inexhaustibly fruitful for popular culture. Even heavy-metal music drew on Scripture. Metallica's song 'Creeping Death' is an exploration of the final plague (the death of the Egyptian firstborns) in what seems to me a fairly apt musical mode. The sheer horror and chaos of this slaughter comes across well, and this is apparently one of Metallica's favourite songs to perform live, with the audience chanting 'Die! Die! Die!' in the song's chorus. The lyrics make a great Sunday school lesson:

> Slaves, Hebrews born to serve, to the Pharaoh.
> Heed to his every word, live in fear.
> Faith of the unknown one, the deliverer.
> Wait, something must be done, 400 years.
>
> So let it be written. So let it be done.
> I'm sent here by the chosen one.
> So let it be written. So let it be done.
> To kill the first-born Pharaoh son.
> I'm Creeping Death.

---

6. Cited at <http://www.ronaldbrucemeyer.com/rants/1102almanac. htm>, accessed 29 Feb. 2008.

Now, let my people go, land of Goshen.
Go, I will be with thee, bush of fire.
Blood, running red and strong down the Nile.
Plague darkness three days long, hail to fire.
. . .
I rule the midnight air, the destroyer.
Born, I shall soon be there, deadly Mass.
I creep the steps and flood, final darkness.
Blood, lamb's blood painted door, I shall pass.

So let it be written. So let it be done.
I'm sent here by the chosen one.
So let it be written. So let it be done.
To kill the first-born Pharaoh son.
I'm Creeping Death.[7]

So what is it about Exodus that makes it a contemporary source
of storytelling, myth-making and artistic appropriation? There are
three features of Exodus that serve to explain its broad appeal.

Three aspects of Exodus' appeal

Grand animation
One of the popular genres for retelling or utilizing Exodus is the
comic, cartoon, graphic novel or animation. Exodus lends itself
to fanciful art, fantastic storyboards and strips of scenes. Dream-
Works's *The Prince of Egypt* (1998) is a film of our times – high
on production values, exciting, but more spectacle than substance.
By making enormous extensions of the biblical storyline and characters, the account of Israel in Egypt becomes a royal romantic
saga with a sentimental theme for children, in fast-moving cartoon
animation with a saccharine pop-music soundtrack.
   Both this film and DeMille's *The Ten Commandments* draw from the
romanticized text *Prince of Egypt*, by Dorothy Clarke Wilson, for

---

7. 'Creeping Death', Metallica, *Ride the Lightning* album (1984).

much of their storyline. Reportedly, the DreamWorks studio consulted 360 religious leaders about this film. One can only guess they were all open to the extra-biblical majority of the story, where the point seems to be sibling rivalry between Moses and Ramses, and God's rescue acts for Israel get lost amid all the chase scenes, silliness and musical numbers. But it is a lot of fun; just not biblical fun, and sadly not the best way for children to construct their biblical knowledge. *The Prince of Egypt* also contains a distracting feminist reconstruction of Zipporah as a kind of biblical Ripley character from the *Alien* films – but such expansion, glamorization and heroic status is commonly conferred on characters in the animation genre.

However, there are more considered and sophisticated uses of Exodus in a comic format. *The Lone and Level Sands* is an example of the increasingly popular graphic novel genre (Lewis 2005). It is an intelligent work, aware of its sources – a fascinating blend of the Bible, the Koran and Percy Bysshe Shelley's poem 'Ozymandias', from which its title is drawn. Ozymandias is the Greek name for Ramses II, and, like Shelley's poem, *The Lone and Level Sands* is told from Ramses' perspective. What emerges is a gripping comic battle between two peoples and their gods, serious in its syncretistic reading of the sources, and serious in its spiritual reflections.

A different kind of comic appropriation of Exodus is found on the Web at 'The Brick Testament: The Book of Exodus in Lego'.[8] This labour of love (or something else) recounts the biblical book scene by scene and in doing so highlights the episodic composition of the narrative; it makes sense to present it as Lego scenes.

Epic scope

The literary category that perhaps suits the appropriations of Exodus most readily (although it doesn't correspond readily to the biblical literature itself) is the epic. The story of Exodus is most often conveyed in the epic mode. Epics always have strong nationalistic content, and their heroes are representative of the hopes and anxieties of the nation. The literary critic Northrop Frye once

---

8. See <http://www.thebricktestament.com/exodus/index.html>, accessed 29 Feb. 2008.

referred to epic as 'the story of all things', a long and episodic narrative that stands for more than a single story; its greatness and grandness elevates it to the status of Story – a story in which other stories can find their shape. The book of Exodus is 'borrowed' in film, literature and music for these epic qualities.

Cecil B. DeMille's 1956 *The Ten Commandments* is the example par excellence. One film scholar describes it as 'a strange mixture of piety and melodrama',[9] a tone common to the epic. The scale of the film is most impressive; it was expensive, ambitious and determined to represent on the big screen the great work of liberation. Everything about it was epic: the exodus-from-Egypt scenes involved fifteen thousand people and twelve thousand animals. The parting of the Red Sea was the most extraordinary special effect ever achieved on film at that point. It is this epic scope of the film, as much as any moral message it conveys, that gives it power; one might fairly offer the criticism that the 'big screen' offers a grand distortion of the remarkable but more shambolic history of Israel's escape from Egypt.

Certainly, nationalistic struggle of many kinds can be presented with an 'Exodus' shape. The entire genre of gospel music is a blend of salvation theology and political liberation. One of the most famous African-American spirituals is 'Go Down, Moses!', with its refrain 'Let my people go'. There is rock-solid identification of the plight of the Negro in slavery with the plight of the Israelites. But in his reception-driven Blackwell commentary, *Exodus through the Centuries*, Scott M. Langston notes that Exodus appeals to oppressed and oppressor alike, and in fact the one power can be both oppressor and oppressed. He writes:

> The book's reception history shows that competing groups have simultaneously invoked its traditions in contradictory causes. This is vividly demonstrated in the appeal to the exodus in the eighteenth and nineteenth centuries by African Americans, white northerners, and white southerners. All three groups claim the authority of Exodus. Enslaved African

---

9. Professor T. F. Williams, online at <http://biblical-studies.ca/pop/OT_on_film2.html#DeMille>, accessed 29 Feb. 2008.

Americans understood themselves as God's people struggling against the
pharaoh of American slaveholders, and abolitionists used it to denounce
the institution of slavery. White southerners, however, considered
themselves as contending against the pharaoh of the North who was intent
on denying them their liberty by taking their property and independence
. . . White American of the revolutionary era has used the Exodus to call
for freedom from Great Britain, but with little thought of its application
to African Americans, despite the latter's concurrent appeal to it. (2006: 7)

Leon Uris's 1958 bestselling novel *Exodus*, and the subsequent
film, charted the upheavals surrounding the birth of the state of
Israel in 1947 and the movements of war refugees and immigrants.
Again, the epic story of one nation's escape from slavery has
become the mythical framework for a range of national and racial
struggles. The epic mode usually involves scenes of great heroism
and symbolic events of huge national significance. Scenes such as
the burning bush, the plagues, the brazen serpent and the parting
of the sea can be presented in a heroic manner. If we allow Moses
to be the hero (although many of his actions are less than heroic!),
we see the many uses to which his character is put in art, culture
and politics.

In his book *Rewriting Moses: The Narrative Eclipse of the Text*, Brian
M. Britt observes that most narratives based on Exodus heroicize
the character of Moses in a way that is hard to match with the
emphases of Scripture itself. He finds around thirty twentieth-
century examples of Moses-based narratives, many of which
impose external literary structures (e.g. Hellenized biography) on
the scant biblical material about Moses himself – an inversion of
Hans Frei's thesis concerning the eclipse of biblical narrative by
historicism (Britt 2004: 6–8).

There are plenty of Moseses to consider in modern politics and
culture. Rastafarian reggae master Bob Marley wades across an
(unparted) sea donning a robe and staff, singing of emancipation
for Africans everywhere: 'Exodus . . . movement of the people'.[10]

10. Online at YouTube, <http://www.youtube.com/watch?v=9s06Q2rh9t8
    &feature;=related>, accessed 12 Mar. 2008.

Nelson Mandela is often referred to as the New Moses. Before him Martin Luther King (MLK) had built a political movement around an interpretation of the book of Exodus. Following Paul Tillich, MLK philosophized the return from exile to the Promised Land so that it came to represent a restoration of human nature itself, the promised 'inner' land of love, peace and freedom. Such a restoration would empower people to change, to rise up and work towards a social order that looks more like Christ's kingdom. In his 1964 Nobel Peace Prize address, MLK described his fight like this:

> The Bible tells the thrilling story of how Moses stood in Pharaoh's court centuries ago and cried, 'Let my people go.' This is a kind of opening chapter in a continuing story. The present struggle in the United States is a later chapter in the same unfolding story.[11]

MLK was not backward in identifying himself with Moses, most famously in his 'mountain top' address the day before he was assassinated, with its stirring climax, 'I have been to the mountain top, I've looked over, and I have seen the Promised Land.'[12]

Moral testing

One of the major uses of Exodus in art and culture is the 'testing' of the divine commandments. Does the law of God survive modern scrutiny? Is it true? Is it relevant? Is it good?

One approach to these questions is to defend the events of Exodus, to see whether God is 'honest' and the exodus in fact took place. Simcha Jacobovici's recent speculative documentary *The Exodus Decoded* (2006), narrated by *Titanic* director James Cameron, constructs a defence of the historicity and scientific viability of the Exodus events. Using dramatic computer-generated effects, it argues various special cases for the dating of the Exodus, the order of the plagues and explanations of other events, in order

---

11. See <http://nobelprize.org/nobel_prizes/peace/laureates/1964/king-lecture.html>, accessed 29 Feb. 2008.
12. Online at YouTube, <http://www.youtube.com/watch?v=ooFiCxZKuv8&e>, accessed 29 Feb. 2008.

to strengthen the case for the 'believability' of Exodus. It has not been taken seriously by scholars, but it represents an acknowledgment that, in an age of infotainment, some apologetic efforts require the visual rhetoric of blockbuster films in order to have an impact on the recipient.

However, these questions are not foremost in the minds of most recipients of the Exodus narrative: their questions are more ethical in nature. While Cecil B. DeMille made such questions specific in his films, they are given contemporary treatment by other film makers. This moral dimension of Exodus is taken up most seriously in the films of Krzysztof Kieslowski, known as *The Decalogue* (1987). In ten one-hour films, Kieslowski contextualizes the commandments for twentieth-century people, emphasizing the human incapacity to avoid sin. A scientist puts his faith in science and logic to govern daily life and loses his son (Decalogue 1: You shall have no other gods). An acting student discovers through a secret letter that her father is not her father (Decalogue 4: Honour your parents). An ethics professor (Maria Koscialkowska) is confronted with the culpability of her actions when asked to harbour a Jewish girl during the Second World War (Decalogue 8: You shall not bear false witness). Two brothers inherit their father's priceless stamp collection, with one vital stamp missing (Decalogue 10: Do not covet). *The Decalogue* is something of a homage to Cecil B. DeMille's 1923 silent film exploration of the lives of six people who attempt to keep the Decalogue. The ten short pieces are concerned with human endeavours to act morally, not with what the rules are; they are existential pieces, primarily interested in the human response, not the God whose law it is that we are to obey.

But it is more common in our culture today to *question* the specific religious content of the divine law. The point at which the book of Exodus is finding its way into culture at present is in the rash of publications gathered under the heading the 'new atheism'. Richard Dawkins, Christopher Hitchens and others have published books promoting atheism, with one of their leading arguments being that the law of God (especially the commands given to Israel in the OT) is either indefensible or simply one expression of the moral law of the (evolving) universe. Dawkins, in his book *The God Delusion*, ridicules the biblical account of the law being given on

Mount Sinai and caricatures God's response to Israel's golden calf idolatry as 'God's jealous sulk' and 'sexual jealousy of the worst kind' (2006: 245, 243). In a similar mocking tone, Christopher Hitchens asserts that 'No society ever discovered has failed to protect itself from self-evident crimes like those supposedly stipulated at Mount Sinai' and 'If god really wanted people to be free of such thoughts [as envy], he should have taken more care to invent a different species' (2007: 100).

Dawkins and Hitchens query not only the historical nature of the Exodus accounts of the giving of the law, but also the goodness of the kind of god who would give such laws and require people to adhere to them. God is deemed capricious, petty and mean. The reputation of the book of Exodus today goes beyond its appropriation for epic storytelling in comics and in film, beyond its power for political movements and its richness of imagery and characters. Exodus remains in the public light because of shock and revulsion at its moral laws from key intellectuals and artists.

The 'new atheist' line is picked up by a number of artists on the CD *Plague Songs*, produced as part of *The Margate Exodus* project. One reviewer described this collection by prominent and alternative British musicians as 'tunes that tend towards a dynamic miserabilism'.[13] *Plague Songs* is filled almost entirely (with the exception of the track by Cody ChesnuTT) with a sense of horror at what God has done. There is little celebration of God bringing justice and liberation for Israel. In fact, there is more sympathy with the animals used in the plagues! The mood of the album is low, a mood of despair, not faith. There is a sense of baffled opposition to God: how could God act this way?

To give two examples, Brian Eno writes on the fourth plague, 'Flies'. There is an incessant buzzing throughout the song, which itself does not rise much above the buzzing in its monotony and emotional opposition to the text of Scripture. The accusation moves beyond Yahweh, to see the plagues from a post-Christ vantage point, but without solace:

---

13. M. McGonigal, <http://www.amazon.com/Plague-Songs-Various-Artists/dp/B000ICLGNK>, accessed 29 Feb. 2008.

If God in Christ would have it so,
The fiery wind would ever blow,
The fire that saves must burn the soul.

This song is not about justice for the oppressed Israelites, but mourning for the oppressor. In his liner notes, Eno writes:

> In another display of His vengeful spite, here we see the Old Testament God turning Nature against Humankind – again. I thought it would be interesting to write something from the point of view of the flies instead of the humans. I imagined these little insects doing an honest day's work, an honest day in which the humans were the unfortunate losers.[14]

The band King Creosote sings a song about the second plague, the frogs, called 'Relate the Tale'. Again, the sympathetic response is to the means of judgment (the frogs themselves) as expressed in the refrain that asks how the 'God of frogs' could have allowed such a thing to take place. It also asks how the God of frogs could have made such a 'mistake'! And finally, it asks how God will then go on to 'relate the tale'. The song depicts Moses (and God) 'getting their own way' at the expense of these creatures. In such songs, we see something of the way the Exodus story is received outside a Jewish or Christian reading: God's goodness and justice are denied.

I confess to feeling slightly appalled to recall choruses such as

I will sing unto the Lord
For he has triumphed gloriously,
The horse and rider thrown into the sea.

I have a Richard Dawkins-like reaction to them when I think of myself as an 8-year-old singing them with glee, lacking the imagin-

---

14. Reproduced by kind permission of Brian Eno/Opal Ltd. Lyrics from 'Flies' by Brian Eno © Opal Music, London.

ation to conceive of what a terrible judgment came upon those horses and riders. But that is the anxious, attentive apologetic mindset overworking; it is not the theologian recalling that the Egyptians were under righteous judgment. This problem highlights the importance of developing our theology of the book of Exodus, working from within the revelation of God, not outside it; working within God's grace, with eyes opened to the truth. From 'inside' the story, the punishment of the unrepentant Egyptian tyrants as they pursued the liberated Israelites is something to celebrate. But from the outside, from the point of view of the twenty-first-century sceptic, these are horrific stories about an unbelievable and wicked god.

The Margate Exodus project and biblical literacy

The *Margate Exodus* project alerted me to the ongoing significance of Exodus for arts, politics and culture. Whereas it could have been a long gaze in the rear-view mirror, this examination of Exodus' influence on culture has uncovered significant uses of the biblical stories, characters, themes and teachings continuing up to this moment. In an age when biblical literacy is very low, it is noteworthy that our artists and intellectuals, even as secularists, are still mining the depths of the OT to explore contemporary problems such as immigration. *The Margate Exodus* brings to life not only the issues of immigration, race, organization of society and justice for the oppressed, but because it uses Exodus as its 'urtext', it puts the biblical story before people once again (or perhaps, for many, for the first time).

This situation presents Bible teachers, preachers, cultural apologists and everyday Christians seeking to engage the general culture with at least three challenges for which they need to be ready, willing and able.

1. Are we ready to help people build a mind-shaping theology of the God of Israel, made known to the Gentiles, that is robust, biblically controlled and as multifaceted and mysterious as the one we find in the book of Exodus? Are we ready to teach them the doctrine within the text?

2. Are we willing to allow for the raw power and aesthetic impact of the incredible stories and characters of Exodus to resonate across a wide range of art forms, with a wide range of applications? Or will we quickly be correcting people's use of the Exodus accounts ('No, that's not a story about immigration') in our anxiety to interpret the Bible in a consistent pattern of biblical theology? Can we begin our discussions of Exodus from these points of contact – be they a Metallica song, a Kieslowski film or the Lego Bible website, and expose our biblically illiterate communities to the word of God, diversely and partially unveiled, as a first step towards exciting people about the Scriptures once more?

3. Are we able to face head-on the moral challenges that arise in a culture where God's administration of justice is seen as juvenile and unfair? If we are to address the complaints raised by a Dawkins or a Hitchens, we shall need to pay careful attention to the biblical story, to detect where the points of moral judgment are, and to guide recipients of these stories in a *theological* manner, teaching clearly and passionately about the God who loves to forgive but who requires that justice be done, and gave his Son to be both just and the one who justifies.

Bibliography

Britt, B. M. (2004), *Rewriting Moses: The Narrative Eclipse of the Text*, Journal for the Study of the Old Testament Gender, Culture, Theory Supplement Series 402, London: T. & T. Clark.

Buford, K. (2000), *Burt Lancaster: An American Life*, New York: Knopf.

Dawkins, R. (2006), *The God Delusion*, London: Bantam.

DeMille, C. B. (dir.), *The Ten Commandments* (1923, 1956, Special Edition 2006).

Hitchens, C. (2007), *God Is Not Great: How Religion Poisons Everything*, Long Branch: Atlantic.

Keneally, T. (1975), *Moses the Lawgiver*, Westerham: Collins. Based on ATV television series, scripted by A. Burgess.

Langston, S. M. (2006), *Exodus through the Centuries*, Oxford: Blackwell.

Lewis, A. D. (writer), mpMann and J. Rodgers (illustrators) (2005), *The Lone and Level Sands*, Fort Lee: Archaia Studios Press.

The Margate Exodus Project, <http://www.themargateexodus.co.uk/home.
    html>, accessed 29 Feb. 2008.
Solomon, J. (2001), *The Ancient World in the Cinema*, Yale: Yale University
    Press.
Uris, L. (1958), *Exodus*, London: Corgi.
Various artists, *Plague Songs* (4AD, 2006).

2. THE CREATION OF ISRAEL: THE COSMIC PROPORTIONS OF THE EXODUS EVENT

George Athas

Contextualizing the exodus

The Margate Exodus is a modern-day appropriation of the biblical Exodus narrative. The grand old story of liberation has been reworked into a context and culture with which we, particularly as Westerners, are more familiar. This is perhaps testimony to the timelessness of the themes and message of Exodus: the longing for freedom; the cry for justice against tyranny and oppression; the reluctant hero; the restlessness of the human spirit.

I believe the reason for such reinterpretations of the Exodus story (not to mention other popular biblical narratives) is that we find ourselves in a time and culture so far removed from the one that originally produced these narratives. Gone are the days when empires sprawled out across the face of a flat earth. Our world today is a globe, characterized by autonomous nation states exerting their right to sovereignty. It is a world where multinational corporations build economic empires, where humans are connected by an information superhighway, and individuals have an inviolable set of human rights, including the right to determine

THE CREATION OF ISRAEL

their own playlist on their own iPod, or maintain their own network on Facebook. The complexion of our world has changed dramatically from the day of the pharaohs. As a result, our mindset has changed with it, and we feel the need to adapt these classic stories to our own time.

It is for this reason that I wish to ask, are we perhaps missing something as we rework the Exodus narrative for modern audiences? Are there subtleties in the text to which our own culture and context have blinded us? And if we have become blind to them, how would we know about them, and how would we go about recovering them?

I would like to suggest that there are indeed such subtleties in the Exodus narrative which the passing of time has obscured from our vision. And I propose that we recover them. My method for doing so is far from radical: it simply involves entering the mindset of the ancients – that is, reading the narratives from the perspective of those earliest readers of Exodus, and asking what they understood when they heard or read these narratives, what impact the narratives had on them.

There is, I believe, a fairly simple way to do this. The ancient culture we are talking about here is that of Israel and Judah – a society (or societies) that produced a considerable corpus of literature, much of which we now have in our canon of Scripture. If we survey these writings, we shall be able to recover something of the mindset that produced the Exodus narratives, and begin to appreciate the way the earliest readers of those narratives responded to them. In essence, what I am proposing here is to use the larger Hebrew canon as an intertext to uncover something of the outlook of the Israelites and Judeans.[1]

However, we can go a little further in recovering this ancient mindset. We must acknowledge that for all their idiosyncrasies

---

1. I am not proposing here to ask the question of the dating of the Exodus narrative to compare it strictly with the literature of the same period. Rather, I am seeking to uncover the more fundamental mindset behind the narrative – a mindset common to a fairly extensive period of ancient Near Eastern history.

and distinctives, Israel and Judah were part of a larger region, which we call the ancient Near East. They did not have email or Internet access, but neither did they live isolated from other communities. On the contrary, they had cultural, linguistic, intellectual and historical affinities with neighbouring communities in the Fertile Crescent. As such, delving into the comparative literature of these neighbouring communities will add more depth to our understanding of the Israelite and Judean mindset. To put it metaphorically, holding Exodus up against the colours of the biblical literature and the comparative literature of its near neighbours should allow us to appreciate the shades and hues in Exodus itself.[2]

Furthermore, we have to come to the book of Exodus with an awareness of its genre. This critical period in the life of Israel has come down to us in the form of a story – a narrative. The astute reader of Exodus will also pick up other genres within the book, such as the legislative material and the extensive description of the tabernacle. However, these are subsumed within a larger narrative framework that conveys the 'story' of Exodus. Sensitivity to those literary devices that shape and define this genre will give further resolution to our view of the book. And this, in turn, can help to sharpen our theology as it arises from the book. As such, in the course of our investigation I shall be appealing to the nature of Exodus as an example of 'story'.[3]

---

2. This is the same basic methodology advocated by W. W. Hallo, who did not want 'to find the key to every biblical phenomenon in some ancient Near Eastern precedent, but rather to silhouette the biblical text against its wider literary and cultural environment' (1991: 24).

3. A caveat is warranted at this point. In placing Exodus within the broad genre of 'story', I am not thereby denying its historicity. A clear distinction must be made between *historiography* and *story*. The former is a dispassionate account of the past, drawing connective links between persons and events, and seeking to answer the questions of 'who', 'what', 'when', 'where', 'how' and, ultimately, 'why'. However, a story has a plot: it presents a predicament and a quest to resolve it. It is not a dispassionate and objective retelling of facts, but rather a consciously selective crafting

Now while this task may take up an entire volume in itself, my observations and comments, for the sake of brevity and integration with the other chapters presented here, will limit itself to Exodus 1 – 18. We shall, of course, make the occasional foray into other parts of the book, but only to get our bearings for this initial portion of the story.

The predicament of Exodus

On the surface Exodus is a story of liberation – how the Israelites were freed from slavery in Egypt under the leadership of Moses. This is, perhaps, the most natural way that we, shaped by our twenty-first-century environment, understand the book. However, if this were the full picture, we should expect the book to end after chapter 15 with the parting of the Reed Sea, the escape of the Israelites, and the destruction of Pharaoh and his army. At that point in the book, Israel's freedom from slavery has been accomplished. Yet, while it is true that the narrative itself reaches a climactic moment with the Israelites crossing the Reed Sea, as we shall observe, the plot continues on to the great theophany at Sinai, the imparting of the law, and the construction of the tabernacle. There is eminently more to the story than just a tale of liberation.

So what is Exodus about?

As an example of the 'story' genre, the book of Exodus presents us with a predicament from which a quest unfolds to resolve it. What, then, is the predicament of Exodus? To answer this, we must look for signs of some kind of tension early in the book. However, I shall first survey the 'stage' on which the narrative takes place so as to ground us in the context of the story itself.

------

of scenes in which characters develop and convey a plot that seeks to move the reader to respond in a particular way. The purposes of the two genres may converge in large part, particularly in the questions they seek to answer, but the devices and techniques used are vastly different: *historiography* is essentially analytical, while *story* is more dramatic or theatrical.

The narrative stage: three domains

The narrative begins with the movement of Jacob's clan from the land of Canaan to the land of Egypt. To be sure, Canaan is not specifically named as the place from which Jacob's clan comes, but it is certainly implied. The opening six verses of the book form a bridge with the narrative of Genesis, where we specifically read of Jacob and his family going down to Egypt (cf. Gen. 46:5–8, 26). Readers of Genesis would bring to Exodus a knowledge of God's promises to the patriarchs, especially the promise to give their descendants the land of Canaan. Yet, the fact that Canaan is not overtly mentioned here in the opening of Exodus is part of the artistry of the narrative, for while the narrative moves initially from an implied starting point in Canaan, the liberation of the Israelites creates a movement from Egypt back to Canaan, to fulfil this patriarchal promise. And yet, the Israelites do not arrive in Canaan before the end of the book. As Alter puts it, Canaan is 'the land that remains beyond the horizon of this book' (2004: 302). Indeed, being described hyperbolically in Exodus as a 'land flowing with milk and honey' (Exod. 3:8, 17; 13:5; 33:3), it is a veritable El Dorado for Jacob's descendants, which always seems to be just out of reach.

Egypt also had a similar reputation in antiquity. Its fertility, stability, wealth and culture were viewed with awe by outsiders. Consequently, it was a haven for those seeking relief from hard times or just a better standard of living. This is evidenced by glyptic art from Beni Hasan depicting a caravan of Asiatics entering Egypt in the nineteenth century BC,[4] as well as the practice letter of a scribe reporting permission granted to *Shasu* (bedouin) tribes from Edom to enter the pasturage of the Nile Delta in the twelfth century BC (Hallo and Younger, 3.5: 1997–2002). Thus, to the ancient ear, the descent of Jacob's clan to Egypt would have

---

4. The wall painting is located in the tomb of a local nomarch's grandson, Khnumhotep II (see Gardiner 1961: 128). The event depicted is dated by the accompanying text to the sixth year of Sesotris II (c. 1880 BC) of the twelfth dynasty. For an excellent colour representation of the wall painting, see Schulz and Seidel 1998: 124 (fig. 35).

sounded very much the way stories of people migrating to Western countries (e.g. USA, UK, France and Australia) sound to us today.

However, within the first chapter of Exodus, Egypt goes from being the land of protection and plenty for Jacob's clan, to the land of tyranny and toil. The popular ancient perception that Egypt was a land of opportunity and stability (a perception we see echoed in Genesis) is turned on its head, and Egypt becomes a land of chaos and disorder.

We have, therefore, two distinct domains in Exodus: once comfortable but now disorderly Egypt, and the unseen but Promised Land of Canaan. Separating the two, however, is a third domain: the desert. And it is in this desert that the majority of the story takes place. It is here that Israel encounters Yahweh, its God, and struggles to come to grips with its newfound freedom. The desert is a place of tension: it is removed from Egypt, the land of disorder, and yet it is a far cry from the Promised Land of Canaan, which flows with milk and honey. It is a transitional domain that on the one hand represents freedom, but on the other represents unfulfilled hopes and promises.

A narrower focus

However, as mentioned previously, Canaan is actually beyond the purview of Exodus. Indeed, Canaan is basically beyond the purview of the whole Pentateuch. Apart from a brief scouting trip and a single aborted attempt at entry (Num. 13 – 14), the descendants of the patriarchs never actually set foot in Canaan before the end of the Pentateuch. Never do they actually come to possess this Promised Land – that must wait for fulfilment in Joshua. For this reason, we could accurately say that Joshua is a book about the fulfilment of divine promise, but the Pentateuch must have a narrower focus.

This, of course, has significant bearings on how we view the book of Exodus. The book itself begins in Egypt and ends, not in Canaan, but in the desert with the establishment of the tabernacle. If we are permitted to see the establishment of the tabernacle as the final climactic moment of Exodus, we may begin to see something of the predicament that drives the narrative.

The tabernacle represents Yahweh graciously taking up residence among his chosen people. It is a symbol of God's presence and his exclusive relationship with Israel. If this is the case, then the theme that drives the narrative of Exodus is the forging of a relationship between Yahweh and Israel. Furthermore, by virtue of who the characters are within the narrative, we understand that this is a relationship between a deity and his servants. It is a cosmic relationship between creator and creature. The first eighteen chapters of Exodus are essentially about the beginnings of this relationship. More specifically, these chapters are about the creation of Israel – the story of how Yahweh begets the nation. This is pivotal to the portrayal of Yahweh as the Father and Creator of the nation, for although Jacob's clan grows to sizable numbers in Egypt, they do not become a nation until Yahweh creates them as such through the event of the Exodus.

With this understanding in place, we may begin surveying the contents of Exodus 1 – 18, noting how the narrative itself unfolds through the characters involved, and looking also for those subtleties the ancient mindset would have noticed.

Before liberation: servitude

Yahweh and Egypt: the makings of a cosmic struggle
The opening chapter of Exodus describes the prolific growth of Jacob's clan to the point where they threaten the Egyptians, in whose land they live. The ancient mindset may have found this a striking claim, for Egypt had a formidable reputation as an ancient superpower. Throughout ancient Near Eastern history, Egypt can be seen campaigning in Syria-Palestine (including Canaan, which the Egyptians knew as Retenu), holding sway over its cities, and even warring against other superpowers. For Egypt, then, to have been threatened by Jacob's growing clan must imply spectacular growth. From the material in Genesis we may assume that this staggering growth is the result of God's intentions to bless and multiply Abraham's descendants. This sentiment is confirmed in the way God deals favourably with the two Hebrew midwives, Shiphrah and Puah. The narrator tells us that the people of Jacob's

clan grew to substantial numbers because God treated the midwives well, giving them families of their own (Exod. 1:20–21), implying that Yahweh was indeed responsible for the people's phenomenal birth rate.

This growth then prompts the Egyptians to subdue the Israelites. Through a series of ever more stringent measures, the Egyptians succeed in making forced labourers of the Israelites – slaves. These measures, however, evidently fly in the face of God's intention to bless Jacob's burgeoning clan. Thus, despite the Egyptians' attempts to curtail their growth, Jacob's clan proliferates even more rapidly under the blessing of Yahweh.

We have, then, in this opening chapter the makings of a cosmic struggle. It is a battle for the control of Jacob's clan, the Israelites. The two main combatants are Egypt (in the person of Pharaoh) and Yahweh. Both lay claim to ownership of the Israelites, but for markedly different purposes. Pharaoh and the Egyptians lay claim to them in order to quash them. It is a claim motivated by fear and hate. The Israelites' slavery and hard living conditions are, therefore, the Egyptians' mark of ownership over them. However, Yahweh lays claim to the Israelites in order to bless them. It is a claim motivated by love and commitment. At this early stage of the narrative, the mark of his ownership is their rapidly increasing numbers. So, with these rival claims of ownership, we have a cosmic showdown in the making between Yahweh and Egypt.

Moses: the embodiment of the struggle

This struggle is perhaps embodied best in the character of Moses. As a fine babe born to an Israelite family (Exod. 2:1–2), he represents Yahweh's blessing and claim to ownership of the Israelites. However, in Egypt's murderous purge of Hebrew boys, he is abandoned to the Nile, a victim of the Egyptians' counterclaim of ownership. Ancient hearers would have been aware that the Nile was both a source of life and of death. In cutting a fertile path through the Sahara Desert, it was the bringer of life, and was worshipped as such by the Egyptians. It was the perennial source of Egypt's fertility and stability. However, it was also the ken of deadly creatures, such as crocodiles, snakes and the occasional hippopotamus. The western bank of the Nile was also the location of the great necropolises, such as the Valley of the Kings. Many a deceased Pharaoh was ferried across the river to be forever interred in a concealed tomb – a crossing over from life to death. In Exodus 1:22, the baby boys born to the Hebrews are to be murdered in the waters of the Nile. Thus in the Nile River we have the juxtaposition of life and death. We see this juxtaposition clearly as Moses himself in his basket is abandoned to this watery chaos, but eventually plucked out and saved. Yet, while it seems that he has crossed over from death to life, he is eventually brought up by an Egyptian woman. He is named by the Egyptian woman (Exod. 2:10), a sign of her authority over him. In all this, he comes to embody the claim of Egypt to own and domesticate the Israelites. It is a kind of living death.

By knowing of Moses' Israelite origins, readers of Exodus are aware that Moses does not belong in the house of the Egyptian woman, who is the daughter of Pharaoh. Her house may be a haven for him, but it cannot really be his home. Just as Jacob's clan found refuge in Egypt in the midst of a life-threatening situation, so Moses finds refuge in the household of Pharaoh. Yet herein lies the predicament: despite this situation, Yahweh has a rival claim, not just upon Moses, but upon all the Israelites descended from Jacob. He is determined to forge a relationship with Jacob's descendants, which will therefore require the breaking of Egypt's bonds over them.

The Israelites: the contested ground

We have seen how the Israelites are basically the contested ground in this cosmic struggle between Yahweh and Egypt. Throughout the early parts of the Exodus narrative the Israelites are portrayed as essentially helpless. Just like the infant Moses, who is unable to affect his own destiny, so the Israelites are unable to determine their own future. Jacob's clan, despite its immense size, is vulnerable and helpless. It cannot throw off the shackles of slavery, because it is a disparate horde that lacks its own order and cohesion. At this stage it still does not exist as a nation: it has no militia, let alone a standing army; it has no leader; it has no organization; it has no land. The Israelites even fight among themselves, as demonstrated by the dispute between two Hebrew men that Moses seeks to adjudicate (Exod. 2:13–14). As slaves subservient to Pharaoh and the Egyptians, the Israelites are a vacuous entity, vulnerable to the whims of their Egyptian overlords and susceptible to their own in-house wrangling.[5] As such, it will take intervention from outside to change their plight, for rescue will certainly not come from Egypt, and it cannot come from within their own troubled and disorganized ranks. Thus Moses has to leave Egypt and then be injected back into the fray to embody this rescue from the outside.

Once again, we see how Moses embodies this plight. Moses himself is not a light shining in the darkness. His earliest active contribution to the story as an adult is a murder. Also, his attempt to adjudicate between the two disputing Hebrew men is cynically rejected, demonstrating the infighting that now characterizes the Israelites. And when he is finally called and commissioned by God in Exodus 3, Moses pleads his own inadequacy. He protests his inability to contribute anything of value for enabling the liberation of the Israelites. This is a far cry from the chorus of the theme song in the 1998 animated film *The Prince of Egypt* (see earlier, pp. 19–20), written by Stephen Schwartz, which speaks of the 'miracles you can achieve', and that these occur 'when you believe'. The next line of the chorus emphasizes this: 'you will, you will when you believe'.

However, that is not the song on Moses' lips, and God certainly does not sing it to Moses in order to encourage his reluctant servant. Just like the Israelites, Moses is incapable of doing anything that can in any way change their plight. It will, therefore, take the direct intervention of Yahweh himself to transform Moses, and, through his agency, to transform the boisterous and browbeaten motley crew that is Jacob's clan into a nation of dignity, unity and, even, holiness.

---

5. This latter feature will become characteristic of Israel's desert wanderings, particular in the challenges to Moses' leadership.

Liberation: the creation of Israel

We have seen how the predicament that drives the narrative of Exodus is essentially about the lengths to which Yahweh will go in order to forge a relationship with the Israelites. In the first fifteen chapters, the major obstacle to this is Egypt's rival claim to possess and control the Israelites, who are themselves something of a chaotic and vacuous entity. In the remainder of the book, it is the Israelites themselves who threaten to undo the relationship Yahweh is forging with them.

It is in the light of this fundamental tension that we must understand the liberation of the Israelites. There are three things to note here: (1) the liberation of Israel represents a disclosure of who God is; (2) by disclosing something of his person, God defines who Israel is; and (3) by breaking Egypt's bonds over the Israelites, the Exodus event is an act of creation that brings the nation of Israel into being. Let us take each of these in turn.

The disclosure of God

If Yahweh is to forge a relationship with the Israelites, they must know who Yahweh actually is. There can be no genuine relationship without a disclosure of who the parties in relationship are. So when Yahweh calls and commissions Moses at the burning bush to return to Egypt and confront Pharaoh, he first identifies himself as 'the God of Abraham, the God of Isaac, and the God of Jacob' (Exod. 3:6 my tr.). Instantly, therefore, we see that this is a God of relationship. He is not merely defined by attributes, but rather in personal terms by his relationships. The first readers of Exodus would naturally have connected this identification with the promises God had made to those patriarchs back in Genesis. Moses' encounter with God is, therefore, a resumption of those promises in a way that helps to frame the present with reference to the past. Just as this God related to the ancient patriarchs, so he now wills to relate to Moses and the Israelites.

However, Moses' encounter with this God represents a new development. Abraham, Isaac and Jacob have long since died, and the promises God had made to them are still outstanding. Yes, the descendants of the ancient patriarchs have multiplied, as promised, but they still do not possess a name of renown, or embody a blessing to the nations, let alone possess the land of Canaan. Thus, in this new encounter, our attention is drawn to what remains unfulfilled.

It is fitting, therefore, that when Moses asks God to disclose his name (a very personal and relational request) he receives in the first instance not a name, but a statement about who God is and what he will reveal himself to be: 'I am who I am' (Exod. 3:14 my tr.). The beauty of this statement in the original Hebrew (Hebrew *'ehyeh 'ăšer 'ehyeh*) is the flexibility of the verb form employed. A short consideration of some of the possible nuances of this verb form (the *yiqtol*[6]) will help us to appreciate the subtleties in this statement.

The essence of the Hebrew *yiqtol* verb is to indicate an action or state of which no one particular concrete instance is on view. Rather, the action or state is viewed in general or conceptual terms. For example, the *yiqtol* can indicate an action that occurred habitually in the past, such as that predicated of Samuel's mother, Hannah: 'His mother *used to make* (Hebrew *taʿăśeh*) him a little cloak, and she would bring it up to him from time to time' (1 Sam. 2:19 my tr.). Alternatively, it can indicate an action viewed as generically true at all times, such as in a proverb: 'A man's heart *plans* (Hebrew *yĕḥaššēb*) his way, but Yahweh *determines* (Hebrew *yākîn*) his step' (Prov. 16:9 my tr.). Yet another alternative is to indicate an action that has not yet come about at the time of speaking, such as a promise or threat: '*I will ruin* (Hebew *'aḥărîb*) mountains and hills' (Isa. 42:15 my tr.).

When God discloses to Moses an identifying statement about who he is, he employs the verb 'to be, become' (Hebrew *hāyāh*) in a first person singular form of a *yiqtol* verb (Hebrew *'ehyeh*) to produce a statement that may be rendered literally as 'I be who I be' (Hebrew *'ehyeh 'ăšer 'ehyeh*). In the light of my brief (and somewhat simplified) grammatical treatment above, there are three possible ways to interpret this identifying statement:

----

6. The *yiqtol* has been traditionally known as the *imperfect* verb. Many grammarians are, however, moving towards this more generic descriptive term, *yiqtol*.

1. 'I have always been who I have always been' (past): This would
   suggest that he has always been the same type of God. In the
   light of the context in which God identifies himself as the God
   of the patriarchs, we could go so far as to say that he is a God
   who embarks on committed relationships.
2. 'I am who I am' (generic present): The implication of this
   nuance would be that God is self-defining such that he cannot
   be altered or unduly influenced by another. He is totally independent.[7]
3. 'I will be who I will be' (future): When understood this way, the
   statement implies that God has a future. In other words, there is
   more yet to come.

As we consider these three possible ways of interpreting God's
self-identifying statement, we must be aware of the exegetical
error of totality transfer. This error consists of importing all the
possible meanings within the semantic range of a word or phrase
into the specific context where that word or phrase is found – that
is, overinterpreting it. It is an error because it fails to acknowledge
that the meaning of words or phrases is primarily determined by
their usage in a given context. Out of all the possible meanings
within the semantic range of a word, only one of those meanings
is usually indicated in a particular circumstance. In other words,
context determines which specific nuance of a word is being
implied. This is especially the case in narrative, such as we have
here in Exodus 3.[8]

As such, we must ask what the context indicates to us with
regard to God's self-identifying statement in Exodus 3:14. There
are a number of important observations we may make to inform
us.

---

7. Augustine understood the statement primarily in this way. See *On the Nature of Good* 19; *Sermon* 6.4.
8. Poetry has greater scope to imply more than one nuance of a word, since it works artistically with words to convey meaning. Thus, while we must also beware not to employ totality transfer in poetry, we should not be as quick to avoid it as we are with narrative.

1. Through the use of an equative verb (*hāyāh*), the statement does not indicate an action but rather a *state*. As such, the context implies no specific or circumscribed deed: the idea conveyed is far more nebulous than that.

2. The *yiqtol* conjugation does not inherently indicate tense. Any temporal significance must be inferred from the context. In this case, the context does not provide much help about *when* the state indicated by the verb comes about. The tense, therefore, remains entirely open. This understanding seems to be reflected in the Septuagint, where the Greek translators used a participle (which has no inherent temporal tense) in the attempt to convey the import of the Hebrew.[9]

3. Equative verbs are usually accompanied by a *predicate* that states something about the subject (e.g. I am *a father*). In the case of Exodus 3:14, the predicate is a relative clause that is essentially reflexive. In other words, the predicate ('I am') says nothing more about the subject than what the subject itself conveys ('I am'). Thus the statement does not actually take us beyond the subject itself to another conceptual category by which we may understand it. The statement is, therefore, quite circular, and so we are forced to dwell not on a newly introduced conceptual category to understand who or what the 'I' in the statement is, but rather on the 'I' itself.

4. The statement itself and the state it indicates function as a name that answers Moses' question in Exodus 3:13 about the name of the God of Israel's patriarchs. This is confirmed by God's directive in 3:14b: 'This is what you are to say to the Israelites: "'I am' sent me to you"'' (my tr.). This specifically answers Moses' question. Thus we have an equation drawn here between the God of Israel's patriarchs (note the past referent) and the statement of 3:14. This equation, however, is not a word-for-word repetition of his identification as the God of the patriarchs (cf. Exod. 3:6). In some way, therefore, this statement in Exodus 3:14 takes us beyond the identification in 3:6. In line with the nature of the equative

---

9. The Septuagint translation is *egō eimi ho ōn*, which equates to *I am the being one.*

verb, we understand this to indicate some kind of state of *being* or *becoming*. This pushes us beyond any one temporal interpretation of the statement.[10]

5. In the context of the chapter, the subject of the statement is the enigmatic God of the patriarchs who now wishes to liberate the Israelites in order to give them the land of Canaan (cf. Exod. 3:6–10, 12). These are past, present and future ideas that all converge upon the subject, 'I'.

6. The three possible nuances (habitual past, generic present, future) mentioned earlier in the discussion are not three independent verbal forms, but rather three legitimate ways to understand the one verb form (*yiqtol*), which is used within the statement of Exodus 3:14.

As can be seen, there is much more than initially meets the eye in this deceptively simple statement in Exodus 3:14. Our observations drive us to consider more than one possible way of interpreting this statement, because there is evidently no one narrow interpretation that stands out above the others. That is, this self-identifying statement of God in Exodus 3:14 is multivalent.

There is good evidence that the statement was taken in just such a multivalent way in antiquity. First, Isaiah 41:4 has God describe himself with a dual characterization as 'the first and the last', followed immediately by the statement 'I am he' (Hebrew *'ănî hû'*). The Septuagint renders this last statement with the same phrase it uses to translate Exodus 3:14 (Greek *egō eimi*; cf. Deut. 32:39). The Jerusalem Targum paraphrases Exodus 3:14 as 'I am he who is and who will be' (Childs 1974: 83). Perhaps the clearest examples come from the book of Revelation in the NT, where God (Jesus included) is referred to as 'the One who was, who is, and is coming' (Greek *ho ēn kai ho ōn kai ho erchomenos* [Rev. 1:4, 8; 4:8; cf. 11:17; 16:5]). This rendering through the use of participles picks up an earlier point which demonstrated that the statement

_____

10. Augustine commented that the statement *I am who I am* is essentially incomprehensible, and it is for this reason that God also identified himself in more comprehensible terms as the God of the patriarchs. See *Tractate on the Gospel of John* 38.8.

transcends temporal categories. By the same token, however, the way it transcends such temporal categories is also by implying all temporal categories (past, present and future).[11] It is, in other words, a bold but simple statement of supreme, factual, dynamic existence that cannot be contained within any one time reference.[12]

We may conclude, therefore, that in this case the syntactical composition, context and circularity of God's self-defining statement in Exodus 3:14 all mean that we are not committing the exegetical error of totality transfer when we attribute more than one nuance to the statement. On the contrary, we would be doing it an injustice if we restricted ourselves to just one narrow nuance in this case.

What then are the implications of all this? On the one hand this simple statement 'I am who I am' says that God is constant and consistent. To pick up the language of James in the NT, in him 'there is no variation or shady bent' (Jas 1:17 my tr.). Thus the God who reveals himself to Moses is no different from the God who revealed himself to the patriarchs and related to them: he is one and the same deity. Yet this God is also self-defining and must be taken on his own terms. Thus, while Moses and the Israelites can relate to God on the basis of the past (the promises to the patriarchs) or the present (his intention to rescue them from Egypt), they cannot change who he is or adapt him to their own desires. Furthermore, this identifying statement invites them to consider who he will prove himself to be in the future.

This ability to point consistently to the past and yet also to the prospective future demonstrates God's intention to be in personal

---

11. Augustine understood the import of the statement somewhat differently when he argued that God's supreme ontology allowed for no past or future, but only an infinite and unchangeable present. References to the past or the future with respect to God are only permitted due to humanity's limited and time-bound perception. See *Tractate on the Gospel of John* 99.5.

12. Gregory of Nazianzus makes a statement to similar effect in the fourth of his five famous *Theological Orations* (4.18).

relationship with Moses and the Israelites. He is not a motionless God who, in his consistent character, is monolithically static. One cannot really talk about a 'personal relationship' (a dynamic phenomenon) with such a static entity. On the contrary, he is dynamic and active; he is consistent, yet not predictable; he is uncontainable, and yet knowable. In other words, with this God one can have a relationship that grows and progresses, such that one can forge a history together with him. He is a living God with whom Moses and the Israelites can interact dynamically. As Fretheim aptly puts it, '*The name shapes Israel's story, and the story gives greater texture to the name.* At the same time, there are stakes in this for God; God has to live up to the name' (1991: 63–64; emphasis his).

That is why Moses' initial encounter with this God at the burning bush in no way exhausts the revelation of who he is. This God divulges himself in a way that allows for relationship, but never in such a way that exhausts that relationship. This is further demonstrated by the fact that after disclosing this identifying statement of himself, God endorses his name as 'Yahweh' (Exod. 3:15). The name 'Yahweh' (Hebrew *yhwh*)[13] is itself some kind of variation on the verb 'to be, become' (Hebrew *hāyāh*).[14] In the light of the statement 'I am who I am', it seems to be a hypocoristicon – a shorthand label that, though not the full essence of one's name or being, still makes some suggestion towards the reality it signifies.[15]

---

13. This transliteration of the Hebrew lexeme gives only the Hebrew consonants, since the exact pronunciation of this word is debated. That is, scholars are ultimately unsure as to which vowels belong with these four consonants because they are not entirely sure of the verb form it is trying to reproduce. The English rendering given here (Yahweh) merely follows the convention of scholarly consensus.

14. More specifically, it appears to be a third person masculine singular ('he . . .') form of the verb. The other grammatical details of the name are debated.

15. Philo had a similar understanding of the relation between the statement 'I am who I am' and the name Yahweh (rendered into Greek by the word *kyrios*, meaning 'Lord'). He argued that the statement conveys the fact that no appellation could be adequately made of God, since God's nature is

This inability to capture the essence of God's identity and yet still be able to relate dynamically to him stands behind the prohibition of idolatry that we encounter later in Exodus. This God cannot be captured and contained in a static creation, for that is a fundamental misrepresentation of who he is.

The implication of this revelation of God's identity is that he must reveal himself as he sees fit, for only he can truly plumb the depths of his own being and express it accurately. Unlike the gods of other ancient Near Eastern communities, Yahweh cannot be manipulated. He cannot be fashioned by a craftsman's chisel, or exhausted by a philosopher's thought. He must be left to reveal himself and so demonstrate who he is in a dynamic way. Moses and the Israelites are, therefore, in some sense, called to be spectators of his being, beholding his frightening glory. Perhaps the most dramatic demonstration of this fact in the first eighteen chapters of Exodus comes as the Israelites find themselves hemmed helplessly between the Reed Sea and the Egyptian armies bearing down upon them:

> Moses said to the people, 'Don't be afraid! Take your positions and watch the salvation Yahweh will accomplish for you today. For the Egyptians you see today you will never ever see again. Yahweh will fight for you – you just stand still.' (Exod. 14:13–14 my tr.)

If the Israelites are called to stand and behold God's glory, the Egyptians, too, are given a disclosure of who Yahweh is. When Moses first comes to Pharaoh with Yahweh's confronting ultimatum that challenges Egypt's claim to the Israelites, Pharaoh responds, 'Who is Yahweh that I should obey him by releasing Israel? I do not know Yahweh, and neither will I release Israel' (Exod. 5:2 my tr.). Whether this is agnosticism or flagrant rejection,

---

simply to be, rather than be described. However, so that humanity might not be without any means of reference to God, the name Yahweh (Greek *kyrios*) was given to Moses. See *On the Change of Names* 1.11; *On Dreams* 1.229–231; *Life of Moses* 1.75. As Childs correctly perceives, Philo's view has a kinship with the tradition of Isaiah 40 – 55 (1974: 83).

Pharaoh's ignorance does not absolve him from the responsibility of having to obey Yahweh. The implication of his own words is that knowing Yahweh leads inextricably to obeying him, be it willingly or unwillingly.

As such, the frightful signs and plagues inflicted on Egypt become a revelation to Egypt of who Yahweh is. It is through these means that Egypt comes to taste the raw power of Yahweh, and thereby acknowledge the legitimacy and truth of his claim over Israel. It is only with the fullness of such judgment that Pharaoh and the Egyptians finally agree to release the Israelites. These ominous signs and plagues are, therefore, how Yahweh deals with his enemies who refuse to acknowledge him and try to counter his own claims.

Tellingly, Israel does not experience these ominous signs in the first fifteen chapters of Exodus. This is not because they are innocent – they themselves in their natural state are not deserving of relationship with God. The fact that they must daub their doorposts with the blood of the Passover sacrifice to stave off judgment (Exod. 12:7, 12–13) demonstrates their inherent unworthiness. They must be spared from judgment themselves and then be made fit for relationship with God. Nonetheless, as Moses and the Israelites behold the frightening revelation of Yahweh's power trained precisely on his enemies, they, too, come to acknowledge Yahweh's sovereignty, power and merciful election. This acknowledgment was to be enshrined in the Passover ritual:

> When your children say to you, 'What does this ritual mean to you?', you are to say, 'It is the Passover sacrifice to Yahweh. He passed over the homes of the Israelites in Egypt when he struck Egypt. But he saved our homes.' (Exod. 12:26–27 my tr.)

Thus in the plague narratives we have a further disclosure of who Yahweh is: he is the God of Israel, and none will deny him the close relationship he seeks with them. And so Yahweh, as it were, fills the stage of the plague narratives. Not one of the Egyptians is mentioned by name. Pharaoh is merely 'Pharaoh' or 'the king of Egypt' (e.g. Exod. 5:4), his courtiers are mentioned only by their titles (e.g. Exod. 7:11), and the gods of Egypt are never named (cf. Exod. 12:12). This is a story about Yahweh, who will not allow anyone or anything to stand in the way of his forging a close and committed relationship with his chosen people.

The definition of Israel

The first reference that Yahweh makes to Israel in the book of Exodus comes in 3:7, where he refers to them as 'my people' (Hebrew 'ammî). Here we see Yahweh's claim of ownership over the Israelites. Ancient readers would probably have interpreted this phrase 'my people' as an expression of Yahweh's patronage of Israel. Most nations of the ancient Near East, especially during the Iron Age (1200–586 BC), had their own national patron deity: the Moabites had Chemosh, the Ammonites had Molech, the Edomites had Qaush, and for the Syrians there was Hadad (better known as Baal). The territory of the nation was viewed as the personal domain of the national god. When one travelled across national borders, one entered the domain of another god and, therefore, one would be expected to pay respect to that god during the time spent in his domain. This is much like the way we use foreign currency whenever we travel today: when we enter another country, we have to use that country's currency. Thus ancient readers of Exodus would have understood this particular term 'my people', and interpreted it in the first instance as Yahweh expressing his patronage of the Israelites.

What is unusual, however, in the Exodus narrative, is that the Israelites do not actually have any territory at this stage. While Canaan has been promised to them, they are at present landless. Thus the foundational category for understanding Yahweh's inter-action with Israel cannot be that of a patron deity and the nation who tenants his land. While such understanding is not completely foreign to the situation between Yahweh and Israel, it is by no means foundational. There is a more fundamental relationship at work here.

We receive an insight into the more foundational category of this relationship in Exodus 4:21–23. There, Yahweh entrusts Moses with the ultimatum he is to deliver to Pharaoh:

This is what Yahweh says: 'Israel is my firstborn son. So I said to you, "Release my son that he may serve me," but you refused to release him. So see, I am going to slay your firstborn son.' (Exod. 4:21–23 my tr.)

Throughout the ancient Near East, the firstborn son was the heir who stood to inherit all that belonged to his father. Yahweh's ultimatum to Pharaoh defines Israel in those filial categories. Israel is to inherit or partake of what is Yahweh's. This understanding helps to explain the language of inheritance employed to describe Israel's later reception of the land of Canaan. It also implies a relationship of close kinship, which explains Yahweh's call for Israel to be holy just as he himself is holy. There is to be a family resemblance, so to speak.

It also frames the concept of 'worship' or 'service' in filial terms. The exodus is not about Israel trading one slave master (Egypt) for another (Yahweh). That is evidently not liberation, but rather becoming a spoil of war – a mere object to be acquired and manipulated for personal gain. Rather, the exodus is about Israel becoming the son of God. The picture we eventually get of this filial relationship is one where the son lives in acknowledgment and thanks of his father's provision, care and unconditional love. This, in turn, leads to free and willing obedience. To serve Yahweh, therefore, is not to experience servility or exploitation, but rather to receive life, freedom and value through an ongoing and dynamic interaction with a loving God.

A caution is warranted at this point, however. While the exodus liberates Israel to serve Yahweh as a son, it is by no means the final word. On the contrary, it is merely the beginning of an important theological trajectory. The theme of sonship develops through the course of the biblical revelation. From its beginnings here in Exodus as a metaphor for the nation of Israel, the category of sonship is narrowed to a particular individual, as Yahweh personally adopts the heir of David as his own son (2 Sam. 7:14). The theme is then given final and definitive expression in the incarnation of God the Son, who serves and worships the Father perfectly, and reveals the inner relations of God. At that point, the God 'I am' who invited Moses and the Israelites to ponder 'who he will be' reveals himself with plenitude to be Trinity. It is in this theological framework that we may also understand Paul's important concept that Christians are constituted as sons of God by adoption through the Spirit and in Christ (cf. Rom. 8:14–17, 23; Gal. 4:4–7). This crucial theological trajectory, which runs through the entire course of the biblical revelation, is first expressed in this initial definition of Israel as Yahweh's firstborn son.

The exodus as an act of creation

In the light of our considerations above, we may now turn to see the exodus as an act of creation. In liberating the Israelites from Egypt, Yahweh begets Israel as his own son. He takes the disparate multitude of Jacob's clan and brings them into being as a nation, forming them into a cohesive people with order, shape and purpose.

In ancient Near Eastern cultures, creation was not viewed primarily in terms of substance, but rather in terms of function. That is, creation was an act of differentiation whereby chaos and disarray were tamed through the imposition of order and purpose. This is not to deny the biblical doctrine of *creatio ex nihilo*; the Christian doctrine of God cannot be logically consistent with the whole biblical revelation if this proposition is denied. However, this was not the prime concern of the ancients. For the ancient person, the world was more frightening, volatile and mysterious than it is for us today with our advanced technologies, scientific knowledge and stable governments with federal constitutions. The ancient situation bred a mindset far more concerned for immediate stability and order than the more philosophical question of whether the universe came to be out of nothing or not. John Walton phrases the issue well:

> As is immediately evident upon even a cursory reading of the texts, very little in these [ancient Near Eastern] cosmologies relates strictly to manufacture of the material cosmos . . . [I]n the ancient world something came into existence when it was separated out as a distinct entity, given a function, and given a name . . . This is in stark contrast to modern ontology, which is much more interested in what might be called the structure or substance of something along with its properties. (2007: 179–180)

In ancient Mesopotamia, the epic *Enuma Elish*[16] depicts the act of creation as a cosmic struggle between Marduk and the chaotic sea-dragon Tiamat.[17] Marduk slays Tiamat (*Enuma Elish* 4.93–104) and out of the pieces of her carcass forms the heavens and the earth (4.135–145). Marduk then takes the blood of Qingu, who is Tiamat's paramour, and forms human beings, giving them the function of working so that the gods may be at ease (6.8, 27–34). Creation is, therefore, conceived in Mesopotamia as a divine conquest over chaos and a subsequent separation into distinct entities with a specific purpose (cf. von Soden 1994: 212–223; Clifford 1994: 90–93).

Similarly, certain Egyptian texts reflect a creation mythology in which the universe begins as a dark watery mass devoid of space or form. Creation is then enacted with the separation of a circumscribed mound and the consequent establishment of life and order.[18] However, the force of chaos and non-being was viewed as still present in such physical realms as the night sky, the ocean or even the desert, for these places smothered human life so that humanity could not function there (Walton 2007: 186).

Readers of Genesis would likewise have been aware of the characterization of the primal chaos as *tohû wābohû* (Gen. 1:2), a phrase difficult to capture in translation. The closest approximation we have in English is something like 'topsy turvey', but this has an almost comical edge, which the Hebrew phrase *tohû wābohû* does not carry. Creation is depicted in Genesis 1 as the separation of various domains out of the dark, vacuous and watery ocean

---

16. For a translation of the epic, see Hallo and Younger 1997–2002: 1:111.

17. It should be noted that though *Enuma Elish* is frequently cited as a creation epic, it is in fact primarily about the rise of Marduk to ascendancy among the gods. The creation of the heavens and the earth is almost an aside to the main plot.

18. The circumscribed mound is usually symbolic of the entire world, and is often identified as a particular god (e.g. Atum). See Clifford 1994: 105–106. For the translation of relevant texts from Egypt, see Hallo and Younger 1997–2002: 1:1, 2, 4, 8, 12. It should also be noted that ancient Egyptians saw creation recurring each day with the rising sun.

chaos. Thus day and night are distinguished from this chaos, and subsequently named and given a function (time). Similarly, sky, sea and land are differentiated, and then appropriately filled with creatures that belong to each of these domains. Out of this watery chaos, therefore, God brings forth order, purpose and stability.

This notion of creation as *distinction* and *imparting of function* would have been part of the mindset the ancients brought to the reading of Exodus. When this is acknowledged, the exodus event can be seen as essentially a creative act, bringing order and function out of chaos. Furthermore, it highlights the exodus as an act of justice. The ancient concept of justice (*mišpāṭ*) was not thought of in purely legal terms, as we largely do today. Rather, justice was setting everything in its proper assigned place so that it may fulfil its assigned function in relational harmony with the rest of creation.[19] In this way, creation and justice go hand in hand: a creative act sets the conditions for justice to prevail. Let us consider briefly how all this is seen in the first section of Exodus.

In the first instance, Yahweh's ultimatum that Pharaoh should release Israel, his firstborn son, so that he may serve him (Exod. 4:22–23) calls for the separation of Israel from Egypt and the bestowal of a function (service) upon Israel. As long as Israel remains subservient to the Egyptians, they are not separated from them, and therefore they cannot fulfil their divinely assigned function of serving Yahweh. This is why Yahweh does not merely reveal himself to Israel and leave them within Egypt, or command them to build a tabernacle in Egypt. That would be an act of injustice, for it would prevent Israel from realizing their own being and function as given to them by God. They must be separated from their oppressors, who unjustly seek to quash their being. In physical terms, this means the removal of Israel from Egypt and their installation in a land of their own where they can fulfil their function of serving God as a son. This is further reinforced during Yahweh's cosmic showdown with Egypt, as three times he

19. This definition of *mišpāṭ* underlies the semantic range of the word, which includes such notions as 'custom', 'norm' and 'pattern', as well as 'judgment', 'verdict', 'sentence' and 'condemnation'.

proclaims that the plagues he inflicts upon Egypt will make a distinction between Egypt and Israel (Exod. 8:23; 9:4; 11:7).

Perhaps the most definitive picture of the exodus as a creative act comes with Israel at the Reed Sea. Here Israel finds itself caught between the watery chaos of the Reed Sea and the armies of chaos consisting of Pharaoh and the Egyptians. With such disorder and mayhem closing in and threatening to drown and expunge them, Yahweh works his salvation for his people through an act of separation: he parts the chaotic sea so that, just as in Genesis 1, the dry land appears. Through this parting, the sea is tamed and Israel is finally delivered from Egypt.

While the biblical literature produced by Israel and Judah does not portray the polytheistic understanding of creation of its ancient Near Eastern neighbours, it nonetheless communicates its understanding of creation through similar conceptual categories:

> By his might he tamed the sea,
> by his expertise he ruptured Rahab.
> (Job 26:12 my tr.)

> God is my king from antiquity,
> a worker of salvation in the midst of the earth.
> You wrenched the sea in your strength.
> You smashed the heads of fanged monsters on the sea.
> You battered the heads of Leviathan.
> You give him as food to the creatures of the wasteland.
> (Ps. 74:12–14 my tr.)

> You crushed Rahab like a corpse;
> with your arm of strength you dispersed your enemies.
> (Ps. 89:11 [English 89:10] my tr.)

> On that day,
> Yahweh will deal his brutal, large and hardy sword
> on Leviathan the fleeing snake,
> on Leviathan the thrashing snake,
> slaying the fanged monster who is in the sea.
> (Isa. 27:1 my tr.)

Wake up! Wake up!
Don the strength of Yahweh's arm!
Wake up as in ancient days, in the generations of old.
Were you not the one who hacked Rahab down,
splitting the fanged monster?
(Isa. 51:9 my tr.)

On two occasions, the OT even identifies Egypt with the fanged monster Rahab:

Egypt's help is vain and empty.
That is why I call her 'Rahab the Failure'.
(Isa. 30:7 my tr.)

I recall Rahab and Babylon among those who have recognized me,
Philistia, Tyre, along with Cush . . .
(Ps. 87:4 my tr.)

In the light of these biblical intertexts, it would be hard to imagine the ancient reader of Exodus not perceiving the parting of the Reed Sea as an act of creation in the midst of a cosmic battle. Indeed, Psalm 106 seems to capture something of this by describing the event as a 'reprimand' of the sea:

He reprimanded the Reed Sea and it dried up.
He had them walk through the watery depths as through a desert.
(Ps. 106:9 my tr.)

Yahweh is here portrayed as taming a hostile entity, the watery depths (Hebrew *těhōmōt*), evoking the fundamental imagery of an act of creation.

Interestingly, the result of this cosmic battle seems to be fore-shadowed much earlier in the narrative. One of the signs Yahweh gives Moses at the burning bush for confronting Pharaoh is to throw his staff (a symbol of leadership) on the ground so that it transforms into a snake (Exod. 4:3–5). However, when this occurs before Pharaoh (Exod. 7:8–13), some of the details change slightly. First, it is Aaron's staff that is thrown down before

Pharaoh (Exod. 7:9). More importantly, though, the Hebrew text uses a different word to denote what the staff turns into. At the burning bush, it turns into a 'snake' (Hebrew *naḥaš*), but before Pharaoh it turns into a 'fanged monster' (Hebrew *tannîn* [Exod. 7:9–10 my tr.]).[20] This change in vocabulary is noteworthy. It is, in the first place, not altogether surprising, for both terms are used as comparable parallels elsewhere (cf. Isa. 27:1, where both words describe the Leviathan). However, the term 'fanged monster' usually denotes the symbol of chaos that thrashes about in the sea and that God vanquishes (cf. Rahab and Leviathan in the verses quoted above). For Moses to be able to pick up such a 'fanged monster' implies the ability to tame chaos. Furthermore, when Pharaoh's magicians are able to replicate the feat (Exod. 7:11), we are told that 'Aaron's staff swallowed up their staffs' (Exod. 7:12). This foreshadows the destruction of the Egyptian army when it is swallowed up by the chaotic Reed Sea tamed by Yahweh (cf. Guillaume 2004: 232–236; Meyers 2005: 81). Thus, if Israel's escape is an act of creation through separation, then the drowning of the Egyptians is an act of uncreation through coalescence. Their existence is undone by the merging of their armies of chaos with the waters of chaos,[21] just as the staffs of the Egyptian magicians are swallowed up by the staff of Aaron. Theirs is a cosmic defeat at the hands of a God who has power to tame chaos.[22]

Thus this act of creation that brings Israel into being occurs in the context of Yahweh vanquishing the forces of chaos. Furthermore, by this creative act Yahweh himself is revealed to the nations

---

20. This fact is often masked in many English versions.

21. This is reminiscent of the flood, in which the world's population (apart from Noah's family) is deluged as the waters above the earth and the waters below the earth converge to obscure the order of creation.

22. Seeing the exodus event in such cosmic proportions allows us to make better sense of the imagery used to characterize Pharaoh and Egypt in various prophetic oracles (Jer. 46:22–23; Ezek. 29:1–16; 32:1–16). I do not concur with Guillaume (2004: 234–235) that Exodus draws upon Ezekiel's imagery. Rather, both Exodus and Ezekiel appear to draw upon a common ancient tradition that characterized Pharaoh and Egypt in this way.

round about, as is celebrated in the famed Song of the Sea (Exod. 15:1–18).

Beyond liberation: service

As we have seen, the creation of Israel implies their liberation and, therefore, their distinction from Egypt. Yet the narrative does not end there. Beyond the Exodus event itself lies Israel's encounter with Yahweh at Sinai, where they are given the law. It is this law that further defines the function of Israel, giving greater resolution and solidity to the order God was bestowing on them: they are to be a kingdom of priests who serve God and relate to him in a dynamic way.

The tabernacle is a physical representation of this relationship. It had defined spaces of specific dimensions within which particular furniture was situated and particular functions took place. It also demonstrated Yahweh's intention of forging a relationship with Israel, as is seen in the final few verses of Exodus, when Yahweh's glory fills the tabernacle (Exod. 40:34–35). These other aspects of Israel's life beyond liberation will be discussed in the following chapters.

Conclusion

In conclusion, I return to my initial consideration and ask what subtleties we have picked up along the way. We first noted that when Exodus is divorced from its ancient Near Eastern mindset and viewed purely through twenty-first-century eyes, it is little more than a story of liberation. Indeed, this is why modern characterizations of the exodus are usually not very interested in what happens after Israel is delivered through the Reed Sea. The imparting of the law does not make for a good liberation story. So what have we gained?

First, by holding Exodus up to its ancient Near Eastern context, we see that it is a story about God's determination to be in relationship with the descendants of Jacob, the Israelites. As such, the exodus is not just any old liberation story with a curious cast of characters. It is actually a revelation of who God is. It portrays him as a God of relationship, who desires to interact creatively and dynamically with the people he has chosen. Indeed, he desires to be the father of this people. Secondly, we have noted how the exodus event is an act of creation that brings Israel into being as a nation who can serve God as a son serving a father.

When we see this creative aspect of Exodus in the light of the revelation of God, and put it in perspective with the grander scheme of the biblical revelation, we see that Exodus represents a significant step in God's transformative or recreative work. That which was lost through sin at Eden is being partially recovered in Exodus. The relationship between God and humanity that was severed through sin is here being overcome, as Yahweh goes to tremendous lengths to regenerate a relationship with his creatures. Exodus is not simply about what God did for an oppressed people, but rather an account of God's efforts to rescue his creation from the chaos of non-being. In Exodus, we see this is miniature, as it were, in the lead up to a grander and more cosmic achievement through the Son of God, Jesus Christ. This is not a story we can simply adapt for our own entertainment or merely to make a political comment. It is, rather, the revelation of a God who desires to be known by his human creatures as Father.

Bibliography

Alter, R. (2004), *The Five Books of Moses: A Translation with Commentary*, New York: W. W. Norton.

Childs, B. S. (1974), *The Book of Exodus: A Critical Theological Commentary*, Old Testament Library, Louisville: Westminster John Knox, repr. 2004.

Clifford, R. J. (1994), *Creation Accounts in the Ancient Near East and in the Bible*, Catholic Biblical Quarterly Monograph Series 26, Washington: Catholic Biblical Association of America.

Fretheim, T. E. (1991), *Exodus*, Louisville: John Knox.

Gardiner, A. (1961), *Egypt of the Pharaohs*, Oxford: Oxford University Press, repr. 1964.

Guillaume, P. (2004), 'Metamorphosis of a Ferocious Pharaoh', *Biblica* 85: 232–236.

Hallo, W. W. (1991), *The Book of the People*, Atlanta: Scholars Press.

Hallo, W. W., and K. L. Younger (1997–2002), *The Context of Scripture*, 3 vols. Leiden, Brill.

Meyers, C. (2005), *Exodus*, New Cambridge Bible Commentary, Cambridge: Cambridge University Press.

Schulz, R., and M. Seidel (1998), *Egypt: The World of the Pharaohs*, Cologne: Könemann.

Soden, W. von (1994), *The Ancient Orient: An Introduction to the Study of the Ancient Near East*, Grand Rapids: Eerdmans.

Walton, J. H. (2007), *Ancient Near Eastern Thought and the Old Testament: Introducing the Conceptual World of the Hebrew Bible*, Grand Rapids: Baker.

3. 'AND GOD HEARD THEIR GROANING': SLAVERY, THE EXODUS AND CONTEMPORARY THEOLOGIES OF LIBERATION

Michael Raiter

Introduction

Of the many problems that beset the human race in the first years of the twenty-first century, one that rarely receives much media attention is the rampant slave trade. The higher profile issues of climate change and Islamic extremism grab the headlines. Of course, it is understandable why people are more focused on these other issues. The consequences of global warming and international terrorism already appear to be affecting each of us. However, 'this immoral trade' (Cox and Marks 2006), as modern slavery has been dubbed, remains at a very safe distance from most in the Western world.

Or, perhaps, we naively think that since Wilberforce won the vote for the abolition of the slave trade two hundred years ago, this practice has finally been been eradicated from our world. Of course, nothing could be further from the truth. Despite the fact that the International Slavery Convention outlawed slavery in the 1920s, today it is conservatively estimated that 27 million people are still trapped in some form of bondage – and the number is growing. Slavery takes many forms, of which the more traditional 'chattel slavery' (where slave owners forcibly capture and maintain other human beings as property to be bought and sold) is just one. There is also debt bondage, children abducted for armed militias, forced labour and women held as sex slaves. In the USA alone, the Central Intelligence Agency estimates that fifty thousand to sixty thousand girls are *annually* brought into the country for sexual exploitation (Cox and Marks 2006: 137).

It seems singularly appropriate in the year of the two hundredth anniversary of the astonishing achievements of William Wilberforce in abolishing the slave trade that we address in this exploration of the book of Exodus the timeless question of human slavery, and the response of the covenant-keeping God to this blight on his creation.

This chapter will, in large part, be a critique of some contemporary theologies of liberation. We shall place their claims under the searchlight of Scripture. We must do this since the abuse or disregard of theology and hermeneutics has the most serious consequences. At the same time such a task is fraught with both risk and presumption for those of us who live in affluent, democratic societies, relatively free from the curse of human bondage. Catholic liberation theologians have some appreciation for those who refuse to do theology because it has no relevance or value for the work of liberation, but they have no sympathy for those who practice theology as an academic discipline in the security of some chamber removed from the traumas of the liberation struggle. Admittedly, most of us are far removed from the physical liberation struggle. Few of us have even visited a village decimated by callous slave traders, let alone immersed ourselves in the political struggles to 'set the captives free'. We gladly acknowledge William Wilberforce as one of our own, an evangelical hero, but would we have been among those like John Newton who persuaded this gifted orator not to enter the ordained ministry, but to continue his service as a parliamentarian because it was too important for the cause of the gospel and the good of humankind?

Slaves in Egypt

The Bible is a book vitally concerned with the liberation of slaves.
Of course, it is much more than a narrative of divine emancipa-
tions. It is theological history. In other words, the authors of Holy
Scripture have little interest in recounting history for history's sake.
They have an agenda. Theological commitments drive the selection and arrangement of their material. This is not to say that they
are unconcerned for historical accuracy. They are historians of
integrity. However, it is to say that there is a larger purpose, or
metanarrative, that drives the authors of Scripture. They are part
of a story recounting God's plan to save his people, a plan promised to Abraham, fulfilled in the Lord Jesus Christ, and to be fully
realized at the end of the age.

At the same time, the Bible describes real people in real life
situations. Whatever else we may say about the Exodus narrative, it
is an account of a people suffering under the oppression of
slavery. While the information the text of Scripture gives us about
the condition of the Hebrew slaves under Pharaoh is relatively
brief, there is enough to indicate the extent of the human tragedy.

Exodus 1 is an account of God's faithfulness to his covenant
people. The Lord had promised Abraham that his descendants
would be as numerous as the stars in the sky, and to ensure that
this word stands, he providentially frustrates Pharaoh's plans to
undermine the divine intention by reducing the Hebrews' numbers.
Nevertheless, for all that, the text does not disguise the suffering
the people endured for generations. Exodus 1 narrates the intensifi-
cation of the oppression of the Israelites by Pharaoh. Alarmed by
the population growth of the fertile Hebrews, the Egyptians
implement a number of policies designed initially to check this
growth, and finally to deal decisively with this perceived threat to
national security. Pharaoh's malevolent policies intensify as the
narrative progresses, yet, remarkably, they appear to be inversely
proportionate to Israel's productivity: the more the people are
oppressed and the more Egypt seeks to exterminate them, the
more 'the people increased and became even more numerous' (v.
20). However, this divine faithfulness does not mitigate the people's
suffering: 'they put slave masters over them to oppress them with

forced labour . . . and worked them ruthlessly. They made their lives bitter with hard labour . . .' (Exod. 1:11–14).[1]

There seemed to be two dimensions to the Egyptians' oppression of the Hebrews. First, there was their disenfranchisement. The text is silent on the actual social status of the Hebrews prior to the implementation of the new Pharaoh's policy of harassment and exploitation. However, it appears that they had lived in Egypt as a recognized and tolerated foreign minority. However, their rapid population increase is perceived by the Egyptians to be a potential threat and so measures are enacted to reduce the Hebrews to the status of slaves required to provide forced labour for their Egyptian overlords. John Goldingay warns us against seeing the bondage of the Hebrews as chattel slavery, whereby men and women are bought and sold in the marketplace. Rather, this was slavery on a national, rather than an individual, level. It was a form of state slavery or serfdom (2003: 295). The Hebrews were conscripted for massive building projects that, as commentator Douglas Stuart points out, would have kept them away from their wives, and thus reduced the possibility of the conception of children. Further, these long absences would mean the Hebrews' own farms would be neglected, again serving ultimately to reduce the productivity necessary for population increase (2006: 69).

When this policy fails to halt the growth of the number of Hebrews, the Egyptians make the labour even more physically exacting, presumably rendering the men too weak and tired to procreate. The cycle of oppression then reaches its nadir with the plan for the extermination of all Hebrew male infants. In summary, for all the people's continued fecundity, the yoke of slavery they bore was a very heavy one; it was 'a cruel bondage' (Exod. 6:9).

---

1. Unless stated otherwise, all Bible quotations in this chapter are from the NIV.

Divine liberation

While scholars differ in their various interpretations of the exodus narrative, across the theological spectrum all agree that the book of Exodus and the event of the exodus itself are foundational and integral to the self-understanding of the people of God. The liberation from the oppression of the Egyptians is paradigmatic for the theology of liberation throughout the rest of salvation history.

As we have noted, the events recorded in Exodus are rooted in history. Whatever else it may have been, the oppression and subsequent liberation of the Israelites was sociopolitical. The enslavement of the Hebrews was a deliberate policy, bordering on genocide, enacted by an insecure and morally bankrupt government. However, God's initiative to bring about the people's liberation was motivated by more than just his compassion for their physical plight. Repeatedly, Scripture affirms that the Lord is rescuing his people in order for them to worship/serve him. The book of Exodus moves from slavery through salvation to worship, or, more particularly, 'from the enforced construction of buildings for Pharaoh to the glad and obedient offering of a building for the worship of God' (Fretheim 2003: 250).

Therefore, both the ancient historian who penned Exodus and those inspired writers who later reflect upon the exodus event saw the event as multidimensional. Most strikingly, the combatants in the battle of liberation are divine and human. Exodus does not present the struggle as a popular uprising led by a charismatic Hebrew leader, a kind of ancient Che Guevera, who challenges the autonomy of the dictatorial Pharaoh. Moses, while not passive, is really the Lord's spokesman. The antagonists are Yahweh and the Egyptian king.

Further, while it is the suffering and groaning of his people that prompts the Lord to 'remember' his covenant with Abraham, and arise and come to their aid, there is clearly more at stake here than a manifestation of God's 'preferential option for the poor'. The constant refrain throughout the narrative is that God is acting 'for the sake of his name'. For example, the Lord tells Moses that he will harden Pharaoh's heart so that he can multiply his signs in the

land of Egypt, in order that '*the Egyptians will know that I am the*
LORD when I stretch out my hand against Egypt and bring the
Israelites out of it' (7:5; my emphasis). Indeed, through Moses the
Lord tells Pharaoh that 'I have raised you up for this very purpose,
that I might show you my power *and that my name might be proclaimed*
in all the earth' (9:16; my emphasis). This is the chief reason for the
prolonged, repeated acts of judgment upon the land of Egypt:
they manifest to Egypt and the surrounding nations the awesome
power of the God of the Israelites (e.g. 10:1–2; 11:9).

Then, when the Israelites eventually leave Egypt, God deliberately leads them into a cul-de-sac with the advancing Egyptians on
one side, and the sea behind them. The narrative then reveals
God's purpose in making his people so vulnerable: 'Pharaoh will
think, "The Israelites are . . . hemmed in by the desert"' (14:3).
Indeed, this response is guaranteed, because the Lord declares, 'I
will harden Pharaoh's heart' (v. 4). From the beginning, God
has engineered both salvation and judgment through the waters of
the sea, so that 'I will gain glory for myself through Pharaoh and
all his army, and *the Egyptians will know that I am the LORD*' (v. 4). The
dramatic destruction of the army of Pharaoh in the waters of the
sea is ascribed solely to the work of the Divine Warrior. Once
again, the Lord announces his purpose in luring the Egyptians to
the sea:

> Then I will harden the hearts of the Egyptians so that they will go in
> after them; and so I will gain glory for myself over Pharaoh and all his
> army, his chariots, and his chariot drivers. *And the Egyptians shall know that*
> *I am the LORD*, when I have gained glory for myself over Pharaoh, his
> chariots, and his chariot drivers. (14:17 NRSV; my emphasis).

The liberation from slavery in Egypt is seen, first and foremost,
as a vindication of the authority of Yahweh over the false gods of
the Egyptians (5:2; 7:8–13, 22–24; 8:6–7, 16–19; 9:10–11). It is also
clear from the narrative that the divine liberation is effected by the
Lord for his people, Israel, on account of the covenant promises
he made to Israel. As Chris Wright (2006: 266) has pointed out,
Yahweh here works as Israel's 'kinsman-redeemer', the *gō'ēl* (6:1–8).
Such a person 'was any member within a wider family group upon

whom fell the duty of acting to protect the interests of the family
or another member in it who was in particular need'. It is critical
to appreciate that the Lord acts for Israel on the basis of the fact
that he has covenantly bound himself to her, and this commits
him to intervene powerfully to effect her rescue and ultimate well-
being.

The exodus motif in the Bible

We must now turn briefly to examine the use of the exodus motif
in the rest of the Bible. The claim of many, if not the majority,
today is that God's initiative in rescuing the oppressed in Egypt is
the paradigm for God's action on behalf of all the oppressed
throughout history. In Egypt, Yahweh revealed his true colours: he
is on the side of the poor and downtrodden and wherever injustice
raises its ugly head, we find God working to liberate 'his people'.
In short, 'the good news of this Exodus story is that God can be
trusted to oppose and defeat all power arrangements directed
against the full experiencing of human well-being' (Birch et al.
2005: 114).

The exodus event stands as the foundational event in the
nation's history. Psalm 136 calls on God's people to 'Give thanks to
the LORD, for he is good', and the refrain 'His love endures for
ever' echoes through every verse of the psalm. The psalmist
describes the two events that demonstrate the Lord's beneficence:
his creation of the world (vv. 4–9) and his deliverance of Israel
from bondage in Egypt (vv. 10–24):

> To him who struck down the firstborn of Egypt
>   His love endures for ever
> And brought Israel out from among them
>   His love endures for ever.
>   (Ps. 136:10–11)

The deliverance from Egypt was the reason for the Lord's
demand that his people 'Observe the Sabbath day by keeping it
holy' (Deut. 5:12–15). It marks her New Year's Day (Exod. 12:2)

and, most importantly of all, it was commemorated annually in the central festival of the Jewish calendar, the Passover.[2]

Throughout the OT the exodus is regularly appealed to as a reminder of God's saving faithfulness to Israel, with the implication that the unchanging God will continue to care for his people (e.g. Pss 77:13ff.; 103:7–8; 135:1–9; Josh. 24:5–7; 2 Sam. 7:23–24). It is also referred to as a rebuke to Israel for her present sin; how can a nation forget all that the Lord has done for her in the past, especially in her liberation from slavery (e.g. 2 Kgs 17:7; Mic. 6:4). Finally, it serves as a cause of hope for the future; as the Lord once redeemed his people, so again there will be an even more glorious new exodus (e.g. Isa. 43:16–17; Jer. 16:14–15; Amos 9:7).

When we come to the NT, we move immediately from the world of historical antecedent and promise, to fulfilment. From the outset, Matthew's Gospel announces that the Lord Jesus will, in some typological sense, recapitulate the history of the nation of Israel. For example, he sees the eventual return of the infant Christ and his refugee family from Egypt back to Israel as a re-enactment of the nation's flight from Egypt centuries before (Matt. 2:13–15). As that initial exodus inaugurated the old covenant, so this next 'exodus' initiates the new one.

Supremely, though, the NT sees the redemptive act of God in the exodus as pointing forward to, and ultimately fulfilled in the sacrifice of Jesus Christ, the Passover lamb (1 Cor. 5:7; 11:25). The book of Hebrews takes this further, presenting the narrative events of the book of Exodus as a foreshadowing of the Christians' life of discipleship. The wandering in the wilderness and the ultimate taking of possession of the Promised Land become the model for the church's life of faith and obedience that, like Israel, will result in her entering her 'rest' (Heb. 4). For believers, ancient and modern, to turn back in apostasy is to repeat the sin of Israel, who, seeing the dangers that lay before them in possessing the land, were tempted to return to Egypt.

The NT, therefore, repeatedly sees the exodus as an event in

---

2. For a useful survey of the importance of Exodus in biblical theology, see Watts 2000: 478–487.

salvation history that actually points forward to, and is therefore fulfilled in, the greater deliverance Christ won for his people on the cross, and the subsequent life of pilgrimage of the followers of Christ. One must not underestimate the importance of how the NT interprets and applies the exodus narrative. It is inaccurate to describe the NT's treatment of these events as a 'spiritualizing'.[3] The correct categories by which we should view the relationship of the history of Israel and the NT is not physical/spiritual but antecedent/fulfilment. However, while some critics have rightly rejected 'spiritualizing' interpretations of the narrative, many would see the approach presented here as similarly reductionistic. It is argued that we must see the exodus as the paradigm for a holistic view of mission. That is, the liberation we must commit ourselves to as Christians must be both spiritual, that is, the forgiveness of sins and reconciliation with God, and political, expressed in working to release those entrapped in concrete conditions of socio-economic bondage.

It is claimed, first, that the parallel between the cross and the exodus does not really fit because 'there is no hint whatsoever that Israel's suffering in Egypt was God's judgment on their sin' (Wright 2006: 278). While it is true that the text does not make such a direct link, there are nevertheless clear indications in the book of Exodus itself that Israel was not guiltless, but rather was complicit in the idolatry of the Egyptians. This is borne out by the incident with the golden calf which demonstrated that idolatry was the nation's automatic default position once they felt weak and vulnerable. Clearly, the nation had deeply imbibed the idolatrous habits of the host nation. Indeed, the OT prophets make this charge of idolatry against Israel during her sojourn in Egypt explicit (Ezek. 20:4–10). Through the prophet God recalls his words to Israel back in Egypt, 'Each of you, get rid of the vile images you have set your

---

3. I am indebted to Hefin Jones and John Woodhouse for this observation. Arguing that the NT 'spiritualizes' OT narratives, in an almost Platonic way places their fulfilment in a realm removed from the material and the historical. Of course, the fulfilment of OT antecedents is thoroughly grounded in time and space.

eyes on, and do not defile yourselves with the idols of Egypt. I am
the LORD your God' (Ezek. 20:7). What is more, the text presents
Israel as a nation only prepared to commit itself to the word of
the Lord spoken through his servant Moses on the basis of dem-
onstrations of wonder-working power (Exod. 4:29–31; 5:20–21).
The plagues may not have been judgment on Israel, but the deliverance was an act of undeserved mercy.[4]

Secondly, those who affirm a holistic interpretation fail to give
due attention to the covenantal dimensions of the exodus. This
was the Lord, the *gō'ēl*, redeeming his people. There is no mention
of any other peoples resident in Egypt at the time whom the Lord
redeemed or any other nations surrounding Egypt that were being
oppressed by similarly despotic rulers. Consistently, it is his people,
and those who by incorporation associate themselves with his
people, that the Lord acts to save. It simply is not true that
'YHWH is ultimately no more concerned for Israel's freedom and
blessing than for other people' (Goldingay, quoted in Wright 2006:
283). Throughout the Pentateuch it is affirmed that the Lord has
committed himself in covenant to this people, and this people
alone. Certainly, a redeemed Israel was to be the means by which
God would bring blessing to the nations in accordance with the
promise to Abraham, but under the old covenant this blessing
came by the nations attaching themselves to Israel, and under the

---

4. It has also been pointed out that the final and most devastating plague on
   Egypt, the killing of the firstborn, was different both in character and
   effect from the earlier plagues. Consistently, the text highlights that the
   other plagues fell on Egypt, but not on the people of Israel. While the
   text is explicit that this judgment also is directed solely at Pharaoh and the
   Egyptians, and not Israel (11:1, 5, 7, 12–13), yet it is striking that in this
   final plague the Israelites are not automatically spared death. It is only the
   covering of the shed blood of a lamb that causes the angel of death to
   pass over God's people. Some have suggested that this is because Israel,
   too, were guilty of worshipping the gods of Egypt and therefore needed
   atonement. The text does not make that link, although it is clear that only
   the blood of the animal sacrifices spares Israel from suffering the same
   judgment as the godless Egyptians (Jeffery, Ovey and Sach 2007: 38).

new covenant it is by the nations attaching themselves to Israel's Messiah. In short, the exodus narrative is not a paradigm for God's preferential option for the poor and oppressed, whoever, whenever and wherever they might be found. It is a paradigm of God's covenant faithfulness, expressed in redemption, and enacted in favour of his chosen, yet unworthy, people.

Introduction to liberation theology

The birth of a movement

In the light of this, we must now turn to examine a very significant contemporary theological movement that has emphasized the political dimension of God's redemptive work, namely liberation theology. In the late 1960s, theologians like Gustavo Gutiérrez, Hugo Assman and Emilio Castro began developing a theological response to the widespread suffering of the poor in many Latin American countries. The plight of these oppressed reached the public eye with the assassination of the Catholic Archbishop of El Salvador, Oscar Romero, on 24 March 1980. Violence perpetrated by the US-backed government had left over 75,000 Salvadorans dead and forced more than a million (out of a population of only 5.5 million) to flee the country. Romero famously wrote to President Jimmy Carter, begging his government to stop sending military aid to the oppressors (the US sent $1.5 million in aid every day for twelve years). Carter never replied and two months later the archbishop was assassinated when leaving an 8.00am Mass, as members of the National Guard opened fire indiscriminately on the worshippers.

Liberation theology in a nutshell

In a nutshell, liberation theology is faith confronted by *oppression*. Charles Bayer writes:

> Liberation Theology is first of all about the oppressed. It views the Christian faith through the eyes of the poor, the wretched of the earth, the non-person. It proclaims God's solidarity with the left out and the destitute, the ratted on and spat upon. (1986: 15)

Even in this brief statement one can feel the author's rage. Proponents of liberation theology are angry and unapologetically so. In the face of the scandal of oppression, whatever insidious form it takes, the only appropriate response is seen to be righteous anger that expresses itself in forceful action. It is said to be the same righteous anger that has motivated God throughout history to identify with the oppressed and marginalized, and to work with them to change and overthrow those sinful structures that keep people locked into their endless cycle of misery, oppression and dehumanization.

Liberation theology has grown and metamorphosed into new forms since the 1960s. From identifying with the poor of Latin America in their struggle for justice, the motif of liberation has been adopted by many groups who sense that they have been marginalized and dehumanized by oppressive regimes and social structures. For example, since the 1980s minjung (literally 'the mass of the people') theology has emerged in South Korea. It is a response to the corporate economic entities who, in their search for profits and economic hegemony, have left in their wake millions of victims. One Korean theologian writes:

> The economic victimization of the people, – Minjung, communities and consumers, – will be absolute and limitless in the global market and dominated by the mammonism of the giant corporate entities, led by the global financial corporate powers. The financial victimization of the people will be noiseless and bloodless but extremely effective. Natural life, human persons, the hungry, the poor and even the not-so-poor middle class people, together with relatively weak economic agencies, will be powerless economic losers in the globally competitive market.[5]

Minjung liberation theology is just one expression of the attempt to build on the work of the pioneering Latin American theologians and apply their insights to the South Korean situation.

---

5. Yong-Bok Kim, 'Minjung and Power: A Biblical and Theological Perspective on Doularchy', <http://www.religion-online.org/showarticle.asp?title=94>, accessed 29 Feb. 2008.

Most notably we have also seen the emergence of a potent Black American liberation theology, feminist liberation theology and, more recently, gay and lesbian liberation theology.

Liberation theology hermeneutics

Supremely, liberation theology is committed to action on behalf of the poor. Charles Bayer writes:

> [Liberation theology] is not overly fascinated with how you interpret the Bible; what the scholarly evidence is for believing this doctrine or that. It is first of all concerned with doing the truth, not understanding it or even believing it . . . [it] is about orthopraxis – right action – not orthodoxy – right belief, or more accurately, right praise. (1986: 16)[6]

One can generalize that for liberation theologians their first act as practitioners of theology is not a study of the Scriptures or the historical traditions of theology. The first act is a commitment to the liberation of the poor. James Cone, the most forceful spokesman for Black theology, asserts that 'our cultural identity and political commitment are worth more than a thousand textbooks on theology' (1999: 148). He goes on to say:

> We do not begin our theology with a reflection on divine revelation as if the God of our faith is separate from the suffering of our people. We do not believe that revelation is a deposit of fixed doctrines or an objective word of God that is then applied to the human situation. On the contrary we contend that there is no truth outside or beyond the concrete historical events in which persons are engaged as agents. (148)

---

6. Interestingly, one finds this same commitment to the primacy of orthopraxy over orthodoxy in the writings of the leading spokesperson for the Emerging Church movement, Brian McLaren (himself a supporter of liberation theology). For McLaren getting theology right 'is beside the point; the point is being and doing good as followers of Jesus Christ, in our unique time and place, fitting in with the ongoing story of God's saving love for planet Earth' (2004: 214).

For writers like Cone, formulating a theology of liberation begins with the social context rather than the biblical texts themselves. Truth is the oppression of the dispossessed. That is the starting point in doing theology. For Cone, truth is not objective; it is subjective. It is a personal experience of God in the midst of the degradation of victimization. For Cone, this contextualized view of truth means that whether an individual is one of the oppressed or an oppressor will determine how you perceive truth and therefore how you do theology. In short, the God of the slave must be a different God from the God of the slave owner. Black religion and white religion are not essentially the same.

One does not turn to the Bible to discover the truth of the human condition; that is revealed as historical events unfold. The Bible then becomes a useful resource that supports this prior understanding of the nature of reality. For example, Korean liberation theologian Yong-Bok Kim candidly admits that the Bible is used as a reference, not as the norm, of minjung theology. Having understood the social context, the theologian's second task is then to scour the pages of Scripture to find any examples of an analogous historical condition, and how the God of Israel and Jesus Christ responded to that condition. For this reason, liberation theologians embrace the account of the exodus and God's work in setting Israel free. In this instance, their search has unearthed in the Bible's reporting of historical events the twin themes of God's identity with the poor and oppressed and his working through these events, synergistically with men and women, for the liberation of those who were marginalized. Of course, this reading of the Bible is avowedly selective. Liberation theologians pay no attention, say, to the book of Joshua, where this same Lord instructs his people to kill or enslave the Canaanite nations.

It follows from all this that linguistic questions like the precise meaning of a particular Hebrew word or phrase, or contextual questions that examine the place and purpose of the passage in the larger narrative, or questions regarding the historicity of the event are largely irrelevant to liberation theologians. The meaning, say, of the exodus event is determined by the modern context. Reality is the scandal of oppression. It is through the lens of this 'truth' that all biblical texts are to be weighed and understood. The correct 'interpretation' of any given passage is that interpretation which illuminates God's attitude towards servitude and tyranny and endorses political efforts to bring about liberation. The text of Scripture, therefore, is quite evidently the handmaid of the interpreter, and it exists to justify his or her own prior theological and political commitments.

There is among liberation theologians a thinly disguised contempt for those whose hermeneutical method begins with the study of Scripture, and then seeks to understand the meaning of a given text, and apply that authoritative meaning to a changing cultural context. This is doing theology the wrong way around. By way of illustration theologians of liberation, while admitting the account of the death of Jesus is open to other interpretations, will emphasize the political dimension of the cross (the oppression of the innocent by the corrupt political power) because this gives the ancient text contemporary relevance. Traditional interpretations of the death of Christ as an atoning sacrifice are not necessarily denied, but largely de-legitimized in the face of the overwhelming contemporary reality of oppression. Of course, such a hermeneutical method means that many parts of the Bible are of little contemporary value and much of traditional hermeneutics has nothing to offer.

The exodus motif in liberation theology

In seeking to find in the Scriptures of the Christian church some justification for their political struggle against oppression, not surprisingly the biblical account of the exodus from Egypt is paradigmatic for liberation theologians. It is the example par excellence of God's expression of compassionate identification with the oppressed, and his action to achieve their liberation. Along with the Gospels' recording of Jesus Christ's identification with the poor and marginalized of ancient Palestine, the liberation of the oppressed Hebrew slaves in Egypt provides liberation theologians with the support they need in affirming God's historical alignment with movements of liberation throughout history. For Robert McAfee Brown, 'If there is a single passage that encapsulates the liberation themes of the Bible, it is the exodus story, describing a God who takes sides, intervening to free the poor and oppressed' (1978: 88).

We can survey only briefly the extent to which various liberation theologians utilize the exodus narrative. They do not engage in detailed exegesis. As we have seen, this event simply serves as historical precedent that legitimizes and inspires similar contemporary movements. Indeed, it is largely irrelevant to such theologians whether or not they are perceived by the biblical academy to have interpreted the text rightly. The only 'text' that needs proper interpretation is the modern text of oppression writ large on the faces of the poor everywhere. That is the truth they are seeking to expound.

Latin American liberation theology

The exodus event is central and pivotal to Latin American liberation theology. In reflecting upon that event, Juan Luis Segundo comments that 'In no other portion of Scripture does God the liberator reveal himself in such close connection with the political plane of human existence' (cited in Nuñez 1985: 187). Gustavo Gutiérrez and other Latin American theologians consider the exodus to be primarily a political event. Most do not deny that it was also spiritual, but this is not where their emphasis lies. The great value of the exodus event for these theologians lies in its presentation of God as the liberator, and the political process of liberation that led to the emancipation of the Hebrews.

Of course, even a fairly superficial reading of the text will demonstrate that this is very much an imposed interpretation. The Latin American liberation theologians' view of salvation is traditionally Catholic; that is, it is the synergistic relationship of human beings and God cooperating together to bring about the mutually desired result of rescue from oppression. Further, it is clear from the narrative that there was no popular uprising in Egypt, no attempt to overthrow corrupt powers, and Israel did not devise a political project to change the structures of society. Indeed, they weren't even told to remain in the society in order to transform it. They were to leave Egypt altogether (Nuñez 1985: 190). And, as we have seen, the focus of the event is the oppression of God's people; the text is silent about the oppression of other peoples.

However, these hermeneutical issues are irrelevant to contemporary theologians. Given the existential reality of oppression, the exegete is free to interpret the text in a way that will address this 'truth'. The only God who can speak to the plight of the marginalized of Latin America and inspire them to confront the oppressors is a God who lifts up the poor and brings down the rich, and the role of the theologian is to search and interpret the Scriptures in order to find and announce such a God.

Feminist liberation theology

Across the theological spectrum women have turned to liberation theology as a means of expressing their own sense of victimization. Of course, one must not give the impression that feminist liberationism is a unified monolithic movement. It takes various forms. Black American women identify their movement as 'womanist theology', while the liberation of Hispanic women is termed 'mujerista theology'. These movements sprang out of the feminist movement of a generation ago that sought to end the historical exclusion of women from those roles and positions in society traditionally dominated by men. Today feminist liberationists seek to emancipate women from any area where it is perceived they are oppressed and dominated by men, even where women themselves might not perceive they are oppressed. Catherina Hawkes identifies one of the great challenges facing feminist liberationists to be convincing women who resist the movement, insisting they are not oppressed: such women 'not only deny themselves but unknowingly deny millions of women who are being sold, raped, and sexually mistreated because of their female body' (1988: 228).

However, for all their differences, they share in common both with themselves and with other liberation movements a common hermeneutic. Their starting point is the present context, which is the reality of patriarchal oppression, and their exegesis is selective. Irrespective of literary context, a given text in Scripture serves as an inspiration for liberation more than a precise identification of the nature of the divine liberation.

Once again, the exodus motif is prominent, in particular the figure of Miriam. For a number of these liberationists she has become significant both as symbol of the lost prophetic leadership of women (Grey 1999: 96), and as the one who led the emancipated people in their song of victory as they left behind their oppression and bondage.

Gay and lesbian

One of the more recent of these advocacy movements is the gay/lesbian/bisexual/transgendered, or what is termed more colloquially as 'queer theology'. They, too, like their peers in other liberation movements, challenge the oppression and discrimination they face, particularly from those within the church. While adopting the nomenclature 'liberation theology', there is less reference to, or dependence upon, the Exodus narrative in their writings. More important for advocates of this movement is to confront the so-called, 'texts of terror', challenging the traditional interpretations that support and make normative heterosexuality.

Black American liberation theology

Independently of the work of Gustavo Gutiérrez and other theologians in Latin America, Black American Christians were beginning themselves to retheologize, and were reaching conclusions that were very similar to those of their Catholic cousins south of the border.

The roots of Black American liberation theology go back much further than those of the Latinos. For Black liberation theologians the material for their theological reflections are 'the twin realities of slavery in the past and the experience of racism in the future' (Antonio 1999: 63). The deeply moving and trenchant *Appeal to the Coloured Citizens of the World* by the nineteenth-century emancipationist David Walker (1785–1830) is considered the founding text of black nationalist thought. Walker, the son of a slave father and a free mother, and himself born a free black, became one of the most articulate, passionate and militant opponents to slavery. He championed the overthrow by force of slavery until he was found dead in 1830, presumed to be a victim of poison.

The purpose of his *Appeal* was to demonstrate that the coloured people of the United States 'are the *most wretched, degraded* and *abject* set of beings that *ever lived* since the world began', and that their treatment at the hands of 'the enlightened and Christian people' is more cruel than that inflicted by any heathens. To support his case he points to the comparatively benign treatment of the Hebrews at the hands of the Egyptians. His treatment of the Egyptian sojourn, and then captivity, climaxes with these impassioned words:

> But to prove farther that the condition of the Israelites was better under the Egyptians than ours is under the whites I call upon the professing Christians, I call upon the philanthropist, I call upon the very tyrant himself, to show me a page of history, either sacred or profane, on which a verse can be found, which maintains, that the Egyptians heaped the *insupportable insult* upon the children of Israel, by telling them that they were not of the *human family*. Can the whites deny this charge? Have they not, after having reduced us to the deplorable condition of slaves under their feet, held us up as descending originally from the tribes of *Monkeys* or *Orang-Outangs?* O my God! I appeal to every man of feeling – is not this insupportable? Is it not heaping the most gross insult upon our miseries, because they have got us under their feet and we cannot help ourselves? Oh! pity us we pray thee, Lord Jesus, Master . . . So far, my brethren, were the Egyptians from heaping these insults upon their slaves, that Pharaoh's daughter took Moses, a son of Israel for her own . . .[7]

The pain of oppression David Walker so eloquently put into prose other black slaves put into poetry and song. Repeatedly, human suffering and oppression is the cauldron in which music and singing is born. The many biblical psalms of lament testify to that. Similarly, black slavery in the United States gave birth to the now widely acclaimed and studied Negro spirituals. In these songs, the Blacks expressed their longing for physical and political emancipation in covert biblical metaphors. The songs were

---

7. D. Walker, *Appeal to the Coloured Citizens of the World*, <http://afroamhistory. about.com/library/blwalkerpreamble.htm>, accessed 10 Mar., 2008.

full of coded messages and hidden meaning (see e.g. Newman 1998). For example, in the popular 'Swing Low, Sweet Chariot' the chariot that takes them across the Jordan is a reference to the Underground Railroad that would carry them to safety across the Ohio River. On the other side they would meet fugitives who would help them find refuge: 'a band of angels coming after me'. The theme of the exodus reappears in these songs of hope and liberation. Many of these spirituals utilized the theme of the crossing of the Jordan, marking the exodus from a life of bondage into a new world of freedom. Just two examples will suffice:

Didn't old Pharaoh get los'
Moses an infant cast away
By Pharaoh's daughter found
Didn't old Pharaoh get los', get los', get los'
Didn't old Pharaoh get los'
In the Red Sea (True believer)
O, didn't old Pharaoh get los', get los', get los'
Didn't old Pharaoh get los'
In the Red Sea.

Go down Moses
Go down Moses
Way down in Egypt land
Tell ole Pharaoh
To let my people go
When Israel was in Egypt land
Let my people go
Oppressed so hard they could not stand
Let my people go
'Thus spoke the Lord,' bold Moses said
'If not, I'll smite your first born dead
Let my people go.'

Contemporary black liberation theologians point to men like David Walker as their inspiration for their own advocacy for justice in today's America. In particular, such early emancipationists

displayed 'the usefulness of the Bible as a support for the liberation of the black poor' (Cone 1999: 63).

Working independently of Gustavo Gutiérrez, yet reaching very
similar conclusions, the ideological leader of Black liberation
theology is James Cone. A Protestant minister from Arkansas,
Cone experienced first hand the dreadful injustice of segregation,
often both perpetrated and perpetuated by white Christians. This
demonstrated to him the bankruptcy of much of Western theology.
Blacks now had to construct their own theology.

We have already observed that for Cone, revelation is God
making himself known in an event, most especially the two
paradigmatic events of the exodus and God's self-disclosure in
Christ. References to the exodus, which demonstrate that God's
revelation is identical with his power to liberate the downtrodden,
appear in virtually all his writings (Antonio 1999: 78). He wrote:

> We black theologians contended that if God sided with the poor and
> weak in biblical times, then why not today? If salvation is a historical
> event of rescue, a deliverance of slaves from Egypt, why not a black
> power event today and a deliverance of blacks from white American
> racial oppression? (Cone 1999: 65)

Reflections on liberation theology, the exodus motif and the gospel for the oppressed

The reality of oppression

Article 4 of the Universal Declaration of Human Rights declares
that 'No one shall be held in slavery or servitude; slavery and the
slave trade shall be prohibited in all their forms.' Sadly, despite
United Nations resolutions, and the fact that this is the bicen-
tenary of the remarkable achievements of William Wilberforce,
slavery has never been as prevalent as it is now. Just a few of the
statistics are sobering, indeed frightening.[8] According to estimates

---

8. I am indebted to Anti-Slavery International, <http://www.antislavery.
   org>, accessed 29 Feb. 2008, for these figures regarding slavery.

by the International Labour Organization (ILO) there are over 200 million working children between the ages of 5 and 14 years, and 49% are girls. For many of these, the work is extremely hazardous, putting their health, education, development to adulthood and even their lives at risk. Many of these children work because their families are poor and their labour is needed for their survival. Employers often exploit children because they are more vulnerable, cheaper to hire than adults and are less likely to demand higher wages or better working conditions.

Today, there are at least 20 million bonded labourers in the world. Bonded labour, or debt bondage, is probably the most widely used method of enslaving people. Such labourers are forced to work to repay debts their employer says they owe. In many cases, entire families are kept like cattle on agricultural estates in South Asia, or women and children are exported into domestic or sexual slavery. According to some reports, seven hundred thousand women and children are trafficked globally each year.

Historically, Christians have been at the forefront of endeavours to eradicate such physical and moral scourges from our world. Thankfully, many today, both religious and non-religious, are campaigning for justice for such victims of oppression. Our theological commitments must ensure that we, as the people of God, partner others in such works, and initiate programmes of liberation in those places where the oppressed are neglected. The people of God ought to honour and support those within their community who pursue this good work.

God's preferential option for the poor

The fact of the scandal of such human slavery has led Christians of all theological persuasions to campaign for social action, and most have found their justification for doing so in the precedent set down for us in the Scriptures, particularly the account of the liberation of God's people from bondage in Egypt. At the heart of all these advocacy movements is the creedal statement affirming God's preferential option for the poor. In this, liberation theology is quite right – and quite wrong. It is remarkable that in virtually all the writings on the Christians' obligations to the poor, nothing is made of the fact that the overwhelming majority of references to the poor in the Bible, and the faithful believer's responsibility to meet the needs of the poor, are focused on the poor within the covenant people of God. Deuteronomy says, 'If there is a poor man *among your brothers* in any of towns of the land . . . do not be hardhearted or tightfisted *toward your poor brother*' (Deut. 15:7; my emphasis). Amos warns the 'cows of Bashan' against oppressing and crushing the poor and needy *within Israel* (Amos 4:1ff.). In the frequently misinterpreted parable of the sheep and goats, Jesus acknowledges that a practically expressed action of love done 'to the least of these my brethren' is an action done to Christ. It is therefore affirmed that Christ is present in the poor, irrespective of their faith commitment. Aside from the enormous theological ramifications of such a claim, it runs counter to the fact that Jesus Christ explicitly identifies his 'brothers' as the disciples in Matthew's Gospel (e.g. Matt. 10:40–42; 12:48–49; 28:10). Paul raised money for poor *saints* in Jerusalem (2 Cor. 8:4). There is no indication that his concern or generosity extended to the unbelieving Jews. When James says that true religion is to care for orphans and widows in their distress, he is probably speaking of the orphans and widows in the Christian community.

All of this is entirely consistent with the apostle Paul's succinct exhortation 'let us do good to all people, especially to those who belong to the family of believers' (Gal. 6:10). The term 'especially' (*malista*) is a superlative, meaning 'most of all' or 'first of all'. There is a very clear prioritizing of the believer's responsibilities to those in need. None of this is meant to imply that we are to disregard the vast majority of other people who are in desperate physical need. This very verse exhorts us to do good to all people. Further, the command to love our enemies, the fact that God sends rain upon the just and the unjust, and the parable of the good Samaritan, all remind us that our concern for those in need must reach beyond the boundaries of the covenant people of God. Indeed, our Christian anthropology must lead us to campaign for social justice and work tirelessly to seek to alleviate the suffering of the poor. Every human being is made in the image of God and is of inestimable value to his Maker. The saving of one life or the deliverance of one man or woman from the bonds of oppression is an act of enormous worth.

However, this should not detract from the fact that the priority in the Scriptures is the poor of the covenant people of God. It is surprising, then, that most Christian social justice agencies take pride in the fact that they are completely impartial in their distribution of aid when, in fact, the Bible explicitly directs us to be partial. Further, the question must at least be asked, 'What other implications for Christian ministry to the unbelieving world flow from this biblical emphasis?' The consistent testimony of Scripture is that God has a preferential option for the poor among *his* people, and this is precisely what we witness in the deliverance of Israel from Egypt.

The new missiological paradigm

Many evangelicals, while sympathetic with the human suffering that has given birth to the theological response known as liberation theology, would distance themselves from its overt emphasis on political action and its deliberate marginalization of the call to evangelism. Mind you, while liberation theologians and advocates of a gospel of social justice have remained unswervingly committed to their social and political agendas, the history of evangelicalism since the 1960s, and in particular since the watershed event of the 1974 Lausanne Congress on World Evangelization, has been a movement away from a traditional prioritizing of evangelism in the mission of the church, to a commitment to holistic mission and, indeed, forms of ministry much more compatible with liberation theology.

It is remarkable that in less than one generation holistic mission has now become entrenched as the new evangelical paradigm. Thomas Kuhn acutely observed in 1962, in the context of scientific revolutions, that established paradigms can be bitterly intolerant of any new (or in this case old) challenges to their ideological hegemony. This is precisely what we observe with holistic mission. Recently a leading American evangelical NT scholar publicly stated how 'distressing' (his words) it is that some other evangelical biblical scholars are seeking to return the biblical theology of mission back to the 'Dark Ages' (my words) of the primacy of gospel proclamation. As illustrative of this disturbing regression he mentioned the recent extensive theologies of mission by Eckhard Schnabel (2004), and Andreas J. Köstenberger and Peter T. O'Brien (2001). Clearly, a commitment to anything but a holistic mission that gives no priority to either the physical and temporal or the spiritual and eternal, irrespective of where the Scriptures might lead, is unacceptable.

Of course, those who advocate holistic mission appear to hold the moral high ground. To argue that, biblically, the mission of Jesus and the apostles was primarily focused on proclaiming the good news of the liberation from sin and slavery to Satan leads to the criticism that such armchair theologians only demonstrate their 'distressing' lack of concern for people's physical, emotional and psychological needs. Mind you, both the history of Christian mission and much contemporary missionary practice bear testimony to the many servants of the gospel who have fervently believed in the primacy of the need for people's reconciliation with God, and yet have laboured tirelessly to minister to the whole person. The 'Father of Modern Mission', William Carey, is just one eloquent example.

So, what does it matter? Are we simply arguing over words? One argues for no priority in physical and spiritual liberation, while another does. If, in the end, both are committed to a Christian ministry of word and deed, isn't this just another Western armchair debate, the very thing liberation theologians have been railing against? Sadly, no. If contemporary mission practice demonstrates that normatively gospel proclaimers have also committed themselves to meeting all the needs of the people to whom they have been sent, it also demonstrates how quickly and easily evangelization and discipleship diminish in importance and urgency when it is affirmed that there should be no prioritizing of physical and spiritual liberation in Christian mission. The sad reality often is that, while rejecting any principled prioritizing of one over the other, so often the ministry of the proclamation of the liberation from sin and the wrath to come is muted in the face of the overwhelming needs of the poor and the urgency of action on their behalf.

Nothing demonstrated that more acutely than the recent Lausanne Forum on World Evangelization held in Pattaya,

Thailand, in 2004. The conferees were told to repent of elevating
the Evangelistic Commission over the Creation Commission,
which esteems daily work, and over the Relational Commission to
love one another. Similarly, tentmakers were publicly called to
repent for not obeying the creation/cultural mandate and for
focusing on evangelism. In plenary reports, only a few spoke of
the need for evangelization; the overwhelming message was the
challenge to meet human physical need. There were cheers and
applause for those who advocated ministry to the poor and needy,
which emotionally strangled and marginalized those who wanted
to argue for the primacy of evangelism.

Perhaps had this been a conference on world mission one could
have understood these emphases (although I would still challenge
them), but this was a Lausanne Forum on World *Evangelization!*
When asked, 'Where is the gospel of the forgiveness of sins,' the
reply consistently came back that, in all that is said, it is implied.
Well, at a conference explicitly on world evangelization it needs to
be more than implied; it needs to be loudly heralded. Too often
the silence of Lausanne 2004 on proclaiming the good news of
the forgiveness of sins in the light of the coming day of wrath was
deafening. Lausanne 2004 was a telling demonstration of the
extent to which holistic mission has established itself as the new
missiological paradigm, and its unyielding intolerance of any perceived overemphasis on the verbal proclamation of the gospel to
lost sinners.

Why hermeneutics matters

There is a great gulf between liberation theologians and evangelical theologians in hermeneutical method. Consequently, there is a
great gulf in their diagnosis of the human condition and, therefore, the nature of our varied engagement with the world. While
acknowledging the importance of ministry to those trapped in the
different kinds of slavery, I would argue that a right understanding
of the place and purpose of the exodus narrative in biblical theology points to another, deeper and far more serious, bondage that
enslaves *all* human beings. Cruel as contemporary slave owners

are, there is another who holds men and women in bondage who is himself quintessentially evil. Tragic as are the consequences of a lifetime spent in the shackles of chattel slavery, sex slavery and debt bondage, almost too terrible to contemplate are the eternal consequences for those who remain captive to sin and the forces of darkness. None of this minimizes the scandal of contemporary expressions of physical slavery, but it magnifies what is the great theme of Scripture. These are not the armchair debates of emotionally distant theologians, but are ever-present human realities.

As we noted earlier, it is critical that we commit ourselves to defending orthodox theology and continue to strive for accurate and faithful understanding of the text of Scripture; otherwise we shall indeed sow the wind and reap the whirlwind. In this regard, it is appropriate that the great William Wilberforce have the last word. Speaking of his own day and the rending asunder of orthodoxy and orthopraxis he observed:

> The fatal habit of considering Christian morals as distinct from Christian doctrines insensibly gained strength. Thus the peculiar doctrines of Christianity went more and more out of sight, and as might naturally have been expected, the moral system itself also began to wither and decay, being robbed of that which should have supplied it with life and nutriment. (Cited in John Piper 2002: 116)

In our day, the 'peculiar doctrines' of the holiness of God, the seriousness of sin, the depravity of the human race, and the terror of judgment and the wrath to come have gone 'more and more out of sight'. It is little wonder, then, that some in the evangelical church have sought to place their energies and priorities in works of liberation compatible with those who historically have not shared our theological and hermeneutical commitments.

Bibliography

Anti-Slavery International, <http://www.antislavery.org>, accessed 29 Feb. 2008.

Antonio, E. (1999), 'Black Theology', in C. Rowland (ed.), *The Cambridge*

Companion to Liberation Theology, Cambridge: Cambridge University Press, 63–88.

Bayer, C. H. (1986), *A Guide to Liberation Theology for Middle Class Congregations*, St. Louis: CBP.

Birch, B. C., W. Brueggemann, T. Fretheim and D. L. Petersen (2005), *A Theological Introduction to the Old Testament*, 2nd ed., Nashville: Abingdon.

Cone, J. (1999), *For My People: Black Theology and the Black Church*, Maryknoll: Orbis.

Cox, C. Baroness, and John Marks (2006), *This Immoral Trade: Slavery in the 21st Century*, Oxford: Monarch.

Fretheim, T. E. (2003), 'Book of Exodus', in T. D. Alexander and D. W. Baker (eds.), *Dictionary of the Old Testament: Pentateuch*, Leicester: IVP, 249–258.

Goldingay, J. (2003), *Old Testament Theology*. Vol. 1: *Israel's Gospel*, Downers Grove: IVP.

Grey, M. (1999), 'Feminist Theology: A Critical Theology of Liberation', in Rowland, *Cambridge Companion to Liberation Theology*, 89–106.

Hawkes, C. (1988), 'Christian Feminism and Liberation Spirituality', *Spirituality Today* 40: 220–236. Also <http://www.spiritualitytoday.org/spir2day/884033halkes.html>, accessed 29 Feb. 2008.

Jeffery, S., M. Ovey and A. Sach (2007), *Pierced for our Transgressions: Rediscovering the Glory of Penal Substitution*, Nottingham: IVP.

Kim, Yong-Bok , 'Minjung and Power: A Biblical and Theological Perspective on Doularchy', <http://www.religion-online.org/showarticle.asp?title=94>, accessed 29 Feb. 2008.

Köstenberger, A. J. and P. T. O'Brien (2001), *Salvation to the Ends of the Earth*, Leicester: Apollos.

McAfee Brown, R. (1978), *Theology in a New Key*, Philadelphia: Westminster.

McLaren, B. (2004), *A Generous Orthodoxy*, Grand Rapids: Zondervan.

Newman, R. (1998), *Go Down Moses: Celebrating the African-American Spiritual*, Lakeville: Clarkson Potter.

Nuñez, E. (1985), *Liberation Theology*, Chicago: Moody.

Piper, J. (2002), *The Roots of Endurance*, Leicester: IVP.

Schnabel, E. J. (2004), *Early Christian Mission*, vols. 1, 2, Leicester: Apollos.

Stuart, D. (2006), *Exodus*, New American Commentary, Nashville: Broadman & Holman, 2006.

Walker, D., *Appeal to the Coloured Citizens of the World*, <http://afroamhistory.about.com/library/blwalkerpreamble.htm>, accessed 10 Mar., 2008.

Watts, R. E. (2000), 'Exodus', in T. D. Alexander and B. S. Rosner (eds.), *New Dictionary of Biblical Theology*, Leicester: IVP, 478–487.

Wright, C. J. H. (2006), *The Mission of God: Unlocking the Bible's Grand Narrative*, Nottingham: IVP, 2006.

4. PROMISES WITH STRINGS ATTACHED: COVENANT AND LAW IN EXODUS 19 – 24

Paul R. Williamson

> Oh the grand old Duke of York, he had 10,000 men
> He marched them up to the top of the hill, and he marched them down
> again.
> And when they were up they were up, and when they were down they
> were down,
> And when they were only half way up, they were neither up nor down.

You may be asking what that profound piece of verse has to do with the book of Exodus. But the similarities between Moses and the grand old Duke of York may be closer than you think. Both men were obviously leaders. Both were responsible for a fairly large group of men. Both had a penchant for going up and down elevated sites. And, most importantly, it is not always clear where either man was at any given time.

As many commentators are quick to point out, tracing the exact movements of Moses in the Sinai narrative can be a little bewildering in places. He goes up the mountain in 19:3; he comes back down to the people in 19:7; he goes up again in 19:8, only to be told to go back down again in 19:10. When he subsequently climbs

back up the mountain in 19:20, he is immediately instructed to go
back down and warn the people not to come up (19:21, 24). Moses
then makes his way back up the mountain yet again in 20:21, and
there he remains until chapter 24. He is then told to bring some
others up along with him. To do so, he must again go back down.
He then brings this delegation up with him in verses 9–11.
However, when we get to verse 12, it appears that they are all back
down again, for Moses is now invited to 'come up', and he leaves
Aaron and Hur in charge of the people during his absence.

So what's going on here? Unlike the grand old Duke of York,
Moses has now gone up and come down some five times, and by
the time we get to chapter 24, it is not quite clear whether he is up
or down! So what is all this ascending and descending about? Is it,
as some would tell us, that the editors have performed a very
shoddy scissors-and-paste job? Have they mixed up their various
sources so that the story is now hopelessly garbled? Or is it that we
have traditionally misread and misunderstood the literary structure of the narrative, as others have suggested? According to
Chirichigno (1987), for example, through the use of 'resumptive
repetition' the compiler offers us a number of literary 'flashbacks'.
In other words, Moses does not really ascend and descend the
mountain as often as it may first appear.[1] Or can we take the text at
face value, and read it in a linear fashion? And if so, does this multiple ascending and descending serve some higher purpose?

Quite possibly, as some have suggested, Moses' movements
serve as rhetorical devices that delineate major structural blocks
in the narrative (cf. Dozeman 1989: 14; Arichea 1989: 244–246;
Davies 2004: 35). But may they also carry some theological
freight?

Before looking at the details of chapters 19–24, it is important to
remind ourselves again of the context. As already noted, the book

---

1. According to Chirichigno's analysis, Exod. 20:1 – 23:33 constitutes a
   resumptive repetition of Exod. 19:16–20, whereas Exod. 24:1–8 constitutes such a repetition of Exod. 19:21–25. Thus understood, rather than
   ascending at least five times by Exod. 24:12, Moses has gone up the
   mountain only three times by this stage.

of Exodus begins with a story of liberation; it recounts how God kept his promise to Israel's ancestors, how he came to their aid and delivered them from an oppressive Egyptian regime through a series of quite extraordinary events. The purpose of this deliverance, and indeed everything Yahweh would do on Israel's behalf, was to make himself known – not only to Pharaoh, Egypt and Israel, but also to the surrounding nations. Thus it is probably not surprising that the story of how Yahweh had rescued Israel from Egypt and sustained them in the wilderness should climax with a visit of a Midianite, Jethro, and his acknowledgment of Israel's God.

With Exodus 19, God's purposes for Israel come into sharper focus. We already know that Yahweh's action in rescuing the Hebrews from Egyptian bondage was prompted by his covenant promise – the oath he had sworn to Israel's ancestors. Moreover, we know that a key aspect of Yahweh's motive in rescuing the Israelites and defeating the Egyptians was to make himself known. As we shall see, this revelatory theme continues in this next section of Exodus, which recounts the establishment of the Mosaic covenant – a solemn agreement that might well be described as 'Promises, with strings attached'.

The contents and structural arrangement of the Sinai narrative (Exod. 19 – 40)[2]

The major sections of the Sinai narrative in Exodus are broadly as follows:

1. Theophany at Sinai (ch. 19)
2. Covenant words and instructions (chs. 20–23)
3. Covenant ratification (ch. 24)
4. Instructions for tabernacle and priesthood (chs. 25–31)

---

2. The Sinai narrative in the Pentateuch obviously continues to Num. 10:10. However, while the laws of Leviticus are also revealed at Mount Sinai (Lev. 26:46; 27:34), their particular setting is in the Tent of Meeting (Lev. 1:1), thus constituting a distinct literary unit within the Pentateuch.

5. Covenant breaking and remaking (chs. 32–34)
6. Preparations for tabernacle worship (chs. 35–40)

With respect to Exodus 19 – 24, this basic outline may be further developed in the following manner:

1. The covenant introduced (19:1–8)
   - Israel's arrival at Sinai (vv. 1–2)
   - Yahweh's word to Moses (vv. 3–6)
     – Reflection (v. 4)
     – Obligation (v. 5a)
     – Promise (vv. 5b–6)
   - Israel's response (vv. 7–8)
2. The Sinai theophany (19:9 – 20:21)
   - The revelatory purpose (v.9)
   - The necessary preparations (vv. 10–15)
   - Yahweh's descent on the mountain (vv. 16–19)
   - The divine exclusion order (vv. 20–25)
   - God's words: the Decalogue (20:1–17)
   - Israel's response (20:18–21)
3. The covenant code (20:22 – 23:33)
   - Prologue: acceptable and non-acceptable worship (20:22–26)
   - Superscription (21:1)
   - Social responsibilities: slaves, injuries and property (21:2 – 22:17)
     – Instructions regarding servants (21:2–11)
     – Instructions regarding injuries (21:12–36)
     – Instructions regarding 'property' (22:1–17)[3]
   - Regulations for worship: capital cultic offences (22:18–20)
   - Social responsibilities: vulnerable and authorities (22:21–27)[4]

---

3. Note, Hebrew verse numeration in ch. 22 is one verse lower than English (22:1 = 21:37 Masoretic Text).

4. Possibly, Exod. 22:21 and 23:9 form an inclusio (so Alexander 2002: 65). However, it is difficult to fit all the material between these two verses into one distinguishable subcategory such as 'safeguarding the weak and the judicial system' (cf. 22:28–31).

- Regulations for worship: respect for God (22:28–31)
- Social responsibilities: lying and injustice (23:1–9)
- Regulations for worship (23:10–19)
  - Sabbatical years (23:10–11)
  - Weekly sabbaths (23:12)
  - Worship Yahweh alone (23:13)
  - Annual festivals (23:14–19)
- Epilogue: instructions for securing the Promised Land (23:20–33)
- Obeying Yahweh's angel (23:20–23)
- Serving Yahweh alone (23:24–33)
4. The sealing of the covenant (24:1–18)
  - Delegation to ascend the mountain (24:1–2)
  - Solemn ratification of the covenant (24:3–8)
  - Delegation's encounter with God (24:9–11)
  - Moses' ascent to receive stone tablets (24:12–18)

As this outline illustrates, the Sinai pericope (Exod. 19 − 24) is a mixture of narrative and law. Indeed, several scholars discern a broad chiastic arrangement of the material in terms of the narrative–law sequence. Sprinkle (2004: 242), for example, has proposed the following arrangement:

A. *Narrative*: the covenant offered (Exod. 19:3–25)
  B. *Laws (general)*: the Decalogue (Exod. 20:1–17)
    C. *Narrative*: the people's fear (Exod. 20:18–21)
  B'. *Laws (specific)*: the book of the covenant (Exod. 20:22 − 23:33)
A'. *Narrative*: the covenant accepted (Exod. 24:1–11)

Such a chiastic structure helpfully illustrates that law is subservient to covenant. Moreover, it also highlights an important function of the theophany at Sinai (to instil a godly fear that would keep Israel from sinning). However, it is perhaps overly reductionistic in the way it groups some of the material. For example, it seems a little forced to group all the material in ch. 19 under the title 'the covenant offered', when this description more accurately applies to verses 1–8 and the rest of the chapter focuses more especially on the Sinai theophany.

Building on the insights of others (cf. Patrick 1977: 145–157; 1986: 64; Dozeman 1989: 59–60), Alexander (1999; 2002: 62–79) has highlighted a number of significant parallels between two important speeches within the Sinai narrative (Exod. 19:3–6 and 20:22 – 24:2):

Exodus 19:2b–8a	Exodus 20:21 – 24:3
[2b] There Israel camped in front of the mountain. {3} But Moses went up to God	[20:21] The people remained at a distance, but Moses approached the thick darkness where God was
And the LORD called to him from the mountain saying,	[20:22] Then the LORD said to Moses,
'This is what you shall say to the house of Jacob and what you shall tell the children of Israel:	'This is what you are to say to the children of Israel:
[4] "YOU [2nd pl.] yourselves have seen what I did to Egypt, and how I carried YOU on eagles' wings and brought you [*sic*] to myself . . ."'	"YOU yourselves have seen that I have spoken to YOU from heaven . . ."'
The main part of the speech	*The main part of the speech*
[7] So Moses came and summoned the elders of the people and put before them all these words which the LORD had commanded him.	[24:3] So Moses came and told the people all the LORD's words and all the laws.
[8] The people replied all together, 'All that the LORD has said we will do.'	All the people replied with one voice, 'All the words that the LORD has said we will do.'

While Alexander focuses mainly on the significance of these parallels for the literary (and authorial) unity of the Sinai narrative, it is possible to develop these further in terms of an overall bifid structure. Thus understood, these chapters (19–24) may be seen to comprise two broadly parallel major parts:

1. Occasion: respective locations of Israel and Moses (19:1–3a; 20:18–21)
2. Yahweh's speech addressing the Israelites (19:4–6; 20:22 – 24:2)
   - introduced with 'thus you will say' (19:3b; 20:22a)
   - opening with 'you yourselves have seen' (19:4; 20:22b)
   - highlighting response incumbent on Israel (19:5a; 20:23 – 23:19)
   - setting forth Israel's prospects (19:5b–6; 23:20–33)
3. Moses reports back to people (19:7; 24:3a)
4. People respond positively (19:8; 24:3b)
5. Preparation for meeting God[5] (19:9–15; 24:4–8)
6. Close encounter with God (19:16–25; 24:9–11)
7. Giving of the Decalogue (20:1–17; 24:12ff.).

As with Sprinkle's chiastic arrangement, the idea of these two parallel panels may seem a little forced in places.[6] However, the fact that there is significant overlap in the way the two speeches are framed and shaped seems to suggest at least some degree of intentionality by the compiler. Moreover, once these two parallel panels are identified, it is possible to trace two key movements in the text (Yahweh's descent towards Israel, and Israel's ascent towards Yahweh),[7] both of which climax with the giving of the commandments.

---

5. Exodus 24:4–8 may not initially appear to be in the same vein as 19:9–15. Nevertheless, the location of this cultic ritual (coming directly between Yahweh's invitation for a representative group to ascend the mountain and the account of their meeting with God when they did so, as well as the fact that it may in some sense be anticipated in 20:22–26) suggests that this covenant-making ritual also served to prepare for the divine–human encounter that followed.

6. E.g. 20:18–20 could equally be viewed as the conclusion of the first main section, with 20:21 providing the occasion for the second. In this case, however, the parallelism suggested above is not quite so neat.

7. This descent and ascent is further reflected in the frequency of the respective Hebrew verbs in chs. 19 and 24.

Israel's commission and the Sinai theophany (19:1 – 20:17)

Chapter 19 marks an important watershed in the book of Exodus. Here an important milestone is reached. The Israelites arrive at a terminus that has been anticipated as far back as chapter 3. At last the liberated slaves have come to Mount Sinai, the place where Yahweh had previously disclosed his plans to Moses. The sign mentioned back in Exodus 3:12 is about to be fulfilled; the first leg of their journey has reached completion; they have arrived at the Mountain of God, the place where Yahweh will manifest himself and reveal how, precisely, Israel may serve him.

Much of the focus in the first half of the book has been on what Yahweh has done for Israel: how he delivered the Israelites from slavery in Egypt; how he humiliated the Egyptians and their so-called gods; how he fulfilled his promises to Israel's ancestors; how he rescued and provided for Israel in some amazing ways. However, when we come to chapter 19, attention shifts from what Yahweh has done for Israel to what Israel must do in response. Admittedly, there have been several hints of this already. We already know that Israel has been 'saved to serve'. Such was the rationale given to Pharaoh: 'Let my people go that they might *serve* me' (Exod. 8:1 my tr.). The exodus, Israel's liberation from Egypt, was never intended to be an end in itself. Rather, it was a means to an end; Israel was set free from the wrong master in order to serve the right Master. The people were set free from serving Pharaoh so that they might be free to serve Yahweh. And here, in Exodus 19 and following, the latter service begins to take shape. In these chapters, Yahweh discloses how he expects Israel to serve him, and in what capacity. Both are delineated in Exodus 19:4–6, a text whose significance has been compared to Genesis 12:1–3. It is certainly a programmatic text in so far as the Sinai narrative is concerned. Indeed, in some respects these verses constitute a microcosm of the book as a whole. Not only do they summarize the key events thus far; they also set out the agenda and rationale for all that follows. We have here in essence what the Sinai covenant and Mosaic law is all about. Thus this is a most important text for opening up our investigation into these central chapters in the book of Exodus. Unfortunately, it is also a problematic text as far as the precise interpretation of some of the details is concerned.

The aim of the covenant (Exodus 19:4–6)

This so-called eagles' wings speech (Exod. 19:4–6) is the first of several messages from Yahweh that Moses has to declare to the Israelites. Significantly, it commences with the theological rationale for serving Yahweh. Yahweh begins by reminding the Israelites why they should serve Him at all: 'You yourselves have seen what I did to Egypt, and how I carried you on eagles' wings and brought you to myself' (Exod. 19:4 NIV). This summary, as Davies suggests, 'is a highly compressed account of Israel's threefold experience to date' (2004: 38). 'What I did to Egypt' obviously alludes to Yahweh's humiliation of the Egyptians through the plagues and their eventual destruction in the Sea. The next clause encompasses God's deliverance of the Israelites and the first stage of Israel's wilderness wanderings – the journey from Egypt to Sinai. The Israelites had been borne along on eagles' wings. Whatever the precise idea conveyed by this metaphor,[8] the main point is clear: Israel's rescue and journey thus far had been facilitated by Yahweh's action, intervention and protection. Without such divine assistance, their escape and survival would have proved impossible. Yahweh had brought Israel safely thus far. Moreover, as the final clause in verse 4 indicates, he had a clear destination in mind: Yahweh had brought this people to himself. Here they were at the Mountain of God, the location where Yahweh had earlier appeared to Moses and said, 'this will be the sign to you that it is I who have sent you: When you have brought the people out of Egypt, you will worship God on this mountain' (Exod. 3:12 NIV). God had thus fulfilled his word and done exactly as he promised. He had delivered Israel from

---

8. Davies (2004: 39) quite rightly dismisses the idea that the fledgling Israelites are learning to 'fly for themselves' as they become less and less dependent on God. However, in his attempt to read the metaphor in the light of the vulture iconography of the ancient world and other biblical texts, insufficient weight is given to Deut. 32:10–12, a text which seems to unpack the metaphor in terms of divine leading and protection.

Egyptian servitude, and brought them safely to himself. His purpose in doing so is spelt out in the following verses.

'Now if you obey me fully and keep my covenant, then out of all nations you will be my treasured possession . . . a kingdom of priests and a holy nation' (Exod. 19:5–6 NIV). It is important to underline that the Israelites are obligated to serve Yahweh because of what he has already done on their behalf. Before telling the Israelites what they must do for him, Yahweh reminds them what he has done for them. And this same note is struck again a little later; the Ten Commandments are premised on the fact that Yahweh is Israel's deliverer (Exod. 20:2). In other words, what Israel must do for Yahweh is grounded first and foremost in what Yahweh has already done for Israel. Thus the covenant obedience Yahweh is calling for here is Israel's response to God's saving initiative. While the Sinai covenant is clearly conditional, obeying God fully and keeping his covenant is not presented as a means of securing salvation. Israel is not charged to obey God and keep his covenant in order to be saved, or for that matter, in order to 'stay saved';[9] rather, Israel's obedience and covenant-keeping is the required response to what God has already done on their behalf.

Having said this, however, these covenant obligations clearly impinge on God's stated purpose for Israel – that which is delineated in the following two verses (Exod. 19:5–6). However we understand the force of the conditional sentence here,[10] the fulfilment of God's purpose for Israel is clearly dependent in some sense on Israel's response. Indeed, such is further attested by the fact that both here in chapter 19, and again just prior to the ratification of the covenant in chapter 24, the Israelites express a willingness to do all that Yahweh has said. In order to enjoy the

---

9. It is clear from Exod. 33 – 34 that the covenant is ultimately maintained not through human effort, but solely by divine mercy and grace.

10. Rather than understanding the apodosis (vv. 5b–6) in terms of a consequence conditional on faithful service ('if you do this, then you will be that'), the protasis may be read as a definitional statement, unpacking what actions the appellations of the apodosis entail ('by doing this, you will be that').

privilege and fulfil the responsibility God intended,[11] Israel must be willing to obey God's voice and keep his covenant.[12]

Yahweh's stated purpose for Israel, according to verses 5–6, was twofold: it involved a unique privilege, and it entailed a special responsibility. The unique privilege is set forth in verse 5. It was God's intention that Israel should be his 'treasured possession'. The underlying Hebrew word (*sĕgullâ*) is a commercial term, referring in its literal sense to acquired and valued personal property. On the two occasions where it is used in a non-figurative sense in the OT (1 Chr. 29:3; Eccles. 2:8), it refers to a king's private treasure – as opposed to that which belonged to the realm. Significantly, cognate terms are used in ancient Near Eastern treaty contexts to describe a vassal's (or servant's) status in relation to his suzerain (or overlord). In its other six occurrences in the OT, the term is used as here, metaphorically depicting Israel's special status before God (cf. Deut. 7:6; 14:2; 26:18; Ps. 135:4; Mal. 3:17). Thus the term conveys the sense of Israel's special status before God in comparison to all the other nations: 'Inherent in the word סגלה is the concept of distinction or separation from other property or relationships. Israel is a סגלה for God in some manner in distinction from . . . all the other nations' (Davies 2004: 54). Such was what an obedient Israel would be: out of all the nations of the earth, Israel would be Yahweh's 'treasured possession', a nation distinguished and set apart from all the rest. If Israel followed Yahweh's instructions and kept his covenant, then Israel would enjoy this privileged status; Israel would be a people distinct from all others, enjoying a relationship with God unique among the nations.

---

11. *Pace* Davies (2004: 97), I shall argue that this text speaks not only of the national privilege held out to Israel, but also of their international responsibility.

12. While the only 'covenant' mentioned thus far in Exodus is the ancestral covenant, the immediate context and the call to obedience suggest that 'my covenant' is used here in a proleptic sense – anticipating the covenant set out and ratified in the following chapters. However, that the Mosaic covenant is closely related to and in some sense a development of the patriarchal covenants is not in doubt.

The nature of this special relationship with God is further explained by what follows. However, as a comparison of the major English translations clearly illustrates,[13] the exact meaning of the final clause in verse 5 is open to several different interpretations. The difficulty lies in knowing what to do with the Hebrew particle *kî*. In its present context, it could be interpreted in a variety of ways:

- It may be introducing a causal clause, supplying the rationale behind God's selection of Israel as his 'special possession' (tr. '*because* all the earth is mine').
- It may be taken in a concessive sense, introducing a statement that qualifies the main clause (tr. '*although* all the earth is mine').
- It may have asseverative force, emphasizing the reliability of the statement that follows ('*indeed* all the earth is mine').
- It may be introducing an explanatory clause, elucidating the preceding statement about Israel's privileged status (tr. '*for* all the earth is mine, but you will be . . .').[14]

Despite the slightly different nuances, the overarching idea in the latter three interpretations is basically the same: each puts stress on Israel's favoured status compared to the rest of the world. The causal interpretation, by contrast, differs quite sharply from the others. Understood in this way, the latter part of verse 5 discloses the purpose of Israel's calling; namely, to benefit the rest of the earth. Adopting such an interpretation, Fretheim argues that the mention of the nations here alludes to 'a mission that encompasses God's purposes for the entire world. *Israel is commissioned to be God's people on behalf of the earth which is God's*

---

13. Cf. NRSV's 'Indeed, the whole earth is mine' with ESV's 'for all the earth is mine' and TNIV's 'Although the whole earth is mine'.

14. For a detailed discussion of the various interpretations of this significant clause, see Davies 2004: 55–60. Davies understands the clause (extending to v. 6a) in an explanatory sense, highlighting 'the twofold notion of Yhwh's ownership of or sovereignty over both all creation in general and Israel in particular' (2004: 59).

(1991: 212; emphasis his). Dumbrell likewise concludes that 'the last clause of verse 5 testifies to the purpose for which the exodus redemption was instituted by God: Israel is called because the whole world ("earth") is the object of Yahweh's care' (1994: 45). Understood in this sense, therefore, verse 5 concludes by drawing attention to Israel's role in relation to the nations, rather than simply highlighting the distinct nature of Israel's privileged status before Yahweh.[15]

Now, admittedly, this would not be the only place in Exodus where Yahweh's dealings on Israel's behalf are brought into a more global perspective (cf. Exod. 9:16; 34:10).[16] In view of this, and the climactic goal of the ancestral promise (Gen. 12:3, mediating blessing to all the families of the earth), the causal interpretation has obvious theological appeal. Indeed, previously I have defended this interpretation myself (see Williamson 2007: 97). The Hebrew syntax, however, appears to favour the explanatory interpretation.[17] Thus understood, rather than giving a reason for Israel's privileged status vis-à-vis the nations, the end of verse 5 should probably be read in conjunction with the following verse as an elaboration or explanation of the statement that Israel would be

---

15. Cf. Davies, who rejects the functional interpretation altogether, and understands vv. 5b–6 as simply elaborating Israel's privileged status as Yahweh's *sĕgullâ*.

16. So Fretheim (1991: 212). In addition, we have already mentioned that the preceding chapter depicts a non-Israelite (Jethro) acknowledging the supremacy of Israel's God (Exod. 18:9–12).

17. From the disjunctive *waw* at the beginning of v. 6, as well as the chiastic arrangement of vv. 5b–6a, Davies cogently argues that the second two lines simply unpack the first two, thus highlighting the privileged status that would be enjoyed by Israel in comparison to the rest of the world:

   A. You will be my special possession
   B. from all the peoples
   B′. for all the earth is mine
   A′. *but* you, you will be mine as a kingdom of priests and a holy nation (my tr.)

God's 'special possession'. It should thus be translated as follows: 'You will be my special possession from all the peoples, for all the earth is mine, but you will be my priestly kingdom and holy nation.' In other words, the point being made is that the whole earth belongs to Yahweh, but Israel is to have a distinct role within it. That role, as spelt out in verse 6, was to be a kingdom of priests and a holy nation.

That first description ('a kingdom of priests') has generated much discussion.[18] This is due in no small part to the ambiguity of this unique Hebrew phrase. This ambiguity is attested not only by ancient translations and early citations,[19] but also by its renditions in contemporary English versions. Should we translate it as 'kingdom of priests' (ESV; TNIV), 'priestly kingdom' (Vulgate; NRSV), 'royal priesthood' (cf. Septuagint and 1 Pet. 2:9), or 'kings/kingdom [and] priests' (cf. Targums/Syriac; Rev. 1:6; 5:10)? And however we translate it, what precisely does the phrase mean?[20]

The most straightforward way to render it is either as 'a kingdom of priests' or 'a priestly kingdom'.[21] Taken either way, the phrase denotes corporate Israel, depicting the latter as a kingdom or royal domain whose citizens are in some sense priests. Thus understood,

---

18. For a comprehensive analysis and critique of the various interpretations, see Davies 2004: 63–100.

19. For a detailed analysis, see Davies 2004: 63–68.

20. See Davies 2004: 68–69. Scott (1950: 216) listed the following plausible interpretations: (a) a kingdom composed of priests; (b) a kingdom possessing a legitimate priesthood; (c) a kingdom with a collective priestly responsibility on behalf of others; (d) a kingdom ruled by priests; (e) a kingdom set apart and possessing collectively, alone among all peoples, the right to approach the altar of Yahweh. As Davies observes, these five options and all feasible subcategories 'primarily divide over their understanding of whether there is a passive or an active force to the verbal notion which underlies ממלקת' (2004: 69).

21. Both translations take *mamleket* as a construct. The second noun may then be read either as an objective or appositional genitive ('a kingdom of [comprising] priests') or as having the characteristic adjectival force that a *nomen rectum* may have in Hebrew (hence 'a priestly kingdom').

the Israelites are to be and/or to serve as priests, and the kingdom they comprise is Yahweh's. While the notion of Yahweh's kingship is admittedly not explicit, the link between Israel's status as Yahweh's *sĕgullâ* and that of a vassal to his suzerain has already been noted; thus the concept of Yahweh as Israel's king is not altogether foreign to this text unit. The one difficulty that remains is that such an interpretation seems to allow little room for the royal or actively reigning dimension reflected in various ancient translations, and carried over into the NT (cf. Rev. 5:10). However, there is at least one way to resolve this. Perhaps, as some have suggested (see Davies 2004: 84–86), 'kingdom' is a deliberately ambivalent term, allowing for both an active and passive connotation. In this case, Israel is both a ruling group and a ruled group, actively and passively participating in the rule (or kingdom) of Yahweh.

If it is correct to understand the first phrase in this way (as a 'kingdom of priests' or a 'priestly kingdom'), we may infer that the term 'kingdom' is roughly synonymous with the term 'nation' in the following phrase; thus the second word in each phrase defines the kind of kingdom or the sort of nation Yahweh wants Israel to become.

So what sort of kingdom is a *priestly* kingdom or a kingdom of *priests*? Indeed, how should we understand this priestly metaphor? Is it to be interpreted merely in an ontological sense or does it carry a functional connotation as well? In other words, is it what priests *are* that Yahweh has in mind here, or is it more what priests *do*?[22] Is Yahweh simply conferring on Israel the status of priests (those with privileged access to the divine presence; so Davies 2004: 98–100), or is he giving Israel the responsibilities of priests (a mediating responsibility of some kind)?[23] Many evangelical commentators interpret the terminology in a functional sense – in terms of Israel's implied 'mission' to the nations. Others, however, reject such an interpretation on the grounds that there is no hint in

22. Davies (2004: 97–98) draws attention to this distinction that has been largely overlooked by others.

23. As assumed by those who interpret this text in terms of Israel's mediatorial relation to the nations.

Exodus of Israel's mediatorial role among the nations being associated with Sinai. Now, while the latter is admittedly not explicit,
the wider Pentateuchal context (cf. Gen. 12:3; 18:18–19; 26:5;
Deut. 4:5–6) may make an implicit association nevertheless feasible. Even so, it is difficult to see why we should restrict this priestly
metaphor here to the idea of mediating the knowledge of God to
the nations. As Motyer has rightly pointed out, 'This [the idea of
mediating the knowledge of God] is certainly not the main understanding of priesthood within the Old Testament' (2005: 199,
n. 8).[24] Moreover, given the specific privilege of priests highlighted
a little later in this very chapter (cf. Exod. 19:22),[25] there are good
exegetical grounds for understanding this priestly metaphor primarily in an ontological sense. While a functional understanding
cannot be ruled out entirely, the difficulty lies in deciding which
priestly functions are to be included or excluded, and on what
grounds. For example, if Israel is being called here to function as
priests, may this not also imply that the Israelites were to represent

---

24. Since it predates the institution of the Aaronic priesthood, it may be
    unwise to read all the latter's responsibilities into the present text.
    However, it appears that the Israelites already had some form of priest-
    hood (cf. Exod. 19:22, 24). Both these latter references may be proleptic,
    referring to those who would subsequently serve as priests. However, the
    warning seems to make more sense if even at this stage there were desig-
    nated individuals or a particular group who officially functioned as priests.
    Moreover, given their time in Egypt, they were undoubtedly familiar with
    the concept of a priest even before their encounter with Jethro, the priest
    of Midian. In other words, even though the Aaronic priesthood had not
    yet been instituted, the Israelites would already have been acquainted with
    the concept of a priest, as well as the privileges and duties such an office
    entailed. In any case, as Davies observes, 'On any view of Pentateuchal
    origins, Israel had a recognized priesthood by the time of the composition
    of the Sinai pericope' (2004: 89). This being so, it can be assumed that
    readers may be expected to interpret the metaphorical concept of Israelite
    priesthood in Exod. 19:6 in the light of the literal phenomenon.
25. This same privilege and function is emphasized in several other passages
    where the role of Israel's priests are defined (cf. 1 Sam. 2:28; Ezek. 45:4).

the nations before God and offer sacrifices on their behalf? On what grounds can we incorporate one priestly function (teaching) in this metaphor, yet exclude others (including the main priestly role of mediating for others before God)?[26]

Not only was Israel called to be a 'priestly kingdom'; Israel was also called to be a 'holy nation'. As previously suggested, these two concepts are broadly synonymous; both phrases express a similar idea in slightly different ways. It may oversimplify it to suggest that 'priestly is to holy what kingdom is to nation'. But the two concepts certainly overlap. The common denominator is Israel's sacredness, sanctity and separation from the nations for the service of God. Israel was to be no ordinary kingdom, but a priestly kingdom, a kingdom of priests, a royal priesthood. However we take it, one thing is absolutely clear. God is promising to confer a priestly standing, a sanctified status on all his people; together, they would comprise a kingdom of priests. Such a status was normally restricted to the religious elite. But here God is promising that the entire nation would enjoy this privileged status. The people as a whole would comprise this priestly kingdom; they would constitute a kingdom set apart by God and for God, consecrated to the service of God and dedicated to his honour and praise, whose primary function was to facilitate the worship of God.

Thus Israel was to be a nation like no other; Israel was to be a holy nation, a nation set apart for God, living *among* the nations yet distinct *from* the nations – if you like, a nation *in* the world, but not *of* the world. Israel was to be a nation reflecting God's value system, modelling God's standards of justice by living according to God's code of ethics, a nation demonstrating God's paradigm for life and society. As Durham puts it, 'they are to be a people set apart, different from all other people by what they are and are becoming – a display people, a showcase to the world of how being in covenant with Yahweh changes a people' (1987: 263). That is, Israel was to

---

26. Stuart's suggestion that 'Israel would intercede for the rest of the world by offering acceptable offerings to God (both sacrifices and right behaviour) and thus ameliorate the general distance between God and humankind' (2006: 423) seems to lack explicit exegetical support.

be a nation set apart from others. On the basis of their relationship with Yahweh, Israel was to be different from the surrounding
nations. As the subsequent laws make clear, Israel was to be
socially and ethically distinct from other nations. As God's holy
nation, Israel was to reflect the holiness of Yahweh himself. Israel
would thus be a light to the nations and mediate blessing to the
nations; Israel would thus serve God and his purposes for all the
families of the earth. As a holy nation, a nation that would reflect
something of God's own character and values to the surrounding
world, Israel would model God's kingdom on earth. But in order
to do so, in order to be the people Yahweh intended them to be,
Israel would have to obey God fully and keep his covenant.

Israel's willingness to do so is clear from what follows. Having
summoned the elders and set before them 'all these words that the
LORD had commanded him' (19:7 ESV), Moses is met with a unani-
mous and positive response: 'All the people answered together and
said, "All that the Lord has spoken we will do"' (19:8 ESV). While
some have dismissed this response as rash or premature, the bifid
structure outlined above would suggest otherwise. Here we see the
people's initial response to the obligations Yahweh places upon them
– a response that remains resolute even after all the details of these
covenant obligations have been disclosed in the theophany and the
subsequent divine address. That the people's compliant response was
indeed sincere and commendable may be further underscored by
Yahweh's words when Moses reports back to him in verse 8.[27] It is
Yahweh's intention to manifest his presence on Sinai so that the
people would hear him speak directly to Moses and thus believe

_____

27. It is unclear whether Yahweh's words recorded in v. 9a were spoken prior
    to or subsequent to hearing how the Israelites had responded to the eagles'
    wings speech. Some (e.g. Stuart 2006: 425) resolve the anomaly of Moses
    apparently reporting the same thing twice (vv. 8b and 9b) by inferring that
    his report was not in fact *delivered* until after Yahweh's further revelation in
    v. 9a. It might also be argued that the *wayyiqtol* of v. 9b should be read as a
    pluperfect: 'Moses *had* declared the people's words to Yahweh' (cf. Exod
    4:19 TNIV). However, while such a translation would make contextual
    sense, it cannot be supported on syntactical grounds; cf. Talstra 1996.

Moses' testimony for ever (19:9). The inclusion of 'for ever' seems to imply some acknowledgment of the people's positive response to the prior revelation. In any case, the theophany that follows is designed to authenticate Moses as the mediator of Yahweh's will for his people and to encourage their ongoing obedience in the future. The people must be left in no doubt about the ultimate source of the covenant requirements Moses will pass on to them (Exod. 19:9). To facilitate this, the Israelites must hear firsthand Yahweh speaking to Moses; thus the entire camp must witness the forthcoming revelation of Yahweh on Sinai.

The God of the covenant (Exod 19:10–24)

Not surprisingly (cf. Moses' experience back in Exod. 3:5), the people's anticipated proximity to Yahweh requires special preparation on their part (19:10–15). A close reading of Exodus 19 suggests that the closest the people in general would be permitted to come was to the foot of the mountain (cf. 19:17), hence the strict limits imposed around it (vv. 12, 23).

Presumably, the 'they' of Exodus 19:13 who would subsequently be permitted to *ascend* (not 'approach' as in TNIV) the mountain (at least part of the way) refers to their representatives: that is, Moses and Aaron (19:24) or Moses, Aaron, Nadab, Abihu and the seventy elders (24:1, 9).[28] In any case, even to stand in the vicinity of the mountain, consecrated because of Yahweh's presence on it (19:23), the Israelites themselves must be 'consecrated'. Precisely what such 'consecration' may have entailed is not made entirely clear,[29]

---

28. Alternatively, Exod. 19:13 may be interpreted as an open invitation for all to ascend, which was subsequently (19:21–24) rescinded. The Septuagint reading 'when the sounds and trumpets and cloud depart from off the mountain, they shall come up on the mountain' looks suspiciously like a harmonistic gloss.

29. Apparently, it is something Moses did to the people (19:10, 14) rather than something they did for themselves (cf. 19:22). Later, the priests and various cultic accoutrements are 'consecrated' (cf. 40:9–13), which seems to involve anointing with oil and setting them apart for exclusive divine service. However, there is no mention of such anointing here in ch. 19.

although arguably this might be spelt out in the subsequent
instructions to set the people apart from Mount Sinai itself
(19:12–13). This seems to make most sense of the warning delivered after the theophany has begun (19:21–24); this is not calling
for some additional act of consecration, now including the priests
as well. Instead, the reiterated warning simply serves to underline
the necessity of keeping their distance for the duration of the
theophany. Thus understood, rather than some undisclosed ritual
act performed by Moses, the consecration (setting apart) of the
people was achieved primarily by cordoning them off outside the
prescribed exclusion zone around Mount Sinai.

In any case, in order to 'be completely ready' (19:11, 15) for this
close encounter with Yahweh, two further actions were required:
they had to wash their clothes (19:11, 14),[30] and they had to abstain
from sexual relations (19:15).[31] Both requirements seem to underline the need for ritual purity in the presence of a holy God.

As anticipated (19:11), the divine advent began at daybreak
on the third day (19:16). Given the arrangement of the text, this
advent appears to be divided into two distinct stages.[32] The first

---

30. As Enns (2000: 390) suggests, 'Perhaps the washing clothes is analogous
    to Moses' removing his shoes in God's presence in 3:5.' In any case, he
    correctly observes that the main point seems to be that 'the Israelites
    cannot simply come as they are'.

31. Literally, 'Do not approach a woman', apparently a euphemism for sexual
    relations, which would render both parties ceremonially unclean and thus
    unfit to be in the presence of Yahweh (cf. Lev. 15:16–18). As several com-
    mentators observe, this prohibition has no moral implications such as 'sex
    is evil or sinful'. Most probably it is simply a ritual requirement here,
    although possibly it highlights that 'different spheres of life – here sex and
    worship – are to be distinguished' (Janzen 2000: 241).

32. While some commentators detect evidence of multiple sources and/or
    redactional layers in vv. 16–25, it is possible to make sense of the text as it
    stands. Yahweh first manifested his presence on Sinai via the theophanic
    features described in vv. 16–19, gave Moses the repeated warning for the
    people to keep their distance (19:20–25), and then continued his descent
    upon the mountain and proclaimed the commandments.

stage is the audio-visual display that heralded Yahweh's descent upon the mountain (19:16–18) and culminated in a divine–human dialogue (19:19). Presumably, this fulfilled the promise of verse 9. However, it seems clear from what follows (Exod. 19:20 – 20:17) that the advent did not end there. Rather, a second stage of the divine advent involved the direct communication of the Decalogue, the general stipulations of the covenant (20:1–17). In using the verb *dbr* (to speak) for God's proclamation of the Decalogue (20:1), the author makes it quite clear that the Israelites have heard God speaking (*dbr*) the Decalogue to them directly (cf. 20:19). Thus Yahweh's advent on Mount Sinai incorporates not just a visual demonstration of his presence, but an audible and direct revelation of Israel's basic covenant obligations (cf. Deut. 4:11–13; 5:4, 22). As Janzen puts it, 'God's self-manifestation to Israel is not only a mystery-filled vision of God's holiness; it includes the communication of God's will for Israel, articulated in clear words' (2000: 267). In other words, the God who reveals himself to Israel is the God who speaks; the God who makes himself known in both act and word.

As noted earlier, these general covenant stipulations are firmly grounded in God's prior act of salvation (Exod. 20:2). Israel is not commanded to observe these stipulations in order to become God's people, but because this was how those who were God's people, those whom he had rescued from oppression, should now behave. As Fretheim puts it, 'the law is not understood as a means of salvation but as instruction regarding the shape such a redeemed life is to take in one's everyday affairs' (1991: 224).

Israel's response and the covenant ratification (20:18 – 24:18)

Israel's response to this 'sound and light' show on Mount Sinai is probably not what we might have expected. There is certainly no thought of anyone forcing his or her way through the perimeter 'fence' to have a closer look (cf. 19:21). Rather, they respond to

this close encounter with Yahweh with abject fear;[33] they are terrified by what they see and hear. Thus they maintain their distance
and beg Moses to speak to them on God's behalf. Moreover, not
only do they ask Moses to do the speaking; they also promise that
if he does so, they will listen. Just as earlier they had promised to
do everything Yahweh said, so now they commit themselves to
obey the words of Moses (20:19; cf. Deut. 5:27). Such was the
effect of this supernatural display of pyrotechnics on its original
audience. Moreover, this was precisely what Yahweh had intended.
His stated intent for this theophany was 'so that the people will
hear me speaking with you and will always put their trust in you'
(19:9 NIV). So far, so good. In this respect, at least, it was 'mission
accomplished'.

Abject fear and godly fear

However, should we infer from Moses' response in verse 20 that
to some extent the people overreacted to the theophany, an over-
reaction that prompted reassurance and correction?[34] Admittedly,
Moses does offer some reassurance here, telling them not to be
afraid. Paradoxically, however, the following sentence suggests that
this theophany was specifically designed to inculcate in them 'the
fear of God'. While there may be an implied distinction here
between two kinds of fear (an abject terror and a godly fear that
facilitates obedience), the distinction may in fact relate simply to

---

33. Possibly, the reading of the ancient versions ('were afraid'; so Septuagint,
   Syriac and Vulgate) is to be preferred here over the Masoretic Text ('saw').
   The unpointed verb forms are identical, but the verb 'to be afraid' may
   suit the context here better (however, cf. Durham 1987: 302–303; Stuart
   2006: 468). In any case, it is clear from 19:16 and from the following
   clauses here in 20:18–20 that the Israelites were indeed frightened by this
   experience.
34. At the extreme end of this spectrum, Sailhamer (1995: 282–289) argues
   that Israel sinned by refusing to ascend the mountain at the appropriate
   moment, and were thus excluded from going up at all (19:21, 23).
   However, this negative reading of Israel's reaction is very difficult to
   square with Deut. 5:23–31 (esp. vv. 28–29).

the object of their fear (when Moses says, 'Do not be afraid', he means, 'Do not be afraid [*of dying*]. God has come . . . so that the fear of God will be with you to keep you from sinning'). Thus understood, Moses is assuring them that, by responding as they had, they were not about to die. God had come to them in this way in order to test their resolve to be obedient and,[35] by instilling in them a genuine *fear of God*, to keep them from sinning. In other words, Israel's response here is the theologically correct and proper response, as would appear to be confirmed by the longer account in Deuteronomy (5:23–29).

And so, rather than intrepidly pressing forward up the mountain, the Israelites remain at its base and maintain their distance from the awesome and terrifying reality of their God. Israel's response so far has thus been exemplary. Their initial response was to resolve to do everything the Lord had said (19:8). Now, having seen and heard from God directly, they demonstrate their obedience by maintaining their position at the base of the mountain, and acknowledging the unique role of Moses as covenant mediator.

The covenant code
Having left the people at the base of the mountain and come to the thick darkness where God is, Moses now receives from Yahweh the detailed stipulations of the covenant.[36] This detailed legislation is bracketed between an introduction (20:22–26) and

---

35. It is not clear what the 'testing' here alludes to, or even if this is the best way of translating the verb in this context; other suggested translations include 'instruct', 'train' and 'experience' (in the sense of 'to give you a taste of himself').

36. As Alexander points out, Exod. 20:22 is the natural sequel to Exod. 20:1–21: 'Since Exodus 20:22 both presupposes a speech uttered directly by Yahweh to the people, and introduces a divine address delivered via Moses, there seems every reason to believe the Decalogue and the Book of the Covenant were incorporated into the Sinai narrative by the author responsible for composing the narrative frameworks that presently surround the divine speeches in Exodus 19:3–6 and 20:22–24:2' (2002: 69).

conclusion (23:20–33), both of which focus primarily on the exclusive allegiance Yahweh demands.[37]

Introduction
The introduction begins with a reminder of what has just been experienced: the Israelites have heard Yahweh speak to them directly.[38] In particular, the first two commandments in the Decalogue are reiterated (20:23; cf. 20:3–6). These two commandments, focusing on forbidden forms of worship, serve here as a foil for the legitimate and acceptable way to worship Yahweh, as set out in the immediately following verses (vv. 24–26).[39] Like several of the other covenant stipulations that follow, these altar laws are presumably designed to distinguish Israelite practice from that of other nations, the indigenous Canaanites in particular.

While some consider these altar laws to be somewhat out of place in the surrounding context, two points should be noted:

---

37. The material in 20:22–26 is clearly distinguished from the covenant instructions that follow by the formal heading for the latter in 21:1. It is also distinct in form and content from the first major section of covenant regulations (21:2 – 22:17; cf. 22:18 – 23:19), which is generally casuistic and focuses on a variety of social responsibilities. The transition to the conclusion is marked by the macrosyntactical marker (*hinneh*) in 23:20 and the switch to a paraenetic style and different focus (Yahweh's assistance in possessing the Promised Land). As Fretheim (1991: 242) notes, another distinctive reflected in both the introduction and the conclusion is the way that command is interwoven with promise.

38. As Durham observes, 'The point of Exod 20:22 is not where Yahweh was when he spoke these instructions, but that the instructions are unequivocally *his*' (1987: 319; emphasis his).

39. While it is possible to take v. 23 as the initial stipulation in the covenant code, the fact that both verbs are plural (cf. the switch to the singular in vv. 24–26) is possibly explained by the fact that this verse is simply a summary reminder of what the people had actually heard Yahweh say previously (in the Decalogue). Indeed, it is quite likely that the first two commands of the Decalogue are here cited as representative of all ten (see Stuart 2006: 470–471).

(1) the nature of Israel's worship was a matter of paramount importance for their covenant relationship with Yahweh; thus it is unsurprising that the covenant code should begin and conclude with regulations concerning such; (2) while these altar laws obviously have much wider ramifications, they may apply in a primary sense to the ratification ritual in chapter 24, which involved both the erection of an altar and the two types of sacrifice prescribed here.[40] Thus understood, these altar laws are more closely connected to their immediate context than is often realized; they highlight how the Israelites may confidently approach Yahweh and secure his blessing (cf. 20:24b), thus overcoming the legitimate fears engendered by their recent experience of his holiness (20:18–19); moreover, these altar laws anticipate, in some measure, the ratification ceremony of chapter 24, after which a representative group of Israelites is permitted to ascend the mountain and survive a close encounter with Yahweh (24:11).

The rulings
The main body of the covenant code (21:2 – 23:19) seems to be a somewhat loosely arranged collection of various laws. While some of the material has obviously been arranged thematically,[41] other sections seem to be more miscellaneous in nature (cf. 22:18 – 23:9).[42]

Significantly, the legislation reflects the two main emphases of the Decalogue itself; namely, loving God and loving one's fellows. Indeed, these laws may be viewed as applying the principles

---

40. So Alexander (2002: 66), who notes in particular that these two texts are the first in the Pentateuch to mention 'burnt offerings' and 'fellowship offerings' side by side.

41. At least some degree of thematic arrangement is discernible in the following legislative groupings: servants (21:2–11), personal injuries (21:12–36), restitution for financial damage (22:1–17), annual festivals (23:14–19).

42. The sudden switch from a casuistic to an apodictic style in 22:18, and the preponderance of the latter throughout 22:18 – 23:9, suggests that these verses comprise a distinct section within the covenant code.

enshrined in the Decalogue to various practical scenarios and situations the Israelites would inevitably encounter.

While much of the covenant code is similar to other ancient Near Eastern legislation, in many respects it is significantly different. For example, the biblical law places a higher value on human life, and does not discriminate in terms of social class. These laws are clearly designed to reflect Yahweh's distinctiveness and values, and thus proclaim such to the surrounding nations.

The conclusion

The covenant code concludes with a more hortatory section that focuses primarily on Israel's journey to the Promised Land and its acquisition (23:20–33). A key to Israel's success in this will be their submission to Yahweh's angel who will accompany them and lead the way. To rebel against this angel would be to invite disaster (23:21), whereas submission will guarantee divine assistance and success (23:22–23).

Blessing in the land would likewise depend on Israel's exclusive worship of Yahweh, and thus every vestige of the Canaanite fertility cult must be eradicated (23:24–26) as Israel gradually displaces the indigenous population (23:27–30). Therefore, while the territorial promise would indeed be fulfilled, it was imperative that Israel safeguard their inheritance by removing all Canaanite influence from the land (23:31–33).

Invitation to ascend

At the end of this extended speech Yahweh again addresses Moses personally,[43] inviting him, on his next ascent, to bring several others along with him (24:1–2). This special delegation is to include Aaron, his two oldest sons, Nadab and Abihu, as well as seventy of Israel's elders; this was evidently a representative group of Israel's civil and religious leadership; and this group is invited to

---

43. While the disjunctive *waw* might signal the start of a new section, the fact that the subject of the verb (Yahweh) is not renominalized (explicitly expressed) would suggest that these verses (24:1–2) are a continuation of the speech that began in 20:22.

ascend the mountain so they may worship God. Once again, however, Yahweh makes it clear that this special privilege is strictly 'invitation only'; this is not a hill-climb open to all and sundry: it is not a trip for anyone who might want to tag along. This ascent was only for those specifically invited; and it had to take place within clearly defined parameters. Even this special delegation cannot get too close; rather, they have to worship God 'at a distance' ('Moses alone is to approach the LORD; the others must not come near. And the people may not come up with him' [Exod. 24:2 NIV]). While this select group will accompany Moses, he alone may approach Yahweh, and the rest of the people must remain where they are. The syntax may be somewhat clumsy,[44] but the main point is clear enough: like the moveable 'Sinai' soon to be constructed, Yahweh's mountain 'dwelling-place' is divided into three distinct parts, reflecting different gradations of holiness. At its base, where the Israelites are encamped, is its outer court; further up, where this delegation will ascend to worship God, is its holy place; and right at the top, where the glory of God settles or tabernacles (24:16) on it – is its most holy place.

Report and response

Rather than assembling this representative group and leading them up to meet God straight away, Moses does something else entirely. First of all he follows the instruction he was given back in chapter 20:22: he relays all the Lord's words and laws to the people. And as before, the people respond positively to what they hear: 'When Moses told the people all the LORD's words and laws, they responded with one voice: "Everything the LORD has said we will do"' (24:3 NIV). One might argue that, had they really stopped to consider and thought carefully about what they were signing off on, perhaps they would have been a little more guarded and a little less confident. However, they certainly weren't in a position to negotiate. This was not the kind of agreement in which there was

---

44. The Septuagint offers a much smoother reading of these verses, reading '*they* will worship the Lord at a distance' (v. 1b) and 'the people must not go up with *them*' (v. 3b).

room for bargaining. Yahweh had set out the stipulations on a take it or leave it basis. But one thing is clear; they could no longer claim ignorance; they could no longer say they hadn't realized what they were getting themselves into. The terms of the covenant had now been proclaimed – both the general stipulations and the detailed stipulations had been spelt out. And now they were all duly recorded; Moses put it all down in writing. This, of course, was a typical thing to do when one was ratifying a covenant in the ancient world. And that explains what happens next, which might otherwise take us a little by surprise. Rather than immediately setting off up the mountain with this delegation to worship God, Moses engages in an elaborate ritual involving the erection of altars and pillars, the offering of sacrifices and the sprinkling of blood.

Sacrificial ritual

He got up early the next morning and built an altar at the foot of the mountain and set up twelve stone pillars representing the twelve tribes of Israel. Then he sent young Israelite men,[45] and they offered burnt offerings and sacrificed young bulls as fellowship offerings to the LORD. Moses took half of the blood and put it in bowls, and the other half he splashed against the altar. Then he took the Book of the Covenant and read it to the people. They responded, 'We will do everything the LORD has said; we will obey.'

Moses then took the blood, sprinkled it on the people and said, 'This is the blood of the covenant that the LORD has made with you in accordance with all these words.' (Exod. 24:4b–8 TNIV)

It is only now (after all this elaborate ritual) that Moses, Aaron and the others may finally go up the mountain to meet God. So what is going on here? Why this altar? Why these sacrifices? Why

---

45. The fact that these young men are not described as 'priests' per se (cf. 19:22, 24) may suggest that they were functioning in a non-professional capacity, or that these young men were Israel's official priests prior to the ordination of the Aaronic priesthood (cf. Exod. 28 – 29; Lev. 8 – 9). In any case, Moses clearly officiates over this ceremony.

all this splashing of blood? What is Moses doing here and why? Some suggest that Moses is simply doing what is more or less implicit back in Exodus 20:24–26. There, as we have noted, the building of an altar was certainly commanded; moreover, these particular sacrifices (burnt offerings and fellowship offerings) were specifically mentioned. However, while both passages share these common features, something more seems to be going on here in chapter 24. Moses is doing more here than simply conducting a normal worship service; there is more going on here than simply offering God acceptable worship. While some of the details are unclear, it is obvious from verse 8 that this ritual was designed to ratify the covenant between Yahweh and Israel. The two parties involved in this covenant are represented by the altar and the twelve pillars. The burnt offerings signify atonement for Israel's sin, and possibly Israel's consecration to God; the fellowship offerings signify the establishment of peace or communion between Israel and God. What is less clear is the precise significance of the next bit; half of the blood being splashed against the altar and the other half being splashed upon the people. Possibly what we have here is an ordination rite, similar to that described in chapter 29, where Aaron and his sons are ordained to serve Yahweh as priests. Thus understood, here all Israel is being ordained to the service of Yahweh; this is a commissioning service for Israel to be the priestly kingdom and holy nation God spoke of back in chapter 19.

But there is probably more to it than this.[46] This blood ritual also underlined that the covenant was a matter of life and death. In the ancient world, such covenants were often sealed in blood. The splattered blood symbolized the death of the covenant makers should they become covenant breakers. The blood of the covenant carried the threat of divine judgment for everyone who broke it. This may be inferred from the two distinct parts of the ritual (splattering half of the blood on the altar and the other half on

---

46. The blood ritual may obviously have more than one significance; the different connotations suggested here are certainly not mutually exclusive. For still other suggestions, see Hilber 1996: 182.

the people), and the way these are separated by a recital of the covenant obligations and Israel's assent to such (24:7).

At the same time, however, the blood was a sign of God's mercy. It not only showed the people what would happen if they failed; it also showed them how God would overcome their failure. Through the shedding of blood their transgressions would be forgiven; through the shedding of blood their sins would be atoned for. As the writer of Hebrews explains:[47]

> In the case of a covenant, the death of the covenant maker must be borne, for a covenant is ratified upon corpses [the animals sacrificed], since it is not otherwise enforced while the covenant maker lives. This is why even the first covenant was not put into effect without blood. When Moses had proclaimed every commandment of the law to all the people, he took the blood of calves, together with water, scarlet wool and branches of hyssop, and sprinkled the scroll and all the people. He said, 'This is the blood of the covenant, which God has commanded you to keep.' In the same way, he sprinkled with the blood both the tabernacle and everything used in its ceremonies. In fact, the law requires that nearly everything be cleansed with blood, and without the shedding of blood there is no forgiveness. (Heb. 9:16–22)

Admittedly, the writer of Hebrews is here drawing from a number of OT passages to make his point; but the point is clear nonetheless: the blood of the covenant signifies the cleansing necessary to ensure forgiveness.

For Israel's representatives to experience this close-up encounter with God, the covenant had to be formally ratified; the people had to be consecrated to God's service; they had to commit themselves to doing God's will; but most importantly, this covenant had to be sealed in blood. Only then, after the blood was splattered on both the altar and the people, could this representative group make their ascent; only then could they enjoy this meeting with God.

---

47. The first sentence (vv. 16–17) is my own translation, defended in Williamson 2007: 203–206. The rest of the quotation cites the NIV.

Delegation's ascent

And so, having sealed this covenant in blood, Israel's representatives make their way up the mountain to have this extraordinary encounter with God. Talk about a 'mountain-top experience'! This one caps them all: they

> went up and saw the God of Israel. Under his feet was something like a pavement made of lapis lazuli, as bright blue as the sky. But God did not raise his hand against these leaders of the Israelites; they saw God, and they ate and drank. (Exod. 24:9b–11, TNIV)

This experience is so amazing that both early translators and modern commentators insist on qualifying it in some way, and undoubtedly some such qualifications are necessary. Even so, however much we qualify it, it is clear that what is being described here is truly 'out of this world'. This group saw in reality what Ezekiel later saw only in a vision. Admittedly, they may not have seen quite as much as the prophet. Possibly, as several commentators suggest, they did not dare raise their eyes above God's feet; maybe seeing the bright blue platform on which God stood was enough; perhaps they instinctively fell prostrate before him in humble adoration. Yet, amazingly, these people ate and drank in God's presence. They shared in some form of communal meal. This covenant or communion meal was thus a further means of signifying that Israel's special relationship with Yahweh had been firmly established. So here they were, eating and drinking in the presence of God, enjoying fellowship with him, seeing the God of Israel – and living to tell the tale.

Conclusions

So then, what conclusions can we draw from this linear reading of the Sinai pericope? Well, for one thing, this narrative complex can indeed make chronological sense as it stands. Recourse to source criticism or literary devices such as 'resumptive repetition' is largely unnecessary. Granted, there may well be an occasional use of 'flashback'. For example, the short narrative located between the Decalogue and the covenant code may indeed take us back to the people's immediate reaction to the theophany described in chapter 19:16–19. However, to try to squeeze the revelation of the entire covenant code between verses 20 and 21 is more problematic. Why is there not even the slightest hint of this very long speech, if it did indeed take place between Moses ascending the mountain in chapter 19:20 and Yahweh speaking to him in chapter 19:21? The speech of Yahweh in chapter 20:22ff. clearly assumes that the people have heard Yahweh speak to them from heaven. But it does not suggest that they heard Yahweh say anything other than the Decalogue. It is therefore difficult to fit the revelation of the covenant code into chapter 19, as Chirichigno attempts to do.

If we read this narrative complex as suggested in this chapter in a linear or chronological fashion, there is no escaping the fact that Moses has indeed gone up the mountain at least five times by the time we reach the end of Exodus 24. What theological significance does this carry? Well, Moses is clearly presented in these chapters as the covenant mediator; and all this going up and coming back down serves to emphasize and reiterate this. By this means 'the inaccessibility of God and the mediatorial role of Moses are forcibly stressed' (Niccacci 1996: 224). Moses was the official go-between, the mediator of this covenant.[48] He communicated Yahweh's instructions to the people; and he communicated the people's response to Yahweh. Every revelation of Yahweh to the people (except for the Decalogue) is associated with another trek up and down the mountain for Moses. Just as earlier Moses undertook a mediating role between Yahweh and Pharaoh, so now he undertakes such a role between Yahweh and Israel – a role that grows in significance, not just in chapters 19–24, which recount the establishment of the Sinai covenant, but also in chapters 32–34, which describe its breaking and remaking.

---

48. While Pratt may be overstating it when he claims that 'Moses wrote Exodus as a defense of his leadership' (1990: 284), it is probably fair to see the divine legitimization of Moses' leadership as one of the book's overarching themes.

Through the mediation of Moses, Yahweh and Israel (a holy God and a sinful people) were at last able to enjoy fellowship with one another. Through the mediation of Moses, a meeting between heaven and earth took place, Israel's unique status was established, and one of the objectives of the exodus was finally realized as Israel's representatives worshipped God, albeit at a distance.

Bibliography

Alexander, T. D. (2002), *From Paradise to the Promised Land: An Introduction to the Pentateuch*, 2nd ed., Grand Rapids: Baker.

— (1999), 'The Composition of the Sinai Narrative in Exodus XIX 1–XXIV 11', *Vetus Testamentum* 49: 2–20.

Arichea, D. C. (1989), 'The Ups and Downs of Moses: Locating Moses in Exodus 19–33', *Bible Translator* 40: 244–246.

Chirichigno, G. C. (1987), 'The Narrative Structure of Exod 19–24', *Biblica* 68: 457–479.

Davies, J. A. (2004), *A Royal Priesthood: Literary and Intertextual Perspectives on an Image of Israel in Exodus 19.6*, Journal for the Study of the Old Testament, Supplement Series 395, London: T. & T. Clark.

Dozeman, T. B. (1989), *God on the Mountain: A Study of Redaction, Theology and Canon in Exodus 19–24*, Society of Biblical Literature Monograph Series 37, Atlanta: Scholars Press.

Dumbrell, W. J. (1994), *The Search for Order: Biblical Eschatology in Focus*, Grand Rapids: Baker.

Durham, J. I. (1987), *Exodus*, Word Biblical Commentary, Waco: Word.

Enns, P. (2000), *Exodus*, New International Version Application Commentary, Grand Rapids: Zondervan.

Fretheim, T. E. (1991), *Exodus*, Interpretation, Louisville: John Knox.

Hilber, J. W. (1996), 'Theology of Worship in Exodus 24', *Journal of the Evangelical Theological Society* 39: 177–189.

Janzen, W. (2000), *Exodus*, Believers Church Bible Commentary, Waterloo, Ont.: Herald.

Motyer, A. (2005), *The Message of Exodus: The Days of our Pilgrimage*, The Bible Speaks Today, Leicester: IVP.

Niccacci, A. (1996), 'Narrative Syntax of Exodus 19–24', in van Wolde, *Narrative Syntax*, 203–228.

Patrick, D. A. (1977), 'The Covenant Code Source', *Vetus Testamentum* 27: 145–157.

— (1986), *Old Testament Law*, London: SCM.

Pratt, R. L. (1990), *He Gave us Stories: The Bible Student's Guide to Interpreting Old Testament Narratives*, Brentwood: Wolgemuth & Hyatt.

Sailhamer, J. H. (1995), *Introduction to Old Testament Theology: A Canonical Approach*, Grand Rapids: Zondervan.

Scott, R. B. Y. (1950), 'A Kingdom of Priests (Exodus xix 6)', *Old Testament Studies* 8: 213–219.

Sprinkle, J. M. (2004), 'Law and Narrative in Exodus 19–24', *Journal of the Evangelical Theological Society* 47.2: 235–252.

Stuart, D. K. (2006), *Exodus*, New American Commentary, Nashville: Broadman & Holman.

Talstra, E. (1996), 'Workshop: Clause Types, Textual Hierarchy, Translation in Exodus 19, 20 and 24', in van Wolde, *Narrative Syntax*, 119–132.

Williamson, P. R. (2007), *Sealed with an Oath: Covenant in God's Unfolding Purpose*, New Studies in Biblical Theology 23, Nottingham: Apollos.

Wolde, E. van (ed.) (1996), *Narrative Syntax and the Hebrew Bible*, Leiden: Brill.

5. LIBERATION AND DESIRE: THE LOGIC OF LAW IN EXODUS AND BEYOND

Andrew Cameron

In this chapter, we shall examine the legal material in Exodus to consider whether modern readers should pattern their lives around any of its substance. An account is offered of the law's function as the divine ordering of various human desires in the social setting of Exodus. A brief review of some related Reformation discussions, and a modest proposal about how the law in Exodus might be read today, then follow.

The very notion that modern persons might attempt to pattern their life around the substance of the Exodus law will evoke various reactions. Some will be unsurprised, having always assumed something similar. Others will be incredulous, having always taken the book as an ancient artefact only. But they may share one assumption: this literature can be understood straightforwardly by modern readers.

Both the Ten Commandments (Exod. 20:3–7, there called 'Ten Words') and the 'Book of the Covenant' that follows (Exod. 21:1 – 23:13) contain a selection of 'apodictic' and 'casuistic' law. ('Apodictic' refers to the more general 'you shall'/'you shall not' form, whereas 'casuistic' describes the more specific case-oriented 'if/when . . . then . . .' form.) At several moments throughout, modern readers intuitively feel some affinity with the material. Here are some examples from the Book of the Covenant:[1]

1. 'Whoever steals a man and sells him, and anyone found in possession of him, shall be put to death' (21:16) was of intense interest in eighteenth- and nineteenth-century slavery debates.
2. Instructions about miscarriages caused by fighting men striking a pregnant woman (21:22) always find a place in debates about the moral status of embryos and fetuses.
3. The 'eye for eye, tooth for tooth, hand for hand, foot for foot' *lex talionis* law of Exodus 21:24 has not gone away in modern discussions about law and justice. The logic of OT retribution still has powerful advocates and detractors.
4. 'If a thief is found breaking in and is struck so that he dies, there shall be no bloodguilt for him' (22:2) reappeared in connection with the 1999 case of Tony Martin, the UK farmer who shot and killed a fleeing intruder.
5. Cases of ox-gorings (21:28–38) and other breaches of agricultural peace (22:5–15) may be alien scenarios for modern city dwellers, yet still represent a gritty and recognizable justice. Indeed, it has been claimed that the ox-goring laws have had a major impact in the philosophy and treatment of animals in Western jurisdictions (Finkelstein 1981).
6. The procedure for handling premarital sex, generally resulting in marriage (22:16–17), drives some serious Christian enquirers to ask whether premarital sex creates an ethical presumption that, ideally, the two will go on to marry.
7. 'You shall not wrong a sojourner or oppress him, for you were sojourners in the land of Egypt' (22:21) suggests a 'spiritual' logic that some apply to hospitality today.
8. 'If you lend money to any of my people with you who is poor, you shall not be like a moneylender to him, and you shall not exact interest from him' (22:25) has ongoing leverage for some in arguments about modern capitalism's interest practices.

---

1. Quotations in this chapter are from the ESV.

Ancient though they may be, something about these texts seems
recognizably to be *ours*. Of the Ten Words themselves, we need
not look far to find the proprietorial sense that many modern
people bring to a discussion of them. Our access seems immediate, and their sense and reference seem plain. Discussions centre
on the extent to which these laws are still binding (Sabbath, or
not?), or on the people upon whom they are still binding (US
public courtrooms, or not?). They are even presented as a universal moral 'gold standard' for well-ordered societies everywhere
(Kuntz 2004). Yet, although these laws can feel proximal to us, we
often drift as we read them:

1. There are institutions we neither understand nor like: 'If [a
   slave's] master gives him a wife and she bears him sons or
   daughters, the wife and her children shall be her master's, and he
   shall go out alone' (21:4).
2. Some practices cause us to recoil: 'When a man sells his daughter as a slave . . .' (21:7).
3. We find some of the penalties extraordinary: 'Whoever strikes
   his father or his mother shall be put to death' (21:15).
4. There are settings and problems that mean little to us: 'If a man
   steals an ox or a sheep, and kills it or sells it, he shall repay five
   oxen for an ox, and four sheep for a sheep' (22:1).
5. Recourse to God is indicated in such ways as we would have no
   idea how to apply, as when a thief's identity is unclear and
   people 'come near to' or 'come before' God to find 'the one
   whom God condemns', who then pays double to his neighbour
   (22:7–9).
6. Crimes are listed that we find hard to measure: 'You shall not
   permit a sorceress to live' (22:18).
7. The fierceness of divine retribution we find hard to compre-
   hend: 'my wrath will burn,' says God (against the mistreatment
   of widows and orphans), 'and I will kill you with the sword, and
   your wives shall become widows and your children fatherless'
   (22:22–24).
8. There are rituals we no longer accept: 'You shall not delay to offer
   from the fullness of your harvest and from the outflow of your
   presses. The firstborn of your sons you shall give to me' (22:29).

9. Some passages (such as the culmination of the Book of the Law, 23:14–33) are quite particular to another time and place, and seem very inaccessible now.

The material is presented for a particular people at the foot of a particular mountain, and any first impression of easy access proves to be illusory. Rather, we do well to ask what makes us feel any affinity with it at all. What constitutes the 'overlap', if there is one, between modern readers and those at the foot of the mountain? That inquiry is interesting and important, and we shall return to consider some of the ways in which theology has construed the overlap that makes some parts of the text seem immanent.

But in an evangelical habit of reading, questions about ourselves are derivative upon whatever was happening on and around that mountain. The prior question becomes 'What does this law have to do with the liberation that is Exodus, and what is the logic of this law for that Exodus?' Only after we have discovered something of this logic may we find what of it remains for subsequent uses of the material.

Of course, centuries of theological and biblical scholarship have been concerned with the logic of OT law and the theologic of its relation to modern readers. It is beyond our scope to survey all that scholarship, just as it is to respond to the moments listed above where laws seem abstruse or morally problematic. The chapter will also include only some brief assertions about other Pentateuchal law, NT Christology, and Pauline theology. In many respects, then, what follows can be considered only a preliminary account of the logic of law in Exodus and beyond, by way of an observation, a summary and some suggestions:

- The observation will be that law appears in Exodus in a very pointed response to two elemental aspects of human life: *desire* and *sociality*. In that setting, the law's first appearance is experienced as a blessing that brings relief. Some details of the Book of the Covenant and the Ten Words will be examined to tease out its logic in its setting.
- The summary will be of some Reformed thought wrestling with the ongoing resonances of these texts. Although this summary

will be well known to readers of Reformed theology, some easily lost distinctions are worth reiterating.
• The suggestions are a modest proposal for Christian reading of the law today, with a few final remarks about its relevance for contemporary legislators.

These will, it is hoped, assist discussion of the law's relevance (or not) for a new generation.

A difficult three months

The story of the law's appearing began long before the mountain came into view. If Sinai dominates the second half of this book, then its first fifteen chapters are dominated by the longed-for liberation, which stands ahead of every word, action and endeavour like the promise of water for a marathon runner, or like the wedding night for a virgin, or like the hope of a cure for the sufferer of chronic illness.

The delay is heightened by Pharaoh's endlessly cruel prevarications, and by the escalating diplomatic tension with Moses (chs. 5–11). The breathless readiness of the final meal, the night and day of flight, and the rumble of horses in pursuit keep us hovering upon the brink of liberation for three more long chapters (12–14). Then, finally, with crashing water and vanquished foes still echoing around us, we arrive at the final exultant ecstasy of freedom in Moses' joyful song and Miriam's exuberant dance.

Yet, after all that, within three days, or one short verse, or four short clauses of text time, 'they found no water' (15:22). After such prolonged anticipation, such an extraordinary consummation and such majestic liberation, simple human creaturely limitation reasserts itself within the blink of an eye. They found no water, and 'so they grumbled'.

History's judgment against their grumbling would be harsh, for it was indeed a harbinger of what was to come. But in terms of the immediate text, such a judgment is premature. This desire for water and the menace of an unhappy crowd will be well known to anyone who has been tasked to manage a social setting, whether

that be a carload of tired children, a conference whose catering
has gone wrong, or a nation under stress. If climate change
reduces dams to a few per cent of capacity, or if a post-peak oil
milieu makes food deliveries intermittent and closes airports,
modern people will react similarly. Few experiences are more com-
plicated and frightening than to have the same strong desires as
those of the mob that surrounds us.

'They found no water' is actually the first of three desperate
moments in the chapters that follow: thirst at Marah (ch. 15),
hunger at Sin (ch. 16) and thirst again at Rephidim (ch. 17). What
we also see in these incidents is a pattern of gracious and generous
divine response, with no hint of judgment.

In the thirst at Marah, God quenches their thirst, then gives
what he calls 'a statute and a rule' that consists in an instruction to
listen to his statutes (15:25–26); then he quenches thirst again at
the springs of Elim. The insertion of statute into a thirst and its
quenching hints that the voice of God quenches thirst as much as
does water.

Likewise, the hunger in the wilderness of Sin is met with manna.
Again, God makes no comment in the judgment, and the voice of
God joins the sating of their hunger with walking in his law (*tôrâ*,
16:4). Their hunger for meat is also sated (vv. 12–13), with no judgment against grumbling.

Further thirst at Rephidim is quenched again, and again without
divine comment on the grumbling. But on this occasion there is
no mention by God of his law. We are left waiting to see if God
will quench and sate them in that other way, through the presence
of his word.

After a quick war (presaging the shape of things to come,
17:8–16), we find ourselves walking with Jethro and viewing Moses'
messy life through his wise and orderly eye (ch. 18). The heady days
of liberation and of Moses' and Miriam's song seem long gone,
and Moses finally unburdens himself about a difficult three months
('Then Moses told his father-in-law . . . all the hardship that had
come upon them in the way', v. 8). But Jethro (vv. 9–12) is able to
see a bigger picture, praising God for this liberation, and in the
brief ceremony that follows we are for a moment transported back
to that exultant moment of release from the oppressor.

But yet again, a new 'hunger' and 'thirst' is upon the people (vv. 13–16) as they stand around Moses, waiting, this time, for the judgment of decisions. God also quenches this 'thirst' when, as Moses puts it, 'I make them know the statutes of God and his laws' (v. 16).

The liberation from Egypt is not simple. It gives rise to a new social setting in all its complexity. The 'liberation' from their brick-making without straw to foot-slogging without water gives this group a slightly desperate edge. The absence at this stage of any judgment against their need and their edginess highlights their status as a frail collective of human creatures with legitimate but unmet desires.

There are few intellectual tasks more difficult to think well about than the interrelation between our desires as individuals, and our need for each other in groups. For any group to remain a group requires some desires to be affirmed and met, with others moderated and resisted. The people's pressing need for water and food gives rise to an equally pressing need for judicial processes. By the time Jethro makes his visit, both participants and readers are wondering what sort of 'liberation' this will become.

'God will be with you'

It is easy, then, to miss the significance of Jethro's speech for what is to follow. When Moses says, 'I make them know the statutes of God and his laws', Jethro replies, somewhat unexpectedly, 'What you are doing is not good.' There is the simple imprudence of Moses tiring himself out. But more is needed, prefigured when Jethro says, 'God be with you' or 'God will be with you' (v. 19).

Jethro proposes a way in which the people, through Moses, may more permanently learn (v. 20) 'the statutes and the laws' and 'the way in which they must walk and what they must do'. Moses takes a new role as mediator between God and people, and good men are appointed to devolve the judiciary and to enable local decisions. As a result (v. 23), God will direct Moses, Moses will survive and the people will find peace. Their 'thirst', we could say, will be 'quenched'. Indeed, the plan succeeds as the restlessness of the crowd is stilled, and there is such order (v. 26) as could almost make it seem the problem is solved.

But there remains a niggling, unresolved silence by God after Rephidim, since which time Moses has sought to deliver God's laws and judgments to the best of his limited ability. Perhaps we expect another small response from God, like the 'statutes' and 'laws' mentioned so far (e.g. 15:25–26), when in his new role, 'Moses went up to God' (19:3).

It turns out, however, that the extent and multifaceted thoroughness by which God is with them defies all expectation. He is 'with' on the mountain, 'with' in words of teaching, judgment and statute, and 'with' in the building of a tabernacle. Jethro's prospect of 'God with you' was directed just to Moses; yet here is God's gracious immanence for all, exceeding their wildest expectations.

This quenching turns out to be such a torrent that later the people will need take cover from it, and put their hope in a representative to meditate it all to them. But not at first: there is a tragically touching moment, both of longing and stilled restlessness, when the people declare, 'All that the LORD has spoken we will do' (19:8). In the covenant on the mountain that follows (ch. 24), we find a second and third tragic protestation of heartfelt participation (24:3, 7). For just a moment, all is as it should be.

The Ten Words (20:2–17)

Israel's presenting problem, it has been suggested, is that individuals with desires must coexist as a society. Each person's desires exist on a spectrum from innocent creaturely need, through to excesses of falsely imagined need that can translate into voracious consumption. The conditions for social harmony will consist in the affirmation and assistance of proper longings, and the resistance of desire's worst excesses.

The Ten Words seem crafted to achieve precisely this end. Obviously enough, the first four reveal God to be the proper object of worship. But we learn something about human desire when we see that three of these four guide *the practices by which* they worship. Desire, it seems, needs not only to be guided toward the worship of God, but also against a kind of misdirection that takes the form of attachment to false objects, whether graven images or the name of God used for improper ends; and it has to be guided away from the kind of preoccupied obsession with work that leaves no room for the expression of affection toward God.

With the proper worship of God set in place as the ultimate target of human desire, attention shifts to five practices. The practice of parental honour puts parents under God as another proper focus for people's affection; and the four boundaries that follow steer their practices away from four arenas most likely to stir improper desire, so filling their horizons as to make a society unsustainable.

It may be unusual to talk in such a manner about the Ten Words. We do not usually think of them as a strategy for ordering desire by helping it to find its proper home. But it is the tenth word that suggests this proposal. It is often singled out as somehow oddly different from the others, most of which seem to concern outward behaviour. But those are not just any outward behaviours: they are eight behaviours that for these people, perhaps for all people, are most likely to be waylaid by the same inner circuitry as drives our hunger and thirst. Hence the tenth word reveals what has been at work all along: the problem of the inner world that drives perjury, theft, adultery, murder, contempt for loving authority, overwork and false or absent worship. The Ten Words are a workable, memorable sketch of what we really need against what we think we need, and although it is not necessarily comprehensive or exhaustive, it is a more than adequate guide for how to manage desire within a society.

In his determination to find the worst in this text, Christopher Hitchens (2007: 100) asserts the bans on murder, adultery, theft and perjury to be ridiculous. 'No society ever discovered has failed to protect itself from self-evident crimes' such as these. Yet on the other hand, he finds the Tenth Word 'absurd' and 'impossible': 'One may be forcibly restrained from wicked actions . . . but to forbid people from *contemplating* them is too much' (100).

According to Hitchens, God should instead 'have taken more care to invent a different species' than the desiring human (Hitchens 2007: 100). Hitchens wants us simply to believe that morality is obvious, and that our desires are basically good. On this view, of course, the Ten Words are unintelligible. But the Ten Words actually reveal the opposite case: morality is not obvious or self-evident when desire is leading us, and a society only succeeds in protection against crime when each member's immediate wants are eclipsed by a common object of love.[2]

The Book of the Covenant (20:22 – 23:33)

Although the Ten Words are easily the best-known example of law in Exodus, in Exodus' own terms, they do not exhaust what needs to be said about law. If we are to do proper justice to the law in Exodus, we need also to familiarize ourselves with the lesser-known material of what becomes referred to as 'the Book of the Covenant' (24:7).

The Book of the Covenant is arranged roughly according to topic, with only some of the Ten Words reappearing clearly in concept. On first glance, the section is a 'ceremonial sandwich' with 'civil filling':

20:22: 'Then the LORD said to Moses'
20:23: repeat of *Word 1*
20:24: about altars
20:25: no dressed stones (*Word 2*)
20:26: no steps
21:1: 'the laws (*mišpāṭîm*) you are to set before them':
21:2–11: slaves and concubinage
21:12–27: kidnaps, deaths, assaults (*Word 5*)
21:28–36: oxen mad or lost
22:1–4: on thieves (*Word 8*)
22:5–15: on restitution
22:16–19: sorcery and sex
22:20: repeat of *Word 1*
22:21–27: aliens and the poor
22:28: on authority (*Word 3*)
22:29–30: sacrifices and firstborn

---

2. I have borrowed the concept of a society's 'common objects of love' from Oliver O'Donovan's Augustinian approach to social and political thought (O'Donovan 2002).

22:31: holiness and torn flesh

23:1–7: lawsuits and stray donkeys (*Words 9, 10*)

23:8: bribes

23:9: aliens again

23:10–12: Sabbath years and days (*Word 4*)

23:13: 'Pay strict attention to everything I have said to you'

23:13: repeat of *Word 1*

23:14–33: Festivals and sacrifices, with special reference to the journey ahead

A more orderly arrangement for the material has been proposed as follows (Staalduine-Sulman 2006: 209–210), although some irregularities remain:

A. *Cult*: the altar as the one place (20:22–26)
  B. *Weak*: slaves and maids (21:1–11)
   C. *Capital charges*: social (21:12–17)
    D. *Bodily integrity*: injuries (21:18–36)
     E. *Theft and ownership* (21:37 – 22:12)
    D'. *Bodily integrity*: cattle and virgins (22:13–16)
   C'. *Capital charges*: cultic (22:17–19)
  B'. *Weak*: strangers, widows and orphans, the poor (22:20–26)
A'. *Cult*: curses and consecration (22:27–30).

Several features of the Book of the Covenant are worth noting:

1. The laws are patchy, covering some areas in detail and others briefly, with many areas of life unaddressed. This law code seems random, even sketchy (as perhaps ours might appear to others).
2. The laws cover a variety of specific cases, which are typical of an agrarian pre-monarchical people, and are consistent with community life in Egypt or with episodes in the patriarchal narratives.[3] These are precisely the kinds of cases that tribal elders

---

3. Calum Carmichael (Carmichael 1992) argues for the origin of the 'Book of the Covenant' in the Jacob narratives.

will be called upon to judge – perhaps not then and there in the wilderness, but soon enough.

3. There is no attempt to distil some aspirational, utopian statement of community life. Even the Ten Words do not do so. Some material in the Book of the Covenant has no obvious connection to the Ten Words; and where the Ten Words are applied, the application is almost random. Not all Ten can confidently be found there, and there is no systematic attempt to present the ones that are.

4. Yet key moral realities, distinctive against other ancient law codes, can be discerned in its layout and themes. Christopher Wright finds here that God is above all else, that people do matter more than objects, and that the needs and circumstances of some people generate a more immediate moral claim than even the legitimate claims of others (Staalduine-Sulman 2006: 211, n. 20; Wright 2004: 306, 309, 312). Paul Williamson has indicated (in this volume) the way they inculcate love for God and neighbour, and do not discriminate according to social class.

   a. In the wider section, there is an intermixing of Hebrew lexemes, which may be glossed as follows:[4]

   b. *mišpāṭ*, a judgment or verdict (15:25; 21:1; 24:3)

   c. *ḥōq*, a canon, rule or regulation (15:25,26; 18:16, 20)

   d. *tôrâ*, an instruction or teaching (16:4; 18:16, 20)

   e. *miṣwâ*, a command (15:26; 20:6). And, of course, in 20:1 (cf. 24:3) what seem like the most momentous statements are simply *dĕbārîm*, 'words' or 'sayings'.

What is the status of this law? It could be 'emergency law' for an unruly desert people; but its expectations of imminent arrival in the land, and its references to situations in agrarian life, suggest that it is no stop-gap measure. It could be 'eternal law' for all people everywhere; but clearly not in the first instance, where it brings order to the passions and desires of a particular group in a particular time and place. Of course, we are not wrong to hear a

---

4. I owe this quick summary of these nuanced terms to George Athas.

resonance with the creation accounts throughout the Ten Words, which lends them some enduring significance. But in the main, this is a first body of law for an emerging nation. However, the story of its establishment is only completed with the narration of the golden-calf incident – surely the most humiliating episode to be found in any people's account of the origins of their national identity.

The denouement (ch. 32)

The opening verse of chapter 32 underlines the short-sightedness of their desire. Instead of waiting with eager expectation for the presence of God in his tabernacle and in his rule of divine law, Moses' delay inflames a desire for replacement gods to bring the security they crave. As Michael Raiter puts it (in this volume, p. 68), idolatry is their 'default position when weak and vulnerable'.

The chapter also underlines the deranging intensity of the group, as the threat of the mob provokes one of the OT's most shocking examples of moral collapse. A tool in the hand would profane the stones of the altar and was not to touch any of them (20:25); yet just such a tool in the hand of Aaron gouges out this bull. The feasting that follows, perhaps even using the meat and manna of Yahweh, spills over into an explosion of revelry. Added together the scene is a cameo of what the NT will later call 'flesh'.

The viewpoint switches to the quietness of the mountain, giving way to the quietly tense confrontation between an interceding Moses and the God who points to the people's corruption. Something ominous and momentous is signalled in the narrative pause to describe

> the two tablets of the testimony in his hand, tablets that were written on both sides; on the front and on the back they were written. The tablets were the work of God, and the writing was the writing of God, engraved on the tablets. (32:15–16)

Why this detail, of which readers have already been twice informed (24:12; 31:18)? As Moses and Joshua descend and the sound of uproar escalates, we know the One whose purpose is to reign supreme through these tablets. So when God's furious

representative delivers them against the foot of the mountain
(the same *taḥat hāhār* as where the people are gathered, 24:4), the
sound of their smashing heralds a new thing, where the law has
hurtled into a collision with the people for whom it was written.
The law, which was to assist in ordering proper affection, has
been greeted with an explosion of passion; and what was once
anticipated with such eagerness as God's way of being with them
to guard their desires and to order their community, now takes its
place as an alien presence. It slices across these short-sighted,
self-justifying and rapacious desires and judges the mob. Nor
does the shattering mean it no longer applies: its republication
(34:1–4) makes clear that in the tablets' shattering, it is *the people*,
not the law, who are somehow shattered.

Resonances beyond Exodus

We began by considering modern readers of this material, and by
asking in what consists the assumption that we understand something so manifestly ancient. The Reformation discussion over the
status of OT law can also be seen as an attempt to answer this
kind of question. This section will briefly explore that discussion.

It is perhaps worth noting that the intermixing of Hebrew
lexemes (with Paul's later rhetorical variations in his use of *nomos*)
is not easily handled in scholastic, Reformed or modern discussions. These expect language to be used with analytic consistency;
but senses and references of the term 'law' generally encompass
many nuances of meaning.[5] This difficulty keeps reappearing and
equivocation over the term remains a difficult problem. There is
little we can do about the problem other than to observe and con-
tinually monitor what sense and referent is on view.

---

5. So in Calvin's *Institutes*, biblical 'law' can refer to the morality of the
   Decalogue (2.8); or to the various collections within the Pentateuch
   (*Institutes* 4.20.14–16); or simply to everything Moses said (2.7.1). But in
   Calvin at least, each sense is generally made clear by definition or by
   context (Calvin 1960: 348, n. 1).

One ancient method of resolving law into some finer distinctions is pithily summarized in the second half of the seventh article of the Thirty-Nine:

> Although the Law given from God by Moses, as touching Ceremonies and Rites, do not bind Christian men, nor the Civil precepts thereof ought of necessity to be received in any commonwealth; yet notwithstanding, no Christian man whatsoever is free from the obedience of the Commandments which are called Moral. (Article 7, 1662)

For moderns, this half-article is too brief and seems to conceal more than it reveals. Its threefold distinction (ceremonial, civil, moral) distils a cluster of long-running theological discussions; but taken at face value these distinctions lose any organic connection to OT law and take on an appearance of arbitrariness, as if each OT verse or sentence can instantly be sorted into one of three hoppers. As Michael Hill rightly observes:

> Many people like to divide the regulations and laws that give shape to God's covenant with Israel into moral, cultic and civil elements. In this way it is hoped that the cultic and civil elements can be jettisoned with the coming of the New Covenant in Christ, and the moral component retained. However the Bible itself does not operate in this way. The Old Covenant is seen as a discrete unified package with a number of aspects, not parts. These various aspects cannot be unravelled and treated as parts. (2002:74)

Such distinctions are often applied to Exodus quite simply. 'Moral law' is equated to the Decalogue, 'civil law' to the large central section of the Book of the Covenant, and 'ceremonial law' to the outside 'sandwich' layers of the Book of the Covenant, and to the tabernacle instructions. But even in Exodus the law is 'a discrete unified package with a number of aspects, not parts'. We can find what looks like 'moral law' and 'ceremonial law' within 'civil law' (22:21–22, 28–31; 23:1–2, 6–9, 12–13). Although the seeming 'moral laws' often take the 'apodictic' form and the 'civil law' often takes the 'casuistic' form, even then we can find exceptions (e.g. an apodictic 'civil' law in 22:18, perhaps a casuistic 'moral' law in 22:22–23, and most apodictic 'ceremonial' law). Nor do the inter-mixed lexemes give us much to work with in order to clarify these distinctions. In short, the material is not easy to codify using the threefold distinction.

Yet to return to Article 7, we should not too quickly pluck it from the theological arguments that gave it intelligibility and a context. For example, the article summarily distances itself from the possibility of an OT-style theocracy. No OT civil law 'ought of necessity to be received in any commonwealth'. In this conclusion, it agrees with John Calvin, who argues that every nation is free to make whatever laws it considers profitable as long as these are 'in conformity to [the] perpetual rule of love' (*Institutes* 4.20.15). For Calvin, particular societies in specific circumstances rightly enact such laws as are needed, provided they are made within boundaries of equity and natural law, and to promote gentleness and love (4.20.15–16).

His conclusion is premised upon a nuanced use of the threefold distinction. Moral law directs our love, first to God and then to one another. It is 'the true and eternal rule of righteousness' (4.20.15), and is 'a testimony of natural law' (4.20.16). From moral law springs ceremonial laws, which tutored the Jews in piety to God and toward their Christological eschaton (as in Gal. 4:3–4). From moral law springs civil laws – those specific 'formulas of equity and justice, by which they might live together blamelessly and peaceably' (4.20.15). Calvin does not fall into the arbitrariness Michael Hill sees in others, for according to Calvin the ceremonial and the civil both expressed morality, instantiating respectively reverent service of God and love for humanity.

Calvin always camouflages his debts to Aquinas, but it is not hard to see a direct influence in this discussion. Aquinas also thought that ceremonial and civil laws were specific manifestations of a more basic natural moral law. It has to be conceded that Aquinas' weakness for seizing on some handy biblical texts risks trivializing his view. When God instructs Moses to teach *miṣwâ*, *ḥûqqîm* and *mišpāṭîm* (Deut. 6:1), Aquinas takes the 'precept' or 'command' (*miṣwâ*) to refer to the moral order, from which springs the ceremonial 'statutes' (*ḥûqqîm*) and the judicial 'rules' or 'judgments' (*mišpāṭîm*). His use of this handy triad sidesteps some semantic complexity; and he simply fails to resist a moment of biblical opportunism that is the occupational hazard of all theologians when 'holy and righteous and good' in Romans 7:12 are merely taken to correspond to 'ceremonial and civil and moral' respectively (Aquinas 1937: 1a2ae.99.a4). But these complaints should not cause us to suppose that Aquinas' overall argument is flawed. He described an underlying divinely ordered moral reality experienced by humanity as a 'natural law', which is then graciously 'republished' for humanity by God in the OT and NT (Pinckaers 1995: 171–185). Calvin was sufficiently persuaded by this approach to deploy it in broad outline. What matters for our purposes is that for both, the morality of moral law pivots upon a conception of a 'natural law'. (An important qualification to this conception is considered below.)

The moral, ceremonial and civil distinction was a tool for exegetical discussion, which tried to map the conceptual logic of the biblical material. But another set of distinctions, three so-called uses of the law, tried to map some modes of the biblical law's relevance for people today. These more uniquely Reformed distinctions do not easily map on to the older moral–ceremonial–civil divide, and the relationship between the 'uses' and the older formulation is confusing at first.

The 'uses' make another threefold distinction. But this new triad is not discussing the whole Mosaic legal code, as the moral–ceremonial–civil distinction does. Rather, the 'uses' of the law are an argument about how we are to receive *only the 'moral' component* of biblical law.

Another point of confusion lies in the unfortunate fact that in various Reformed documents, the first two uses were often reversed. Terminology of 'first use' and 'second use' was never quite settled. In Calvin's exposition of the moral law's uses (*Institutes* 2.8):

- Its first use (2.7.6–9) is a 'theological use': it acts as a 'mirror', convicting both believers and unbelievers of sin, driving them to repent and find grace through faith.
- Its second use (2.7.10–11) is a 'civil use', a 'bridle' upon wilful sinners, so enabling communities to live in relative harmony.

(Calvin cites 1 Tim. 1:9–10 in support, although the text could equally support the moral law's theological use.) We must note that for Calvin and for Article 7 (and for the Westminster Confession 19.4), it is this *second use of the OT moral law, not the OT civil law as such*, that is to form the basis for any modern system of justice.

There was a broad Reformation consensus upon these two uses of moral law. Even the antinomian John Agricola could agree to the *civil* use of the moral law. (His complaint was against its theological use.) In contrast, we would probably find a less clear consensus among Christians of Reformed lineage today about either use. (It would be interesting to map the history of the change.)

But the main Reformation dispute was over the so-called third use of the law, summarized in Article 7 as that 'no Christian man whatsoever is free from the obedience of the Commandments which are called Moral'. Calvin is in no doubt:

> The third and principal use, which pertains more closely to the proper purpose of the law, finds its place among believers . . . Here is the best instrument for them to learn more thoroughly each day the nature of the Lord's will. (*Institutes* 2.7.12)

In Calvin's startling metaphor, this use is 'a whip to an idle and balky ass' and 'a constant sting' upon the believer – always with the proviso, of course, that no believer is condemned by law or justified by its works.

Noticing the psalmist's love of the law, Calvin asks, 'what would be less loveable than the law if . . . it troubled souls through fear, and distressed them through fright?' In the law is also found a promise of grace 'which alone sweetens what is bitter' (2.7.12).

Calvin's disagreement with Luther about this third use seems pointed and irreconcilable. Luther finds only the first two uses, both blended in the following statement of absolute finality (with archaisms of the English translation slightly modified):

> the law is also a light, which shows and reveals, not the grace of God, not righteousness and life; but sin, death, the wrath and judgment of

God. For, as in the mount Sinai the thundering, lightening, the thick and
dark cloud, the hill smoking and flaming, and all that terrible show did
not rejoice nor quicken the children of Israel, but terrified and
astonished them, and showed how unable they were, with all their purity
and holiness, to abide the presence of God speaking to them out of the
cloud: even so the law, when it is in his [sic] true sense, does nothing else
but reveal sin, engender wrath, accuse and terrify men, so that it brings
them to the very brink of desperation. This is the proper use of the law,
and here it has an end, and it ought to go no further. (1953: 302)

But if Exodus is anything to go by, has Luther gone too far?
After all, the nuance of that narrative is to say that despite their
awestruck fear of God on the mountain, this is also that brief
interlude where the law is loved, representing relief and order.
There is not yet a warrant for Luther's sharp distinction of gospel
and law, for, after all, the representatives of the people 'saw the
God of Israel . . . And he did not lay his hand on the chief men of
the people of Israel; they beheld God, and ate and drank' (Exod.
24:10–11). Does Calvin's third use better reflect that moment
where the community gratefully offers to do everything for the
God who is with them, ordering their desire, creating community,
meeting their needs with sayings and judgments?

There is rarely much to be gained by playing Calvin and Luther
against each other. In this case, there really is a profound sense in
which both are right. Exegetically speaking, Luther may have been
a little quick to see disaster prefigured at Sinai; but theologically
speaking, he is in good company with the author to the Hebrews
in seeing disaster prefigured there (Heb. 12:18–21), just as the
psalmist sees disaster prefigured in the murmurings in the wilderness (Ps. 95:8–9). For exegetically speaking, the disaster does strike
when the tablets of the law shatter among the people, and law
becomes precisely the arch-enemy of which Luther speaks.

Calvin's and Luther's opposing position on the third use of
moral law reflects a dialectic present in the text of Exodus, where
the law is both a friend and an enemy to the people. It is a friend
because it offers to order their desires and to build their community. It is an enemy because it judges a community whose desires
explode in every direction. But where does that dialectic leave *us*?

In what way should we look to the law, if at all? Obviously, this discussion did not stop at the Reformation, and we shall return below to touch on three recent proposals.

A modest proposal

However, in this section another proposal for the Christian reading of the law will be presented, although the thought is far from new. The proposal is simply that Christians now read the law to grow in Christian wisdom. It no longer comes to us with the force of direct command. In the overall 'story-arc' of the Bible, we receive it in the same way we receive a proverb, a psalm or some other biblical wisdom; and we receive this wisdom 'in Christ', reading with the kind of faith in him that converts it into *Christian* wisdom. It helps to inform us about moral reality understood Christianly.

It must be conceded that there is some difficulty in detailing how this hermeneutical project should proceed. That difficulty may be an artefact of the way that in general, true 'wisdom' cannot easily be described in advance. Nonetheless, four lines of evidence can be offered in support of the proposal:

1. A 'natural law', properly understood as the God-given order of creation, undergirds both law and wisdom.
2. There are moments in Exodus that look 'wisdom-like', where laws are premised on the basis of this order.
3. Some Jewish intertestamental thinkers argue for similarities between wisdom and law, despite their different origins.
4. Moments from Exodus are used to build Christian wisdom in the NT.

Each of these lines of evidence will now be examined in turn.

'Natural law'
We observed that for Aquinas and Calvin, OT ceremonial law was a specific instance of the moral law to worship God; and OT civil law was a specific instance of the moral law to order human

desires and human society. On their view, 'moral law' is an expression of 'natural law'.

'Natural law' is a concept that generates some heat among Protestants when it connotes an uncomplicated autonomous capacity to read morality from creation. But this sense is emphatically not what Calvin (nor probably even Aquinas) had in mind. Calvin simply meant to refer to moral realities that God has embedded into that creation which is divinely described in moral terms as 'very good' (Gen. 1:31).

By discerning a 'moral law' in OT law, theologians do not mean to be arbitrary. They simply refer to the aspect of it that is intelligible because of our common pattern as humans: our shared interdependence with the earth and with each other, the similar desires we have, and the need to know God that resides within us all. Law names, articulates and guards the moral structure of things, just as wisdom literature does in its own way. Biblical literature does so with a precision and to an extent that no human mind could achieve unaided.

Could Luther live with this conception of natural law as undergirding the structure of moral law? He speaks of the moral law's 'total power and force' (Luther 1960: 116; 'Law', §34) and its applicability to the 'whole world' (Luther 1960: 114–115; 'Law', §§7, 13). Nothing in Luther's writing ever suggests that the Christian is released from moral reality, and to that extent he would approve a qualified conception of a 'natural law' as undergirding OT law.

Moments of moral order in Exodus

George Athas (in this volume, p. 53) has explained that ancient *mišpāṭ* justice set 'everything in its proper assigned place so that it may fulfil its assigned function in relational harmony with the rest of creation'. What he showed as occurring in the first section of Exodus becomes explicit in the *mišpāṭîm* of the Book of the Covenant, when we see a few instances of what might be called 'wisdom-based law'.

The clearest example is where 'you shall take no bribe, for a bribe blinds the clear-sighted and subverts the cause of those who are in the right' (23:8). This divine command actually takes its warrant from a wrong but persistent pattern of human behaviour, and even though the language is different, its logic bears striking resemblance to some wisdom aphorisms (e.g. Prov. 17:23; Eccles. 7:7). Arguably, up to six other such 'wisdom moments' appear (20:26; 22:21, 27; 23:2, 9, 12).

But, more significantly, it is possible to show that the Decalogue itself alludes throughout to the creation and fall narratives.[6] The uncreated otherness of God; the telos of the earth in rest; a son's slaughter of his parent's son; the one man to one woman relationship; the theft of the fruit; the shifting of blame; the desire that drove it all – in response to each of these, each saying in the Decalogue guards and restores what began as very good.

We have warrant on both fronts, then, to discern a moral aspect to the Exodus laws that finds its origin in the creation's moral order. (The law against bribery, premised on a wrongful pattern of human behaviour, might not at first seem to reflect divine moral order. But this regularly recurrent *pattern* of human behaviour is a corruption of the predictability of human desire, which is itself an aspect of the divinely ordered cosmos.) This ordering may peek through here and there in the material: perhaps the kindly reminder to the priest not to ascend the stairs before the invention of underwear recalls the goodness of our sexuality for our marriage. But there is no need to find everything grounded in created moral order. For example, there may be an arbitrariness to the refusal of torn flesh as a symbol of holiness (22:31).

The main point is that the creation's moral order grounds some of the Exodus laws just as it grounds some later wisdom. To quote Moses' words in Deuteronomy 4:6: 'Keep them and do them, for that will be your wisdom and your understanding in the sight of the peoples, who, when they hear all these statutes, will say, "Surely this great nation is a wise and understanding people."'

Intertestamental thinkers
Even though the wisdom literature is a different OT stream than the legal and salvation-historical material, Eckhardt Schnabel sees

---

6. So Carmichael argues, although he also thinks that the first table derives from the golden-calf account (1992: 22–50).

a convergence between law and wisdom in Jewish intertestamental literature:

> both law and wisdom are repeatedly linked with the concept of life as 'walking' in (good) 'ways' . . . Similarly, both law and wisdom are often compared with 'light' . . . Both law and wisdom are intimately linked with righteousness, holiness, and purity as goal of the enlightened walk in the proper way. (1985: 344–345)

Indeed, in Ecclesiasticus (Sirach) 24.23, wisdom is explicitly identified with Mosaic law in general, and with the Book of the Covenant in particular.[7] Of course, many intertestamental developments are not directly relevant to a Christian reading of the Bible; but Schnabel's point is that in some respects, Paul's use of the law reflects the intertestamental convergence of law and wisdom. But rather than testing Schnabel's argument, we can arrive at a similar result by observing the uses of the Exodus law in the NT.

NT usage of Exodus

What might it look like to use OT law in the NT as data there for Christian wisdom? At least a few 'tests' can be imagined:

- We may see law peppered unsystematically throughout moral discussion, or allusions to it threaded throughout moral discussion, since it would function only as one of a number of sources for Christian wisdom.
- We may see the purpose or ground of any given law functioning as the primary moral datum, rather than its deontic force per se.
- When law does appear, we may expect to see its inner logic expanded, and/or amplified, and/or reapplied.

With one exception, these are precisely the features we find in NT usage of Exodus laws. Its appearances are few, but when it does

---

7. See Levenson for another discussion of this verse and of law as a form of wisdom (Levenson 1980: 25 and *passim*).

appear, its function in moral discussion is unpredictably creative. Its depths are often plumbed in a kind of Christian wonderment.

The absence of the first four Decalogue 'words' from the NT would be almost incredible, except that their logic is richly interwoven throughout the NT, possibly at the level of several subtle allusions. The direct quotation of the seventh word in Ephesians 6:2–3 about parents appears to be the exception subverting the thesis here presented, for it is a direct quote in support of an apostolic instruction. But in this passage no other law is used in this way, and this one is singled out for the promise attached to it. It is at least plausible that the Christian child is being asked to grow in wisdom about the moral realities of honour to parents, rather than being commanded merely on the basis that the seventh word exists.

In James 2:11, the fifth and sixth words about murder and adultery are used to illustrate the problem of a restricted use of Mosaic law, and we are quickly pointed to a 'law of freedom' (v. 12) that seems to govern the subsequent moral instruction of this letter. The anthropological depths of the words about murder and adultery are searched out and strengthened in Jesus' teaching (Matt. 5:21, 27), and Paul's use of the ninth word about coveting adds to his exposition of human anthropology in Romans 7:7.

The one clear exception to this wisdom-enhancing usage of law is seen in Jesus' discussion with the young man about the second table of the law (Matt. 19:18–19; Mark 10:19; Luke 18:20). But then at this point in salvation history, the Jewish people are still 'under' this law.

In sharp contrast, the second table of law is used in Romans 13:9 to strengthen and extend Christian wisdom about love, which of course is repeatedly and provocatively the new Christian 'law'. It is probably the law's fulfilment by love (Gal. 5:14) that is renamed 'the law of Christ' in Galatians 6:2. This theme of the law's fulfilment by love is repeated in James 2:8 and 1 John 3:23 (which is perhaps a Christocentric reworking of the two great commandments). Obviously, the theme derives from Jesus' use of Deuteronomy 6:5 (cf. 10:12 and 30:6) and Leviticus 19:18 as the hermeneutical keys to law. The law was always an exposition of love (Mark 12:30–34; Matt. 22:37–40; cf. 19:19; Luke 10:27). In this new kind of Christian 'law', the person and work of Christ have become the organizing centre and the interpretative matrix for moral reality.

The Book of the Covenant makes only three direct appearances, when Jesus refuses to allow two of its civil laws to distort personal relationships (Matt. 5:38–39 on Exod. 21:24; and probably Matt. 5:40 on Exod. 22:26–28); and in Paul's almost mischievous use of Exodus 22:28 in Acts 23:5.

In short, there is ample reason to think that NT readers of the Exodus law are very interested in allowing it to inform their moral reasoning, but not at all interested in allowing it to define or control that reasoning. In other words, it has become for them a contributor to Christian wisdom.

The 'third use' is wrong, then, if taken to mean that Christians are forensically bound by OT 'moral' laws. We are not 'under the law' (Rom. 3:28; 6:14; 1 Cor. 9:21; Gal. 3:25; 5:18; and cf. 4:5), and no OT command can be quoted as the sole basis for Christian moral motivation. But NT thinkers did not seem to imagine that 'freedom from law' entailed Marcion's error, as if OT laws should no longer be read as part of the canon of Scripture.

Certainly, in Christ 'are hidden all the treasures of wisdom and knowledge' (Col. 2:3); yet this statement should not be taken in an *ontological* sense, as if we need no longer refer to anything else in the cosmos, whether the writings of the OT, or the general ordering of the cosmos. The statement is *teleological*, describing the way it is that only through Christ and his eschatological purposes may we properly 'decode' the texts we read and the order we think we see. Paul may mean something like this when he speaks of faith somehow upholding the law (Rom. 3:31).

Nor did any serious Reformation thinker imagine that to be 'freed from the law' was to be 'freed from moral reality'. Luther does declare that if it came down to a choice between Christ and the law,

> the law would have to be let go, not Christ. For if we have Christ, we can easily establish laws and we shall judge all things rightly. Indeed, we would make new decalogues, as Paul does in all the epistles, and Peter, but above all Christ in the gospel. And these decalogues are clearer than the decalogue of Moses . . . (1960: 112–113; 'Faith', §§51–54)

This surprising assertion is no mere rhetorical flourish. Luther expects faith in Christ to make whole new realms of moral insight possible. Yet, ironically perhaps, Luther is one of the best examples of wise Christian use of the law. His *Treatise on Good Works* (Luther 1966), and his two Catechisms, are classic instances of a wise Christian mind 'at play' among the Ten Words. We see Luther quarrying for wisdom at this seam that yields knowledge of our hearts, and knowledge of our neighbour's needs. He does so in knowledge and love of the Christ who meets every tabernacle yearning, and who also meets every legal yearning. (For laws do have yearnings, however well they may be hidden: the yearning for a new person whose desires are right; the yearning for a people who love each other well; the yearning for a people who patiently wait upon the God who is with them. All of these yearnings are consummated in Christ, the firstfruits and the lastfruits of the law's proper longing.) Armed with joyful faith in Christ, Luther reaches into the inner depths of law, knitting its logic together with the knowledge of Christ. He therefore achieves everything in this Treatise that any 'third use' could ever hope to achieve.

In an important sense, then, the 'third use' *is* correct. Spirit and Word free us properly to receive moral reality, so we may now 'wisely' receive the law in Christ, discerning much in it about love for God and others. But we can offer no formula in advance for how the Christological reading of a given law (or proverb) will proceed. That there is some difficulty in detailing this hermeneutical project is not a strong defeater of it, for the entire witness of Scripture is that true 'wisdom' is a lifelong process that must be pursued heuristically, and in humble partnership with God.

Beseeching our legislators

As a kind of postscript, I offer some brief comments on three recent discussions of the law and its use. I shall conclude with some suggestions about how the law in Exodus might be seen to offer wisdom for modern legislators.

Covenantal nomism

In 1980, Jon Levenson complained that the generally welcome rediscovery of the concept of covenant in OT studies was getting carried away, to the point where OT law was being explained entirely as arbitrary conditions imposed by the divine suzerain upon his people (Levenson 1980). Levenson complained that this move ignored the wisdom evidently embedded in OT law.

Covenantal nomism, whether a real belief system or one imagined by scholars, takes this trend to its logical extreme. Law obedience is primarily for covenantal inclusion.[8] But this preoccupation strips law of any real connection to a natural moral order, and so covenantal nomism seems to assert a radical voluntarism, where God simply commands in order to test for covenantal obedience, and people simply obey in order to effect covenantal membership. On this view, there really can be nothing to say from the OT for human affairs; it is of antiquarian interest only.

Theonomist reconstructionism

Diametrically opposed is theonomist reconstructionism, which seeks for substantial aspects of OT law to be reconstructed in modern life. Although some propose the reconstruction of the OT cult, Greg Bahnsen confines his attention to the reconstruction of modern civil law along OT lines (1996). Wright summarizes some of the major objections to this project (2004: 403–408). But one of its mistakes is to equate the written OT civil law with moral reality. In an attempt, then, to commend moral reality to modern legislators, reconstructionism commends OT civil law. But the Reformed conclusion is to be preferred: moral reality can be defended and upheld by different civil laws in different times and places.

---

8. 'Briefly put, covenantal nomism is the view that one's place in God's plan is established on the basis of the covenant and that the covenant requires as the proper response of man his obedience to its commandments, while providing means of atonement for transgression' (Sanders 1977: 75).

Biblical relationism

Another project seeks to find what it calls 'paradigms' for social life in OT biblical law. Its proponents do not think of themselves as 'reconstructionists', and they are not (Schluter and Ashcroft 2005: *passim*; Wright 2004: 408–411). They would agree with Michael Hill's statement: 'The basic shape of God's rule, and God's just order established at creation, is confirmed and further delineated in the Law [which] gives us, as Christians, a glimpse of God's just order' (2002: 74).

Biblical relationism optimistically quarries the law for 'divine wisdom', we might say, about human society. Various social structures and interactions are drawn from its pages, and reforged into modern-day public policy suggestions. However, the text always seems to constrain these suggestions: we should have a Sabbath, no interest and a return to clan-based security. Each suggestion has merits, but this interesting project does not always demonstrably read OT law 'Christologically'.

We have already seen that a 'Christological' reading is hard to specify in advance, and proponents of biblical relationism may reasonably be reserved about an expectation that they should do so without any specification of how to proceed. Nonetheless, NT soteriology and eschatology do bring new insights into moral reality, resulting (for example) in merciful civil judgments, the good of chaste singleness, the total error of modern holy war, or the distinction between church and state. To read OT law only on its own terms may predispose us to some errors of moral judgment.

Avoiding these errors, then, what wisdom might be on offer for a modern legislator from the law in Exodus? The following suggestions are ad hoc only, and far from exhaustive.

First, we may observe how surprisingly brief the Exodus law is. Modern parliaments now operate as legislative factories, multiplying law upon law in an overbearing effort to regulate human society. Admittedly, there are many more of us, our society is more complex, and different times do require different laws. But a wisdom formed by Exodus might conclude that sometimes less is more, and that excessive 'positive law' (legislation) does not always assist local leaders to judge, lead and help shape communities.

Secondly, our legislators may note the way the Exodus law is not *idealistic* law. Not even the Ten Words finally map out and hold people to some complete utopian specification of the good society, and the Book of the Covenant is quite patchy in what it regulates. Presumably, it regulated whatever needed regulating, and beyond that, allowed community life to look after itself. But in some respects modern Western law may be tempted to espouse the kind of grand moral vision that no law is capable of. (Some implementations of human rights law may labour under such a temptation, although other instances of it are more appropriately circumscribed.)

Thirdly, anyone interested in the morality of law needs to try working with the grain of this material. In this volume, Greg Clarke has pointed to some recent mockery of it; but quite apart from these authors' decision always to see the worst in these pages, they simply cheat. They presume that modern liberal morality would have been self-evident to any reasonable atheist such as themselves – whether ancient or modern. They presume ancient societies should use modern liberal punishment practices and punish similar crimes. But this self-righteous finger wagging simply ignores the way OT law had to regulate a particular time and place without the relative luxuries we enjoy. This kind of modern liberalism also avoids any consideration of whether this law, and the gospel's fond farewell to it, have flowed together through the millennia to create some of the modern liberal luxuries that make us who we are. Surely no modern legislators can blithely go about their business without wrestling with that great story.

Finally, the law in Exodus is connected to human desire, and has in mind the good of communities. Of course, good modern legislators do think about human desires and the good of communities. Nevertheless, we may urge them to keep looking to those channel-markers in their law making. A modern legislator, crushed under a weight of technical and political concerns, may simply forget that his or her task is to take human desire into account, assisting its best longings and resisting its worst excesses, so that a community may dwell together in relative peace. What we need is a peaceful society, not a body of law. Even the modern legislator will find his or her wisdom sharpened by reading from this law, and of the Christ who fulfils it.

The psalmist once prayed:

> Give me understanding, that I may keep your law
>   and observe it with my whole heart.
> (Ps. 119:34)

Perhaps the corresponding prayer today is, 'Give us understanding, that we might learn wisdom through your old law, and discern what is the best through faith in Christ, who is the fulfilment and end of that law.'

Bibliography

Aquinas, T. (1937), *Summa Theologica*, London: Benzinger Brothers.

Bahnsen, G. L. (1996), 'The Theonomic Reformed Approach to Law and Gospel', in S. N. Gundry (ed.), *Five Views on Law and Gospel*, Grand Rapids: Zondervan, 93–143.

Calvin, J. (1960), *Institutes of the Christian Religion*, vols. 1–2, Philadelphia: Westminster.

Carmichael, C. M. (1992), *The Origins of Biblical Law: The Decalogues and the Book of the Covenant*, Ithaca: Cornell University Press.

Finkelstein, J. J. (1981), *The Ox That Gored*, Philadelphia: American Philosophical Society.

Hill, M. (2002), *The How and Why of Love: An Introduction to Evangelical Ethics*, Kingsford: Matthias Media.

Hitchens, C. (2007), *God is NOT Great: How Religion Poisons Everything*, Crows Nest: Allen & Unwin.

Kuntz, P. G. (2004), *The Ten Commandments in History: Moral Paradigms for a Well-Ordered Society*, Grand Rapids: Eerdmans.

Levenson, J. D. (1980), 'The Theologies of Commandment in Biblical Israel', *Harvard Theological Review* 73: 17–33.

Luther, M. (1953), 'Galatians', in P. S. Watson (ed.), *A Commentary on St Paul's Epistle to the Galatians Based on Lectures Delivered by Martin Luther at the University of Wittenberg in the Year 1531 and First Published in 1535*, London: James Clarke.

— (1960), 'Theses concerning Faith and Law [1535]', in L. W. Spitz (ed.), *Luther's Works*. Vol. 34: *Career of the Reformer IV*, Philadelphia: Muhlenberg, 109–120.

— (1966), 'Treatise on Good Works [1520]', in J. Atkinson (ed.), *Luther's Works*. Vol. 44: *The Christian in Society I*, Philadelphia: Fortress, 21–114.

O'Donovan, O. M. T. (2002), *Common Objects of Love: Moral Reflection and the Shaping of Community*, Grand Rapids: Eerdmans.

Pinckaers, S. (1995), *The Sources of Christian Ethics*, Edinburgh: T. & T. Clark.

Sanders, E. P. (1977), *Paul and Palestinian Judaism*, Norristown: Fortress.

Schluter, M., and J. Ashcroft (2005), *Jubilee Manifesto: A Framework, Agenda and Strategy for Christian Social Reform*, Leicester: IVP.

Schnabel, E. J. (1985), *Law and Wisdom from Ben Sira to Paul: A Tradition Historical Enquiry into the Relation of Law, Wisdom and Ethics*, Tübingen: Mohr.

Staalduine-Sulman, E. van (2006), 'Between Legislative and Linguistic Parallels: Exodus 21:22–25 in its Context', in R. Roukema (ed.), *The Interpretation of Exodus: Studies in Honour of Cornelis Houtman*, Leuven: Peeters, 207–224.

Wright, C. J. H. (2004), *Old Testament Ethics for the People of God*, Leicester: IVP.

6. HEAVEN ON EARTH: THE SIGNIFICANCE OF THE TABERNACLE IN ITS LITERARY AND THEOLOGICAL CONTEXT

Barry G. Webb

Introduction

The tabernacle does strange things to people. In some, it engenders an almost manic fascination (as indicated by the Internet sites devoted to it).[1] In others, it barely produces a yawn. The majority find what the OT says about it so impossibly remote and repetitious they feel the only sensible thing to do is ignore it. Only those who believe that reading the Bible from cover to cover is a particularly meritorious work push on doggedly through the tabernacle like a ship in thick fog, which begins to dissipate only when Israel leaves Sinai in Numbers 10:11 and things at last start to *happen* again! Most of the contemporary Christian church has simply run out of patience with the tabernacle. But the fact is that quite a big chunk of the OT is devoted

---

1. A quick search will find reconstructions, models, pictures, study material (e.g. 'The Tabernacle: God's Prophetic Program'), do-it-yourself tabernacle kits, conferences etc.

to it, and the NT letter to the Hebrews treats it as a rich source of gospel truth.

In Exodus, the importance of the tabernacle is evident from the fact that thirteen whole chapters are devoted to it, and a further five are intimately connected with it: nearly half the book in all. Furthermore, it is clear from the narrative flow of Exodus that the building of the tabernacle at the end is not an appendix but a climax. Exodus moves from 'service' (slavery) to Pharaoh in Egypt, to the 'service' (worship)[2] of Yahweh at Sinai, with the connection between the two nicely made by the terse command to Pharaoh in 7:16: 'Let my people go that they may serve me.'[3] Chapters 25–40 are all about this second kind of 'service'.

Its importance is also indicated by the unusual way the tabernacle is spoken about. It is common these days to speak of the remarkable economy of Hebrew narrative: as few words are used as possible, with dialogue carrying most of the significant content. But the material dealing with the tabernacle (which *is* a narrative) is completely different from this. There is minimal dialogue, and a great deal of repetition. Almost everything is said twice, first as instruction about what is to be done (chs. 25–31); then as description of the instructions being carried out (chs. 35–40). It is the commentaries rather than the text itself that normally try to achieve some sort of economy by treating the two blocks of material simultaneously rather than in succession (e.g. Enns 2000b: 506). The uncharacteristic wordiness of the biblical material itself, however, has the effect of slowing the narrative down, and focusing our attention on the tabernacle in a particularly sustained and detailed way. In view of this, the manic fascination referred to earlier is the lesser of two evils: at least it is not dismissive of something the author considers important.

But here we meet the problem that lies at the heart of this chapter. How can we move beyond respectful *attention* to *understanding*? Or to put the matter more baldly, 'What does it all mean?' And how can we pursue that question without going insane? The

---

2. The same Hebrew expression, *'ābad*, is used for both (Exod. 1:13–14; 3:12).

3. Quotations are from the ESV unless stated otherwise.

problem is not just that the tabernacle belongs to a world far removed from us, but that the text which deals with it, for all its wordiness, is at the same time surprisingly reticent – especially in the area that most concerns us. What is directly presented to us, for the most part, is details of the physical structure the tabernacle: dimensions, numbers, materials, colours and furniture of various kinds. Only rarely does one find any statement of a theological nature. The few that *are* made are important, of course, and we shall attend to them in due course. But generally speaking, the theological significance is conveyed more by the context and shape of the material than its fine detail, and has to be inferred rather than read directly off the surface of the text. Consequently, it seems wiser to take a top-down rather than bottom-up approach, letting the broad features of the material establish the parameters of our study, and extending interpretation to the details only as far as the limitations of a short treatment such as this permit. Much light is shed on the tabernacle by considering it in its literary setting in Exodus and the rest of the OT. Some things of value can be gleaned from looking at it in its ancient Near Eastern setting. Of course the final, definitive word on the tabernacle is spoken in the NT, but the luxury of viewing it from that vantage point lies beyond my brief and must be left to another contributor to this volume.

We shall take as our starting point the overall shape and content of the material in Exodus, dealing with the plan and construction of the tabernacle.

The shape of the material

A. 25:1–9: the presence of God foreshadowed
  B. 25:10 – 31:11: instructions given for making the tabernacle
    C. 31:12–17: the Sabbath
      D. 31:18: the tablets of the law
        X. 32:1 – 33:23: THE GOLDEN CALF
      D'. 34:1–35: the tablets of the law
    C'. 35:1–3: the Sabbath
  B'. 35:4 – 40:33: instructions carried out: the tabernacle built
A'. 40:34–38: the presence of God realized

As this chiasm shows, the tabernacle material of Exodus extends from the beginning of chapter 25 to the end of chapter 40, and is arranged symmetrically around the incident of the golden calf in chapters 32–33. It symbolically frames and contains the apostasy associated with it. This design throws certain things into prominence at once.

The tabernacle and the law (and therefore the covenant)

The instructions for making the tabernacle conclude with Yahweh formally handing over to Moses the two tablets of the law (31:18). These are smashed when Moses sees the golden calf (32:10), but replaced with two new tablets before the tabernacle is built (34:1). When it is completed, these tablets of the law are placed inside it, in the ark of the covenant (40:20). So, as a repository for the law, the tabernacle represents revealed religion as opposed to man-made religion (Moberly 1983: 512). The smashing of the two tablets of the law in 32:10 dramatizes the irreconcilable conflict between the two. The writing of a new set of tablets and the building of the tabernacle after the golden-calf episode shows the triumph of true religion over false. The built tabernacle, with the law at its centre, is a powerful sign that the covenant between Yahweh and Israel is still intact, despite Israel's sin.

The tabernacle and the presence of Yahweh

The purpose of the tabernacle is to be a dwelling place for Yahweh. This is foreshadowed in 25:8, 'Let them make me a sanctuary, that I may dwell in their midst' (NIV), and realized in 40:34, 'The glory of the LORD filled the tabernacle' (NIV). We shall return to this below.

The tabernacle and the sabbath (and therefore creation)

A command to keep the sabbath occurs at the end of the instructions for making the tabernacle, and again at the beginning of the account of its construction (31:12–17 and 35:2–3). The importance of keeping the sabbath is indicated, not just by the repetition of the command, but by the use of the emphatic particle 'ak (surely) in 31:13: '*Surely* you shall keep my sabbaths' (my tr.).[4] Given the

---

4. I take the plural, 'sabbaths', to refer to the one sabbath day, week after week.

connection between the sabbath and creation in the Exodus form of the Decalogue (20:11), this double command to keep the sabbath in the tabernacle material entails a connection between tabernacle, too, and creation, as is widely recognized (e.g. Wenham 1994; Enns 2000a; Dumbrell 2002; Williamson 2007). This connection is reinforced by features of the design of the tabernacle reminiscent of the garden of Eden, such as the presence of God (25:8/Gen. 3:8), the treelike menorah (25:32/Gen. 2:9), the guardian cherubim (cf. 25:18–20/Gen. 3:24), and the single entrance on the eastern side (38:13/Gen. 3:24).[5] Like Eden, the tabernacle is a sanctuary (*miqdāš*, 28:8), a holy place set apart from the created world in general, where God and human beings meet in harmony (Wenham 2003: 76).

The Sabbath also carries with it the concepts of completion, rest and covenant, all of which are significant for the theology of the tabernacle. Enns has noted that the expression 'Yahweh said to Moses' occurs seven times in the instructions for the building of the tabernacle in chapters 25–31, the last of which introduces the command to keep the Sabbath (2000b: 149). This can hardly be accidental. It implies that, as the Sabbath of the seventh day marked the completion of God's work of creation, the building of the tabernacle was meant to mark the completion of his work of redeeming Israel from slavery in Egypt. As humanity was told to rest in God's finished work of creation, Israel is told to rest in God's finished work of redemption.[6] Finally (and this is particularly stressed in Exodus), the sabbath was intended to be an enduring sign of Yahweh's unique covenant relationship with Israel (31:13, 17). Similarly, the tabernacle was to be a sign that Yahweh's covenant with Israel stood firm, in spite of Israel's sin. So the connection between the command to build the tabernacle and the command to keep the Sabbath is an entirely natural one.

---

5. Note, too, James Palmer's observation (following G. K. Beale) that 'Leviticus 26:11ff. uses the language of the LORD walking amongst his people in connection with the Tabernacle. This strongly recalls the Genesis account of Adam and Eve (Gen. 2:15; 3:8)' (2004: 15).

6. This connection is made explicit in the alternative form of the sabbath commandment in Deut. 5:15.

The connections between the tabernacle and creation also suggest that the tabernacle had universal significance: it was a sign of God's ongoing commitment to humanity as a whole, despite the fall. We shall return to this below when we look at the connection between the tabernacle and eschatology.

The literary context of the material

Here the scope of our study expands as we consider the significance of the tabernacle in its broader OT context.

In the Pentateuch

After the preface in Genesis 1 – 11, the Pentateuch is the story of an epic journey, from Ur to Haran, to Canaan, to Egypt, to Sinai, and on to the plains of Moab.[7] It is an unfinished journey, because it ends with Israel at the border of the land that has been promised to them, but not yet in it. Within the Pentateuch itself, the most significant stopping point on this journey is Sinai. The description of what takes place there straddles three of the five books, from Exodus 19:1, where the Israelites arrive at Sinai, to Numbers 10:11, where they leave it. For just over fifty-eight chapters the forward movement of the narrative is arrested, and of those fifty-eight, just short of forty-three are devoted to the plan, construction and rites associated with the tabernacle. In short, the tabernacle looms very large in the Pentateuch and stands close to the centre of it. Only the making of the covenant itself in Exodus 19 – 24 is arguably more important. However, as we have seen, the tabernacle is not another reality competing with this for importance, but another form of the same reality. The tabernacle was built to confirm and maintain the relationship the covenant making had established. In fact, if we take the programmatic statements of the first part of Exodus as our cue ('Let my people go that they may *serve* me' [7:16; 8:1, 26]), then the tabernacle, and the 'service' associated with it, is the real, vital centre of the

---

7. Clines (1997) compares it to *Gilgamesh*, the *Odyssey* and other classic travel stories.

Pentateuch. The journey to Sinai is a journey towards this kind of service, the happenings at Sinai are the establishment of it, and the journey on from there is the living out of it. In theological terms, we might say that what the tabernacle material of Exodus teaches is that the worship of God is both the goal and foundation of the redeemed life. That is its great contribution to the theology of the Pentateuch.

In the Old Testament in general

In the context of the OT as a whole, the tabernacle is on a trajectory that runs from Eden, through the tabernacle itself, to Solomon's temple, and from there to the prophetic expectation of a new temple, which is realized only partly and symbolically in the second temple of the post-exilic period (Dumbrell 1985). The story that unfolds around this theme is largely taken up with the struggle to keep the kind of worship prescribed at Sinai at the heart of Israel's national life. As Israel comes of age and takes its place among the nations of the world, the danger that it will become simply *like* them is a constant one. Israel's religion is always in danger of being politicized, and becoming simply a state religion, manipulated by the king to support whatever foreign policy he deems most expedient to pursue.[8] But the tabernacle, even when only a memory, continues to be a reminder that Israel is fundamentally a theocracy, ruled by a divine King, whose will must be deferred to in all aspects of her national life – including politics. It is noteworthy in this respect, that when Ezekiel projects the ideal future, he does so in terms reminiscent of the tabernacle, with the residence of Yahweh, the divine King, in the centre, and the twelve tribes arranged around it (Ezek. 40 – 48; cf. Num. 2).

Symbolism

The tabernacle and its furnishings are clearly symbolic in some sense: the golden lampstand, for example, is not simply a light in

---

8. As when Ahaz decided to submit to Assyria, and had an Assyrian-style altar installed in the Jerusalem temple (2 Kgs 16:10).

the sense that a modern light bulb is. That is to say, it has a significance that is not exhausted by its utility in a literal, straightforward
sense. As well as *being* something, it *represents* something. The same
is true of the table that stood opposite it, the curtain that divided
the interior of the tabernacle into two sections, and so on.

The modern reader of the biblical material has at least two
problems: first, for the most part the symbolic significance of
these things is not directly stated, and secondly, we are not familiar
with the symbolic world to which they belong. But neither are we
left entirely in the dark. The biblical material does at least provide
us with some starting points. What can be known about temples
of the second millennium BC context in which the tabernacle had
its being is also helpful.

The symbolism of the tabernacle in the biblical material itself

We begin with the spatial and directional language in which the
revelation of the tabernacle to Israel is described. Yahweh
'comes down' on to the summit of Mount Sinai (19:20) and
Moses 'goes up' to meet him there (19:20; 24:9, 13, 15, 18). So
the summit of Sinai becomes the meeting point of heaven and
earth, and it is precisely at this interface between the 'above' and
'below' that the tabernacle is revealed. Moses is 'shown' the tabernacle (25:9; more of this in a moment), and 'goes down' (32:15)
to the foot of the mountain, where the tabernacle is built according to the 'pattern' Moses has been shown (25:9, 40; cf. Num.
8:4). So the tabernacle is the realization on earth of what has
been brought down from heaven and shown to Moses. For the
purposes of this revelation Sinai becomes a kind of Jacob's
ladder, linking heaven and earth, with Yahweh at the top, and
Moses, his messenger, going up and down it.[9] The built tabernacle, which results from this revelation, partakes of both heaven
and earth.

---

9. Compare the pyramids of Egypt: 'The step-pyramids had the shape, not
   only of a hill but (at least in their most ancient form) of a staircase. Spell
   267 of the Pyramid Texts reads: "A staircase to heaven is laid out for him
   [the king] so that he may climb up to heaven thereby"' (Keel 1978: 113).

But here we meet some riddles difficult to solve. Is the 'seeing/ showing' language literal, implying that Moses literally sees either an architectural plan, or even the heavenly archetype of the taber- nacle? Or is it simply a metaphor for the act of revelation, leaving the precise form of the revelation unspecified?[10] I doubt that this is resolvable from the text of Exodus itself.[11] However, it is clear from 1 Kings 8 that the Jerusalem temple, the eventual successor to the tabernacle, was understood to be a representation on earth of Yahweh's true dwelling place in heaven. Solomon's words in his prayer of dedication are quite explicit about this: 'Listen to the plea of your servant and of your people Israel, when they pray towards this place. And listen *in heaven your dwelling place*, and when you hear, forgive' (1 Kgs 8:30 NIV; my emphasis).

The same tradition is reflected, for example, in the account of Isaiah's call, in Isaiah 6, and given what we have already observed in Exodus, it is likely that this tradition was not a novelty of the ninth and eighth centuries, but part of Israel's tabernacle/temple theology from the beginning. If so, this is the basis of the symbol- ism associated with the tabernacle. It is a vertical symbolism in the sense that the tabernacle points upward to a greater heavenly reality. This is not to say that the presence of Yahweh in the taber- nacle is not real, but that there is something greater than it, to which it corresponds. We may call this its 'archetype'.

The symbolism of the tabernacle in its ancient Near Eastern setting

The symbolism we have identified in the biblical text is related to 'the ancient oriental idea of a mythical analogical relation between

---

10. 'As human beings are the kind of physical beings God would be if God were a physical being, so the sanctuary is the kind of dwelling heaven would be if heaven were a physical place' (Goldingay 2003: 395).

11. But note Cole's comment on the term *tabnît* in Exod. 25:9: '*The pattern* means almost "architect's model". Gudea of Lagash (3000 BC) claims that he saw in a dream the very model of a temple, which he later built meticu- lously. Moses is commended for similar obedience, both in Exodus (39:5) and Hebrews (3:2–5)' (1973: 198). Cf. 2 Kgs 16:10–11; Heb. 8:5.

the two worlds, the heavenly and the earthly, the macrocosm and the microcosm, so that lands, rivers, cities, and especially temples have their heavenly originals' (Goppelt 1964–76: 256–257). Temples were regarded as sites where heaven and earth met. For example, 'The ziggurat of Larsa [southern Iraq] bears the beautiful name, "house of the bond between heaven and earth"' (Keel 1978: 113). In keeping with this general belief, temples were normally built on mountain tops or, where no mountain was available, in the form of a mountain (e.g. the ziggurats of ancient Mesopotamia and the pyramids of Egypt).

At first sight the tabernacle seems to have no connection at all with this tradition: it is not built on a mountain and does not have the shape of one. But the difference is practical rather than ideological. Unlike temples in general, it is a portable structure, designed to travel with the Israelites and be erected and dismantled as required. Nevertheless, as we have seen, there is a very strong link between the tabernacle and a holy mountain. The cloud and fire associated with Yahweh's presence on Sinai also cover and light the tabernacle when it is completed (40:34–38), and continue to appear over it on the journey to Canaan (Num. 12:5; Deut. 31:15). It maintains Israel's link with Sinai, and projects it forward into its subsequent experience. It is a kind of portable Sinai, a travelling holy mountain (Childs 1974: 540; Sarna 1991: 237).

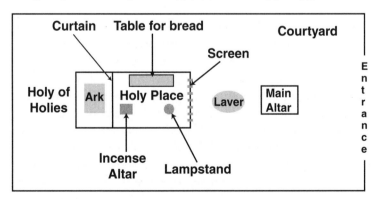

Figure 6.1 *The tabernacle*

Kitchen (1993: 123) has shown that, in terms of its basic design, materials, construction, ornamentation, even to some extent its rituals, the tabernacle belongs to the Late Bronze Egyptian-Semitic world. In particular, the

> basically rectangular layout of the Hebrew camp [with the tabernacle in the middle] directly resembles Egyptian usage of the 13th century BCE, as illustrated by the Battle of Qadesh reliefs of Rameses II, whose tabernacular, fenced-off tent was in the middle of a rectangular camp.

This corresponds precisely to the biblical picture of Yahweh, Israel's divine king, 'camped' in the midst of his people as they set off on what on is intended to be a military campaign to conquer Canaan (Num. 1 – 2). Like Kitchen, Wenham and others have noted that, in terms of its interior layout and ornamentation, the tabernacle

> resembled a royal palace with its throne-room, the holy of holies, right at the heart of the structure. It thus expressed the idea that the LORD as Israel's king dwelt among his people. Its drapes of purple suggested royalty and its blue curtains suggested heaven. The sequence of metals, from bronze in the outer court, silver around the base of the tent, and pure gold covering the furniture inside the tent, indicated increasing nearness to the divine king. (Wenham 2003: 75–76)

In general, then, the tabernacle was a powerful sign of the presence of Yahweh, Israel's divine king and warrior, among his people on their march to the Promised Land of Canaan.[12]

Time and space (and in some cases lack of data) prevent us from attempting a more detailed treatment here of the symbolism of the tabernacle. We have already noted how a number of its features recall the Garden of Eden, and shall look below at some aspects of the symbolism of the atonement rituals of the tabernacle. I shall limit myself here, though, to some comments about the symbolism of the ark with its cherubim.

---

12. Cf. Num. 23:21: 'The LORD their God is with them, and the shout of a king is among them.'

In terms of its construction and purpose, the ark belongs to a category of sacred furniture well known from extra-biblical sources. 'Such boxes, borne on carrying-poles passing through rings . . . were commonplace in Egypt' (Kitchen 1993: 125). Kitchen and others (e.g. Sarna 1991; Enns 2000a) refer, for example, to a box of similar size and design that was discovered in the tomb of Tutankhamun (1333–1323 BC), which, like the ark, served as a repository for holy objects – in this case ritual libation vessels. Cherubim, too, belonged to a class of winged, celestial beings well known in ancient Near Eastern religious art and architecture as attendants and guardians of sacred persons and places. In the tabernacle, their spread wings protect the ark, and serve as a seat for Yahweh, who is invisibly enthroned above them (Exod. 25:20; 37:9; cf. 2 Kgs 19:15). A striking parallel is found in 'a series of scenes at the Deir el-Bahri memorial temple of Queen Hatshepsut (c. 1470 BCE), where an empty "lion-throne" repeatedly occurs in festival processions, its absent or invisible occupant symbolised only by a feather-fan' (Kitchen 1993: 125). Many other examples could be given of how the symbolism of the tabernacle would have made perfect sense to any Israelite of the exodus and wilderness period.

Typology

If what we have looked at so far can be described as 'vertical' symbolism, typology is 'longitudinal' or 'horizontal' symbolism. In the former case, the greater reality, the archetype, is located above, in the heavenly sphere; in the latter case the corresponding greater reality, the antitype, is located in the historical sphere. The two kinds of symbolism converge when the heavenly archetype comes down to earth. We may represent this as shown in Figure 6.2 at the top of the next page.

We have already noted how the tabernacle is located on a temple trajectory that stretches from Eden to Solomon's temple and beyond. At certain points along this trajectory, the biblical text draws our attention, explicitly or implicitly, to something that has occurred as a moment of fulfilment. In terms of the definition

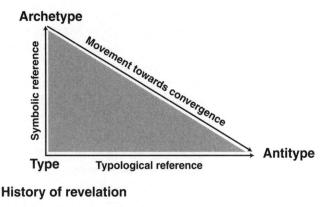

Figure 6.2 *Symbolism and typology* (adapted from Clowney 1961: 110)

just given, these are the logical points for us to look for the antitype of the tabernacle, in whole or in part.

The tabernacle and the sanctuary at Shiloh

The first definite moment of this kind is in the book of Joshua,
when we are told that 'Not one word of all the good promises that
the LORD had made to the house of Israel had failed; all came to
pass' (Josh. 21:45). This is closely related to the setting up of the
tabernacle at Shiloh (18:1), and the casting of lots there to distrib-
ute the land among the various tribes (18:2 – 21:43). The primary
reference, of course, is to the fulfilment of the promise God had
made to Abraham to give his descendants the land of Canaan. But
since the text speaks here of 'all' the promises being fulfilled, and
the erection of the tabernacle at Shiloh is prominent in the
context, there is justification in principle for seeing this as the antitype of the erection of the tabernacle at Sinai.

However, the same context severely qualifies such a perspective.
First, what is erected at Shiloh is the tabernacle itself, so we have
not yet moved beyond the tabernacle to something greater, as true
typology would require. Secondly, the book of Joshua qualifies the
note of fulfilment so boldly affirmed in 21:45, by going on to
speak of 'remaining' nations, and of land still to be possessed
(23:4, 5; cf. 13:1). In other words, the story will go on, and the ultimate fulfilment has not yet come. The erection of the tabernacle

at Shiloh is a staging post on the movement from type to antitype, not the point of arrival in an absolute sense.

The tabernacle and Solomon's temple

The planning, building and dedication of the Jerusalem temple is another significant point on the temple trajectory of the OT narrative, and is dwelt on at much greater length by the biblical writers. Here what is built is clearly beyond the tabernacle of earlier times, and greater in size and grandeur. Furthermore, this time the temple itself is the primary point of reference, and occurs in a context where the theme of 'every promise fulfilled' returns in the transparent allusions to the promises God had given to Abraham:

> Judah and Israel were as many as the sand by the sea. They ate and drank and were happy. Solomon ruled over all the kingdoms from the Euphrates to the land of the Philistines and to the border of Egypt. They brought tribute and served Solomon all the days of his life. (1 Kgs 4:20–21)

The reference to Solomon having 'rest on every side' (1 Kgs 5:4) shows us that the incompleteness of the Joshua situation has now been overcome, and the fulfilment of what God had promised can now be spoken of without qualification. Here we seem to have precisely the situation where we may look for the antitype of the tabernacle with complete confidence.

Furthermore, Solomon's prayer of dedication shows that the temple was understood to be not just another tabernacle, but something greater, as an antitype always is. In its solidity and grandeur, it was a symbol of Israel's new status as a nation among nations, and the opportunities and responsibilities this entailed. Solomon specifically speaks of the temple as a place of prayer, open to people of all nations, and a witness to all nations that Yahweh is the only true God (1 Kgs 8:60) – the realization of Israel's destiny as spelled out in both the Sinaitic and Abrahamic covenants (Exod. 19:5–6; Gen. 12:1–3).

But this ideal is barely realized before it is compromised by Solomon's apostasy. By the end of his reign the temple coexists, in Jerusalem itself, with shrines to rival gods, and in the period immediately following his reign major alternative shrines are created in the north. The reappearance of the golden calf as an alternative to the temple returns us, effectively, to the situation of Exodus 32, and eventually the compromised temple is destroyed in 587 BC. The tabernacle/temple trajectory would have ended at this point, in oblivion rather than fulfilment, were it not for two divinely engineered rescue strategies: the eschatology of the eighth-century prophets (which was already in place), and the restoration of a remnant community to Jerusalem in the early Persian period.

The second temple and the new temple of prophetic eschatology

While the post-exilic prophets rightly attached great importance to the second temple, its modest size and the political climate in which it existed meant that, at best, it could be only a sign and promise of the new temple earlier prophets had spoken about, rather than the full realization of it. So, at the end of the OT period, the true antitype of the tabernacle is still a hope rather than a historical reality.

The antitype that the OT is always looking for is a meeting place between God and his people that will endure, where redeemed human beings will offer pure worship in the presence of God for ever. In the broadest terms, this is a recovery of the situation that existed at the beginning, in Eden, purged of all defilement, free from all the effects of the fall. While human kingship plays a significant part along the way, particularly that of David and Solomon and reformers of their line such as Hezekiah and Josiah, the final hope of the temple theme is of *divine* kingship fully realized on earth – the theocratic ideal of the original tabernacle expanded to embrace the entire world (Dumbrell 1985: 37–76). The revelation and construction of the tabernacle in the time of Moses, however, is a key defining moment in this temple trajectory that stretches from Eden to the new temple of prophetic hope.

While the thematic structure identified above provides a *framework* for more particular typologies to emerge, this never actually happens. While there is a developing typology of the temple as a whole, there is no corresponding typology of its various parts: the golden lampstand, for example, or the ark of the covenant, or the table with its symbolic loaves of bread. In fact, the ark of the covenant (arguably the most important single element of the tabernacle furnishings) disappears entirely – something Jeremiah could apparently view with complete equanimity: 'And when you have multiplied and increased in the land, in those days, declares the LORD, they shall no more say, "The ark of the covenant of the LORD." It shall not come to mind or be remembered or missed; it shall not be made again' (Jer. 3:16). So while the OT does clearly support a typology of the tabernacle as a whole, it does not appear to support a typology of its individual parts. The one possible exception is the golden lampstand in the vision of Zechariah 4:1–9. However, it is doubtful that it is in fact a menorah, but if so, it is probably to be understood as a symbol of the second temple as a whole (Stead 2007) or of Zechariah's community (Webb 2003: 90–93). If the former, it confirms that there is no typology of the menorah itself in the OT; if the latter, it is a hint that the menorah, like the ark, is destined to disappear completely. In either case, a new temple as a whole is on view in Zechariah, not a new menorah.[13]

The doctrinal significance of the tabernacle

So far we have considered the theology of the tabernacle, first in terms of its vertical symbolic significance, and second in terms of its horizontal symbolic significance (its typology). In this final section of the chapter, we shall consider how the tabernacle provides materials for some major biblical doctrines.

The doctrine of God

His holiness
The tabernacle gives classic, institutional expression to the fact of God's holiness. The noun *qōdeš*, 'holiness', occurs thirty-seven times in Exodus in connection with the tabernacle. Everything about it is holy: its two inner parts (the holy and most holy places),

---

13. There is no menorah in Ezekiel's new temple vision of Ezek. 40 – 48.

the veil that separates them, the garments the priests wear, the golden plate on the high priest's turban, the gifts the people bring in worship, the altar on which they are offered, the altar itself and all the other furnishings, the anointing oil used by the priests, the incense, the sabbath observed in connection with it. Of course, only God himself is *intrinsically* holy; everything else, including the whole material structure of the tabernacle, is holy only in a *derivative* sense, after being ritually cleansed and set apart from ordinary use (40:9).[14]

One of the ways, then, that the tabernacle contributes to the biblical doctrine of God is by giving powerful, symbolic expression to the fact that God is not 'ordinary', and cannot therefore be engaged with casually, but only on his own terms and in accordance with a strict protocol that he himself determines. He cannot be taken for granted.

His transcendence and immanence
We have seen how, from the beginning, the tabernacle partakes of heaven and earth. It belongs to a symbolic world in which there is an 'above' and 'below' that correspond to one another. In theological terms, this means that the tabernacle gives concrete expression to the truth that God is both 'up there' and 'down here', transcendent and immanent. But his immanence is a choice, an expression of his freely made, covenant commitment to be with/among his people on earth: to 'dwell' among them as their divine king (Exod. 25:8). So the tabernacle signifies both the proximity and distance of God, his separateness and his accessibility, the fact that he can be housed but not contained. This theology of transcendence and immanence is later given classic

---

14. Interestingly, however, the first *explicit* statement that God himself is holy does not come in Exodus, in connection with the tabernacle and its rituals, but in Leviticus 11:44, in the context of instruction about what must be done and not done in daily life. The term used *directly* of God himself in Exodus is *kĕbôd*, 'glory' – his manifest power and presence, at the Red Sea, on Sinai, and in the tabernacle (Exod. 14:4; 16:10; 40:34–35).

expression in Solomon's prayer at the dedication of the Jerusalem temple:

> But will God indeed dwell on the earth? Behold, heaven and the highest heaven cannot contain you; how much less this house that I have built! Yet have regard to the prayer of your servant and to his plea, O LORD my God, listening to the cry and to the prayer that your servant prays before you this day, that your eyes may be open night and day toward this house, the place of which you have said, 'My name shall be there,' that you may listen to the prayer that your servant offers toward this place. And listen to the plea of your servant and of your people Israel, when they pray toward this place. And listen in heaven your dwelling place, and when you hear, forgive. (1 Kgs 8:27–30)

'My name shall be there' (v. 29) nicely captures the tension between transcendence and immanence.[15] The temple, like the tabernacle before it, was the place par excellence that God chose to be immanent, without compromising his transcendence. The placing of his 'name' there indicated his willingness to be approached and addressed there by his people.

The doctrine of sin and atonement

Definitions can be helpful in clarifying discussion, but must not pre-empt it by imposing on the material to be studied concepts alien to it. In short, definitions need to arise from usage in the text(s) under discussion. In the material we are looking at in Exodus, 'sin' (ḥaṭṭā't) is an activity, such as idolatrous worship, which is contrary to the will of God – in the present case, the will of God made known to Israel in the Decalogue. Atonement (kippōret) is a process by which alienation from God is dealt with, and right relationship with him is restored. Sin and atonement are clearly central issues in Exodus 25 – 40. Words from the 'sin' (ḥṭ') word group occur twelve times, and words from the 'atone/cover'

---

15. It is the Deuteronomic equivalent to the 'glory' language of Exodus (Exod. 40:34; cf. 3:13–15).

(*kpr*) word group occur twenty-two times, fifteen of them in relation to the *kappōret*, 'mercy seat/ atonement lid', on the top of the
ark in the most holy place. Atonement is spoken of in relation to
both people and things.

Atonement for sin

The most revealing treatment of this in the material before us
comes in chapter 32, after the apostasy of the golden calf. The
issue is raised by Moses' declaration of intent: 'You have committed a great sin. But now I will go up to the LORD; perhaps I can
make atonement for your sin' (v. 30 NIV). He then proceeds to do
so by pleading with Yahweh to forgive them (vv. 31–32). Several
things are worthy of note:

1. This is done only after the people have been challenged, on pain
    of death, to stand with Moses (and Yahweh) against the golden
    calf and those who maintain their solidarity with it. Those who
    respond are spared; the rest are killed. Only then does Moses try
    to make atonement.
2. Moses' attempt to secure atonement by simply asking for it is
    rejected, even when he offers himself as a victim in place of the
    people (vv. 31–32).
3. While the people are permitted to continue their journey to the
    land Yahweh has promised them, he will still judge them on an
    unspecified 'day' in the future (vv. 33–34).
4. Even before they set out on this journey Yahweh sends a plague
    that kills some who have survived the previous purge (v. 35).
5. The tabernacle, with its promise of atonement through sacri-
    fice, is subsequently built, and God's glory fills it (35:8 – 40:36).

The implication is that atonement is possible, but not by prayer
alone, and not without renunciation of sin. Positively, it is possible
only through the sacrificial system instituted by God himself, and
made available to sinners in the tabernacle. It is a gift of God
rather than a human achievement (Lev. 17:11). Moreover, while it
averts breakdown of the covenant relationship, it does not rule out
punishment *within* that relationship.

Atonement for things

As part of the commissioning of the tabernacle, atonement had to be made for the bronze altar (29:36–37), and the altar of incense (30:10), and also, by implication, for the garments worn by the priests at their ordination (29:21, 33). The reason why these material things needed to have atonement made for them is not given. However, in Leviticus we are told that on the Day of Atonement, atonement had to be made for the tabernacle itself and everything in it, 'because of the uncleannesses of the people . . . their transgressions . . . and their sins', and because the tabernacle 'dwells with them in the midst of their uncleannesses' (Lev. 16:14–16). The idea seems to be that the sin of the people contaminates their entire environment, including all that has been used in making the tabernacle. So these things themselves have to have atonement made for them before they can be used to make atonement for the people. In every case, the prescribed method is by sprinkling the thing in question with the blood of a sacrificed animal.

Given the clear link between the tabernacle and creation, already noted above, the logic underlying this atonement theology is probably grounded in the Genesis account of the fall and its consequences. Since Adam and Eve were commissioned to rule the earth, their sin had severe consequences for the earth itself, which now resists their rule by producing thorns and thistles. It is no longer a pure environment. Therefore materials derived from the earth are not automatically fit for use in making atonement. They are made *potentially* fit by being offered to Yahweh and used to make the tabernacle according to his instructions. But they are not ready *to be used* in making atonement for human beings until their own 'fallenness' is acknowledged and dealt with by having atonement made for them. The sacrificial blood to be used in making atonement is a gift of God (Lev. 17:11).

Here, as in everything related to the tabernacle, we are dealing with symbols, and so the efficacy lies in what is symbolized rather than in the symbols themselves. But the meaning is clear: the tabernacle does not support the notion of 'non-violent atonement' (atonement without the shedding of blood as a divine requirement) as advocated, for example, by Weaver and others (Weaver 2001);[16] nor does the NT.

The doctrine of the last things

By its portability – a tent for taking on a journey – the tabernacle pointed forward to something promised but not yet realized. By its creation symbolism and association with the sabbath, it promised rest and an eventual return to Eden. By its vertical symbolism it pointed to a heavenly reality greater than itself, and therefore not yet fully found on earth. And through its existence, and the atonement it provided, it brought these realities into the present, and made it possible for faithful Israelites to taste them in the here and now. In all these ways, the tabernacle provides important materials for biblical eschatology. The OT prophets already draw on it in this way (Isa. 4:6; 16:5; 33:20; Ezek. 37:27). Its full eschatological significance is revealed in the NT, as the next chapter in this volume shows.

Bibliography

Childs, B. S. (1974), *Exodus: A Commentary*, Old Testament Library, London: SCM.

---

16. For Weaver, the OT atonement sacrifices were acts of self-dedication (the symbolic offering of one's whole life to God). They 'did not involve the destruction of an animal in place of killing a person' (2001: 59). The death of Jesus was inevitable (given the nature of the world into which he came), but 'was not a payment owed to God's honor, nor was it divine punishment that he suffered as a substitute for sinners'. It was the rejection of the rule of God by forces opposed to that rule. His resurrection 'displayed the power of the reign of God to triumph over death, the last enemy'. The 'nonviolence of the rule of God [was] revealed and made visible by the life, death and resurrection of Jesus' (2001: 44). As Weaver himself shows, similar non-violent views of atonement feature in certain kinds of liberation, feminist and womanist theology.

Clines, D. J. A. (1997), *The Theme of the Pentateuch*, Sheffield: Sheffield Academic Press.

Clowney, E. P. (1961), *Preaching and Biblical Theology*, Phillipsburg: Presbyterian & Reformed.

Cole, R. A. (1973), *Exodus: An Introduction and Commentary*, Tyndale Old Testament Commentaries, London: Tyndale.

Dumbrell, W. J. (1985), *The End of the Beginning: Revelation 21–22 and the Old Testament*, Grand Rapids: Baker.

— (2002), *The Faith of Israel: A Theological Survey of the Old Testament*, Grand Rapids: Baker.

Enns, P. (2000a), *Exodus*, New International Version Application Commentary, Grand Rapids: Zondervan.

— (2000b), 'Exodus', in T. D. Alexander and B. S. Rosner (eds.), *New Dictionary of Biblical Theology*, Leicester: IVP, 146–152.

Goldingay, J., *Old Testament Theology*. Vol. 1: *Israel's Gospel*, Downers Grove: IVP, 2003.

Goppelt, L. (1964–76), 'Tupos as the Heavenly Original according to Ex. 25:40', in G. Kittel and G. Friedrich (eds.), *Theological Dictionary of the New Testament*, 10 vols., Grand Rapids: Eerdmans, 8: 256–257.

Keel, O. (1978), *The Symbolism of the Biblical World: Ancient Near Eastern Iconography and the Book of Psalms*, London: SPCK.

Kitchen, K. A. (1993), 'The Tabernacle – A Bronze Age Artifact', *Eretz-Israel* 24: 119–129.

Moberly, R. W. L. (1983), *At the Mountain of God: Story and Theology in Exodus 32–34*, Sheffield: JSOT Press.

Palmer, J. (2004), 'Exodus and the Biblical Theology of the Tabernacle', in T. D. Alexander and S. J. Gathercole (eds.), *Heaven on Earth: The Temple in Biblical Theology*, Carlisle: Paternoster, 11–22.

Sarna, N. M. (1991), *Exodus = Shemot: The Traditional Hebrew Text with the New JPS Translation*, Philadelphia: Jewish Publication Society.

Stead, M. (2007), 'Zechariah and the Former Prophets: An Examination of the Re-Use of the Prophetic Tradition in the Book of Zechariah', PhD thesis, Gloucester: University of Gloucester.

Weaver, J. D. (2001), *The Nonviolent Atonement*, Grand Rapids: Eerdmans.

Webb, B. G. (2003), *The Message of Zechariah: Your Kingdom Come*, Leicester: IVP.

Wenham, G. J. (1994), 'Sanctuary Symbolism in the Garden of Eden Story', in R. S. Hess and D. T. Tsumura (eds.), *'I Studied Inscriptions from before the*

Flood': Ancient Near Eastern, Literary, and Linguistic Approaches to Genesis 1–11, Winona Lake: Eisenbrauns, 399–404.

— (2003), *Exploring the Old Testament*. Vol. 1: *The Pentateuch*, London: SPCK.

Williamson, P. R. (2007), *Sealed with an Oath: Covenant in God's Unfolding Purpose*, New Studies in Biblical Theology 23, Downers Grove: IVP; Nottingham, Apollos.

7. FROM EARTHLY SYMBOL TO HEAVENLY REALITY: THE TABERNACLE IN THE NEW TESTAMENT

Constantine R. Campbell

Introduction

> Generations of Christian scholars have attempted to discern in the
> tabernacle a theological significance for the church of their own time. For
> Clement of Alexandria, Jerome, and others, the tabernacle represented
> the universe. Origen, Bede, and medieval exegetes maintained that it
> illustrated the virtues of Christian life, while various interpreters from the
> seventeenth through the early twentieth centuries presented the
> tabernacle as a type of Christ and the church. (Koester 1989: ix)

The tabernacle for our time?

What does the tabernacle mean for the writers of the NT, and for
us today? There are many theological connections to be made
between the tabernacle and various other themes in the NT. For
example, it is related to *church*, to *salvation*, to *sacrifice* and *forgiveness*,
to the *person and work of Christ*, to *union with Christ*, to *the intratrinitar-
ian relations within the Godhead*. It is impossible to explore these
connected themes in any depth here. What will be explored,
however, is the basic trajectory of NT thought regarding the tab-

ernacle – its essential outline. In doing this, two pertinent questions are raised: 'What is the relationship between the tabernacle and the temple in New Testament theology?' and 'Who or what *is* the tabernacle in the New Testament?'

Tabernacle or temple?

It is commonplace in NT theology to consider references to the tabernacle to be indistinguishable from those to the temple, since the latter is regarded as a development of the former. This would make for a neat trajectory within biblical theology (tabernacle to temple to Christ, for example), but the issue is not quite so clear-cut. Not only did distinctions between the tabernacle and the temple persist within the intertestamental literature, but such distinctions are evident within the NT itself. For example, Stephen seems to have viewed the tabernacle favourably, yet denounces the temple (Acts 7:47–50). John uses tabernacle language to describe the incarnate Word (John 1:14), but employs temple language in reference to Jesus' resurrection body (John 2:19–22) (Koester 1989: 2). Revelation depicts the dwelling place (tabernacle) of God with men (Rev. 21:3), but there will be no temple there (21:22).

What, if anything, can be made of this apparent distinction between the tabernacle and temple within NT thought? Are the two concepts roughly synonymous, or is the distinction intentional and meaningful? How can we know?

Christ, God's people, and the individual

As the NT appropriates the concept of the tabernacle/temple, there seems to be a multiplicity of referents to which it is applied. In biblical-theological terms, the temple is superseded and fulfilled by Christ (e.g. John 2:19–21). On the other hand, the people of God are equated as being the new temple (e.g. Eph. 2:19–22). And yet again, in one case the bodies of individual Christians are described as the temple of God (1 Cor. 6:19; see below).

In order to understand properly the tabernacle/temple in its biblical theological context, we must attempt to reconcile these various referents. How do they fit together? What is the new tabernacle/temple, according to the NT? In the approach that follows, I shall attempt to outline the trajectory of thought by dealing with NT passages representative of the various strands of teaching, without trying to deal with all the material that might be addressed. I wish to preserve *some* detailed analysis of various passages, but the wider aim is to represent the broad sweep of tabernacle theology in the NT.

Intertestamental period

Understanding something of the literature between the OT and NT may assist in understanding the context in which NT writers engaged with the concepts of the tabernacle and temple.

While the tabernacle was understood in a variety of ways through the period 200 BC to AD 150, there were nevertheless parallels with the OT understanding of the tabernacle. Koester summarizes:

> (1) The tabernacle's role as a place of revelation was mentioned in Pseudo-Philo, was depicted as the place of apocalyptic vision in the *Testament of Moses*, and was associated with the wisdom and virtue that bring one closer to heavenly realities in Philo's works. (2) The tabernacle was remembered as a place of sacrifice by most authors, although Philo noted that sacrifices were not *essential* to the worship represented by the tabernacle. (3) The tabernacle also reminded readers how God acted faithfully toward Israel, by correcting Israel's apostasy during the wilderness period (*1 Enoch*), by promising and giving Israel the land (*T. Moses*), and by choosing Jerusalem (4QDibHam). Such faithfulness provided a basis for hope that God would redeem his people in the future, as in the hidden tabernacle traditions. (1989: 73)

In short, the writings of the intertestamental period understood Solomon's temple to be the legitimate successor to the tabernacle, though appraisals of the second temple varied (Koester 1989: 73). As such, it may be an appropriate speculation to suggest that references to the tabernacle in the Second Temple period were somewhat in lieu of a temple that was regarded as bona fide.

Furthermore, intertestamental apocalyptic literature envisages a heavenly temple, as MacRae sets forth:

> In the apocalyptic literature we find the notion of a temple in heaven full
> blown and even taken for granted. A few examples will suffice. In
> Ethiopic *Enoch* 14, Enoch enters heaven in a vision and passes through a
> large house, then a second house in which God is enthroned. [. . .] The
> *Testament of Levi* is quite unequivocal: 'And thereupon the angel opened
> to me the gates of heaven, and I saw the holy temple, and upon a throne
> of glory the Most High' (5:1; cf. 18:6). [. . .] Among the Qumran
> sectarians apparently we also have the notion of a temple in heaven in
> which there is an angelic liturgy . . . (1978: 183–184)

Related to this is the link between creation and the tabernacle that
is seen in the literature of the Second Temple period. Philo and
Josephus, for instance, held the view that the tabernacle was a
microcosm of creation, a 'heaven on earth' (Palmer 2004: 15). We
shall return to this concept below.

Gospels and Acts

Matthew
In Matthew 12:6, Jesus declares that 'something greater than the
temple is here!' According to Alan Cole, the only fact that can suit-
ably explain this startling claim is that 'God's presence is more
manifest in Him than in the Temple. On Him, not the Temple,
now rests the Shekinah, as later Judaism was to see it resting on
those who studied Torah' (1950: 12–13). Beale expands further on
the significance of this claim in Matthew:

> Therefore, not only is Jesus identified with the temple because he is
> assuming the role of the sacrificial system, but he is also now, instead of
> the temple, the unique place on earth where God's revelatory presence is
> located. God is manifesting his glorious presence in a greater way than it
> was ever manifested in a physical temple structure. (2004: 178)

The tearing of the temple curtain at the point of Christ's death
is of pointed significance in Matthew (27:50–52). Not to be left
without interpretation, this event follows the mockery that Jesus
endured relating to his claim that he would destroy the temple and

rebuild it in three days (26:60–61). Beale notes the irony of this interchange: Jesus is mocked for claiming that he would destroy the temple, and at virtually the same time we are told that Jesus was in fact doing exactly that when he died (2004: 189).

Finally, while the temple had been a symbol of the exclusion of Gentiles, Christ's replacement of the temple is significant in Matthew's Gospel for the inclusion of Gentiles (Cole 1950: 12–14).

John

Within his first two chapters, John employs both the tabernacle-cognate *skēnoō* and the temple-cognate *naos* with reference to Jesus, and then does not employ either cognate group again in the Gospel.[1]

With reference to the tabernacle language in John 1:14, Beale suggests the following explanation as to why this, rather than temple language, was used:

> In the first century neither Jews nor Samaritans worshiped in a tabernacle. By portraying Jesus as the tabernacle, the evangelist may have wanted to show that the Christian community had a center that was distinct from the Jerusalem temple and from Gerizim, yet had continuity with Israel's cultic heritage. (2004: 108)

Frankly, however, this explanation does not solve the problem. The fact that in the very next chapter Jesus explicitly connects himself to the temple, not the tabernacle, would seem to undermine Beale's case. If John's intention in 1:14 was to create a distinction from the Jerusalem temple, he quickly undid this by connecting Jesus to that same temple in 2:19–21.

---

1. The *hieron* cognate group is employed more frequently in John, but is in no instance used as a way of referring to Jesus as the fulfilment of the temple (see John 2:14, 15; 5:14; 7:14, 28; 8:2, 20, 59; 10:23; 11:56; 18:20). Thus only *skēnoō* and *naos* are used with reference to Jesus' fulfilment of the tabernacle or temple. Salier (2004: 126–127) points out the background of Exodus 32 – 34 to John's use of *skēnoō*, and the context in which it is found. See also Spatafora 1997: 111.

It would seem more likely, rather, that the tabernacle language is used because it primarily refers to *dwelling*, which is the point at issue in 1:14. The Word became flesh and dwelt among us. It is this fluid and dynamic nuance that the verb *skēnoō* allows, which makes it a suitable choice here – more suitable than temple language, which lacks dynamicity and refers instead to some kind of locative permanence.

As for the use of *naos* in John 2:19–21, this is no doubt related to the capacity of this word for double entendre. While *naos* may refer to the physical structure of a temple, it may also refer to the body (e.g. Philo, *De opificio mundi* 136–137; Tatian, 15.2). The double entendre is evident in 2:19–21, in which the Jews understood Jesus to be referring to the physical temple, whereas the author reveals that Jesus was, in fact, speaking of his body. The point here is that, while *naos* is capable of such a double meaning, the more standard temple language is not.

Suffice to say, John 1 and 2 connect the fulfilment of the tabernacle and the temple to the incarnation, death and resurrection of Jesus. He is the Lord who dwells among his people, and he becomes the location of true worship.

Acts

During his speech in Acts 7, Stephen summarizes the history of the tabernacle with language that recalls the Septuagint (Acts 7:44–46). Clearly, Stephen presents the tabernacle favourably, as being made in accordance with the pattern given to Moses from God (7:44).

Even more clearly, Stephen roundly denounces Solomon's temple, describing it as a house made with hands (7:47–48). His condemnation of the temple does not here seem to be related to the subsequent corruption and destruction of the temple. Rather, the problem with the temple was that the Most High does not dwell in such man-made houses, since heaven is his throne and earth his footstool (7:48–49; cf. Isa. 66:1–2).[2]

---

2. Koester's (1989: 84) suggestion that Stephen's condemnation of the temple was due to the fact that it was not prescribed by law or established by a prophet, and therefore was not a legitimate sanctuary, is unconvincing.

As evidenced by his reference to Isaiah 66, Stephen is not making a new claim about the temple. He is simply reiterating the declaration of the Lord that he is not limited by his choice to inhabit the temple building. Admittedly, by his grace the Lord chose to dwell in a special way in Solomon's temple, but this fact should never be seen as an indication that Yahweh is a localized god, limited to his temporal and physical surrounds. Just as Israel is criticized by the prophets for its duplicitous and faithless engagement with the sacrificial system, so, too, its attitude toward the temple is at fault. The sacrificial system and temple are both instituted by God, and are instruments of his grace, but in both cases they are abused and mistreated by rebellious Israel. The people might well have performed the outer ritualistic requirements, yet their hearts were far from the Lord. This sense is immediately continued within Stephen's speech, in which his opponents are declared to be stiff-necked 'with uncircumcised hearts and ears' (7:51–53).

Through this analysis, we are able to understand Stephen's endorsement of the tabernacle, on the one hand, and his vilification of the temple on the other. The issue is not whether one was ordained by God or not, but simply how each came to be treated by Israel. God's presence in the tabernacle did not lead Israel to misconstrue his omnipotence. The temple, however, became a focal point of false religion and of mockery toward the Holy God.

Paul

1 Corinthians
The movement from the Gospels and Acts to Pauline material witnesses the first inclusion of God's people as constituting the new temple.[3] Interestingly, K. G. Kuhn has pointed out that, of all the

---

3. Bonnington (2004: 152–158) argues that Paul's agenda in 1 Corinthians is not to articulate a 'temple-replacement' theology; rather, the language relating to the temple has to do with holiness and purity. However, while

documents contemporaneous with the NT, only the writings of
Qumran apply the imagery of the temple to a community (cited in
Coppens 1973: 59). Whereas the Gospels firmly assert that Jesus
has replaced the old temple, in 1 Corinthians 3:16–17 Paul encour-
ages his readers with these words: 'Do you not know that you are
God's temple and that God's Spirit dwells in you? If anyone
destroys God's temple, God will destroy him. For God's temple is
holy, and you are that temple.'[4]

The second person here is of course plural, indicating that corporately these Corinthian Christians constitute the temple of God.
Without going into detail, Paul makes it clear why he describes
these Christians in such a manner: it is because 'God's Spirit dwells
in you'. Since God dwells by his Spirit among these people, they
are, by definition, God's temple. If the presence of God is the
feature that most essentially defines the temple, the indwelling of
his Spirit so defines this congregation. This enables Paul to make
his case for preserving the holiness of God's people: the temple is
holy, and that is what they are.[5]

Only a few chapters later, Paul again associates God's temple
with the Corinthians, but this time in a seemingly more intimate
way. Speaking of the dangers of sexual immorality, Paul says, 'Do
you not know that your body is a temple of the Holy Spirit within
you, whom you have from God? You are not your own, for you
were bought with a price. So glorify God in your body' (1 Cor.
6:19–20).

There are obvious parallels between this and the previously
quoted passage, but this time the referent appears to be the indi-

---

Footnote 3 (*continued*)

Bonnington is correct in observing that the context of the relevant passages clearly has holiness and purity issues in mind, it seems hard to avoid
some kind of temple-replacement motif, even if this is not Paul's primary
concern.

4. Bible quotations in this chapter are from the ESV.

5. Rosner (1991) argues that this passage, and its connection between temple
and holiness, lies behind Paul's command in ch. 5 to expel the incestuous
man: there is no room for such within the holy temple of God.

vidual believer rather than the congregation. Both references to the body (*sōma*) are singular, though the possessive pronouns are plural (*hymōn*). Syntactically, this could indicate that 'body' here is functioning collectively, referring to the one body that belongs to all concerned (the corporate temple). On the other hand, everything in the context seems to indicate that Paul indeed has the individual in mind, since he has been addressing the issue of prostitution and how any individual joined to a prostitute is one with her (6:16),[6] and 'the sexually immoral person sins against his own body' (6:18). As such, the plural pronouns most naturally indicate the multiplicity of individual bodies that make up the Corinthian congregation.

It would seem, then, that 1 Corinthians 6:19 does indeed refer to the individual believer's body as a temple of the Holy Spirit. As with the 1 Corinthians 3 passage, the rationale behind this assertion appears to stem from the fact that the Holy Spirit dwells within each believer. Since God dwells within each individual by his Spirit, it is appropriate to describe each body as a temple of the Spirit.

The OT temple was to house God's glory, and these Corinthians are to glorify God in their bodies (6:20). As Beale comments, 'Just as God's glory uniquely dwelt in Israel's old temple, so the glorious attributes of God are to be manifested in the Corinthians both individually and corporately, since they are the new temple' (2004: 252). Thus, in this way Paul employs temple language in order to highlight the seriousness of holiness for the Christian community. God will destroy the one who ruins the temple; the Corinthians must not jeopardize the holiness of the new temple through sexual immorality.

Ephesians

With Ephesians 2:17–22 we witness one of the most important texts relating to the temple in the NT corpus. It is worth citing here in full:

---

6. Most likely Paul has in mind temple prostitution in particular (Rosner 1998).

And he [Christ] came, and preached peace to you who were far off and
peace to those who were near. For through him we both have access in
one Spirit to the Father. So then you are no longer strangers and aliens,
but you are fellow citizens with the saints and members of the
household of God, built on the foundation of the apostles and
prophets, Christ Jesus himself being the cornerstone, in whom the
whole structure, being joined together, grows into a holy temple in the
Lord. In him you also are being built together into a dwelling place for
God by the Spirit.

The passage is set in the context of the unification of Jews and
Gentiles in Christ, which is possible because salvation is by grace,
through faith (2:8). Those not having the law are now able to par-
ticipate in the promise in Christ, because he has 'broken down in
his flesh the dividing wall of hostility', which is the law and its
regulations (2:14–15).

Thus Christ proclaimed the good news to those far away, and
peace to those near (2:17), and through him *both have access in one
Spirit to the Father*' (2:18). Here in 2:18 we detect the first hint of
temple-related language – that of *access*. In the next verse, this hint
becomes stronger, as Gentiles are included with the saints as
members of *God's household*. This hint gives way to the full-blown
exposition in 2:21–22, where we are told that this building is
growing into a holy temple in the Lord, being built together for
God's dwelling in the Spirit. While the OT temple was, among
other things, a symbol for the exclusion of Gentiles, the new
temple in Christ is built with Jews and Gentiles. It is thus the
temple imagery that here underscores the wonders of salvation by
grace – Jew and Gentile *together* constitute this holy temple in the
Lord.

Here also we receive the clearest picture as to how the various
referents of temple language in the NT are to be understood as
fitting together. The temple is built upon the foundation of the
apostles and prophets, with Christ himself as the cornerstone
(2:20). In him, the building grows and is built together (2:20–21).
The whole building, which consists of Christ, his apostles and
prophets, and all Jews and Gentiles who belong to Christ, is God's
dwelling place in the Spirit (2:22).

Since this passage has given us the most complete picture of the new temple thus far, it is worth pausing in order to reflect upon how we may integrate the material investigated to this point. It would seem that Jesus is the 'original' replacement of the old temple, as the Gospels indicate. God dwells in Jesus; he replaces the temple and is the sole location at which people may meet God. However, those united to Christ by faith become part of his body (Eph. 4:16; 5:23–32). His body persists as the dwelling place of God, but now we are included in that body. Since we are part of Christ's body, the Spirit of Christ is in us, and because we each individually belong to this body, his Spirit indwells each individual. As Peterson affirms, '*Christians in union with Christ* fulfil the Temple ideal' (Peterson 2004: 165). In this way, the rich tapestry of temple language in the NT is sewn together: Jesus is the temple, his people are the temple and each individual is a temple of the Spirit.

Hebrews

Hebrews uses tabernacle language more than any other NT book, with ten references in all (8:2, 5; 9:2, 3, 6, 8, 11, 21; 11:9; 13:10). Interestingly, temple-cognate language is entirely absent. The immediate question raised, then, is, 'What is the significance, if any, of the *tabernacle* language in Hebrews, with reference to the absence of *temple* language?'

Beale argues that the choice of the author to the Hebrews in his use of tabernacle language simply reflects the supposition that the tabernacle is virtually synonymous with the temple: 'the temple in Jerusalem was the permanent form of the mobile tabernacle and . . . the two are so closely related that, for all intents and purposes, they are functionally identical' (2004: 293). While this solution is possible, it seems unlikely given the distinction between the tabernacle and temple that we have observed thus far, throughout both the intertestamental and NT literature. May we really assume that the author to the Hebrews was unaware of the distinction, or deliberately collapsed the two categories? It is preferable to suggest an alternative solution.

The first tabernacle reference in Hebrews speaks of the true tabernacle, which has been established by the true high priest (8:1–2). While the passage 8:1–6 does not explicitly link this true tabernacle with heaven, the implication is clear. The high priest is seated at the right hand of the throne of Majesty in the heavens (8:1), and his heavenly priestly activity contrasts that of earthly priests (8:4). The author goes on to say that the earthly priestly activities are only a copy and shadow of the heavenly things, as Moses said when he was about to complete the tabernacle (8:5). The true tabernacle is heavenly, which is where the true high priest may be found.

Most of the other tabernacle references in the book are found in chapter 9. In this chapter, we witness the most profound exposition of the relationship between the Exodus tabernacle material and the new covenant. After a detailed description of the Exodus tabernacle (9:1–5), the author points out the ultimate inadequacy of this earthly symbol (9:6–10).

This tabernacle-focused section segues into the covenant ministry of the Christ, which involves his ministry within the 'greater and more perfect tent not made with hands, that is, not of this creation' (9:11). Christ offered his own blood in the holy of holies (9:12), and is the mediator of a new covenant (9:15).

Later in the chapter we are told that the Christ 'has entered, not into holy places made with hands, which are copies of the true things, but into heaven itself' (9:24). While the word *hagia* (holy places), rather than explicit tabernacle language, is used here, the parallels to 9:11 are striking. In 9:11, the author speaks of the 'greater and more perfect tent (not made with hands)', while 9:24 indicates that the Christ did not enter the 'holy places' 'made with hands (only a model of the true one)'. Clearly, therefore, the 'holy places' in 9:24 can be read for 'tent [tabernacle]' in 9:11. As such, the contrast between the earthly tabernacle and heaven itself is clear in 9:24.

Hebrews 9 not only indicates that the true tabernacle is heaven, but equates all of the priestly activity connected to the earthly tabernacle with the heavenly high priest, whose sacrifice and intercession is the reality to which the earthly symbols pointed. The pastoral implication of all this is that believers have true and unfettered access to the very presence of God through Jesus, our mediator.

While Hebrews draws on a matrix of OT antecedents, chapter 9 is indubitably based upon Exodus 25 – 31, 35 – 40. This Exodus background is no doubt the clearest explanation behind the tabernacle language in Hebrews.[7] It is the fulfilment of the earthly ministries of the priest, sacrificial system and tabernacle that are on view throughout Hebrews 7 – 10, all of which belong to the Exodus material. Tabernacle language, as opposed to that of the temple, is therefore entirely appropriate here, and use of the latter would simply be anachronistic. Thus the author to the Hebrews is not necessarily driving a wedge between the tabernacle and the temple in Israelite history, but neither is he necessarily collapsing the two categories into one. It seems far more likely that his employment of tabernacle language suits the parallels he wishes to make between Christ and the old covenant.

Revelation

Revelation employs both tabernacle and temple language, and both in ample measure.[8] The tabernacle word group occurs seven times, making Revelation second only to Hebrews in its frequency of reference in the NT (Rev. 7:15; 12:12; 13:6 [twice]; 15:5; 21:3 [twice]). Temple language (*naos*) occurs sixteen times, making Revelation the leading NT book for references to the *naos* word group (Rev 3:12; 7:15; 11:1–2, 19 [twice]; 14:15, 17; 15:5–6, 8 [twice]; 16:1, 17; ; 21:22 [twice]).[9] We shall investigate three key passages.

---

7. Motyer (2004: 180) suggests that the absence of temple language in Hebrews is due to the hostility of Jewish audiences to a Christocentric reinterpretation of the temple. This, however, seems rather less likely than the suggestion put forth above, which deems tabernacle language as more appropriate to the Exodus background to Hebrews.

8. See Briggs 1999 for a helpful treatment of the Jewish background and sources to Revelation.

9. Acts, however, contains twenty-five references to the *hieron* word group.

Since Revelation employs both tabernacle and temple terminology, it seems reasonable to conclude that the writer makes a deliberate distinction between the two. If such a distinction is indeed legitimate in Revelation, the author nevertheless explicitly links the two concepts in Revelation 7:15, 15:5 and chapter 21.

Koester points out that chapter 7 contains several connections to chapter 21, including God's tabernacling with his people (7:15/21:3), the end to thirst (7:16/21:6), the absence of the sun (7:16/21:23), springs of living water (7:17/21:6) and wiping away tears (7:17/21:4) (Koester 1989: 118). A further connection between the two chapters is their references to both tabernacle and temple. In 7:15, we read,

> Therefore they are before the throne of God,
> and serve him day and night in his temple;
> and he who sits on the throne will shelter them with his presence.

We are told in the first half of this verse that the people who are robed in white (v. 13) serve God before his throne in his temple (*naō*). We are then immediately told that the one sitting on the throne will spread his tent over them, or literally 'tabernacle upon them' (*skēnōsei ep'autous*). Whatever it means to 'tabernacle upon them', we see clearly that the result of this action is protection and care extended to God's people: they will no longer hunger or thirst; they will be protected from the sun; they will be shepherded by the Lamb, who will lead them to living waters; God will wipe away their tears (7:16–17). Furthermore, this tabernacling will occur in the temple. That is where these people are located, as they serve God night and day, and it is where God sits on his throne as he performs this act.

Before exploring how this connection between tabernacle and temple in chapter 7 resonates with chapter 21, it is worth investigating the second passage in Revelation that links the two concepts. After those who had been victorious over the beast sang the song of the Lamb (15:2–4), we read in 15:5, 'After this I looked, and the sanctuary of the tent of witness in heaven was opened'.

This verse explicitly connects the 'tent of witness' to the temple; in fact, the two terms are in apposition. The next verse reverts to temple language ('out of the sanctuary came the seven angels'), which further confirms that indeed the temple is still in view.

Thus these two passages provide a strong case for regarding the usage of temple and tabernacle language as overlapping, if not synonymous, in this book. If that is the case, then chapter 21, in the first instance, appears to create some tension to this.

Revelation 21:3 declares that God's tabernacle is with men. He will live with them; they will be his people and he will be their God. And yet, towards the end of the chapter, it is reported that John did not see a temple in the new city, because the Lord God and the Lamb are its temple. If, as has been suggested above, temple and tabernacle language are virtually synonymous in Revelation, these two statements at the beginning and end of chapter 21 might appear to be contradictory. This apparent contradiction, however, only pertains to the surface level.

Verse 22 says that John did not *see* a temple in the city. This does not mean that there was no temple, but that there was no physical temple made of stone (Quek 2004: 165). The temple, verse 22 makes clear, is the Lord God and the Lamb. They are regarded as the temple because central to the concept of the temple was the dwelling of God with his people. Once his people are with him in the New Jerusalem, they are in the temple par excellence – they are with God, in his presence, completely and fully.

By the same token, God's tabernacle with men (21:3) does not refer to an actual physical tabernacle, but to the actual presence of God with his people. He dwells with them directly. Koester argues that, by implication, the city that has just descended from heaven is the new tabernacle. He supports this by recognizing several similarities this new city bears to the tabernacle: 'Like the holy of holies, the new Jerusalem is a cube (21:16) in which the glory of God appears (21:11) and in which the faithful serve with God's name on their foreheads like high priests' (1989: 121). Dumbrell argues similarly, claiming that 'Since the New Jerusalem comes down from God and is filled with his glory, it is at once a temple and a city' (1994: 344). Spatafora, however, disagrees with this correlation, arguing that the cubic shape of the city suggests a 'great degree of holiness permeating the city because of the divine presence within it' (1997: 240). Whether or not we are supposed to regard the city as the new tabernacle (though I think we are), it is clear that this city is God's dwelling place, and so in that regard it performs the key function that defined the tabernacle.

Thus we see that 21:3 and 21:22 do not stand in tension at all – in fact, they are saying the same thing. There is no physical temple because God dwells with his people directly and fully in the New Jerusalem.

Finally, an important theme in Revelation 21 – 22 that has not yet been addressed has to do with the connections to creation that the temple/tabernacle language reveals. As several scholars have noticed, these chapters invoke creation and the Garden of Eden, casting them in connection to the temple/tabernacle (Quek 2004: 2). There is reference to 'a new heaven and a new earth' (21:1), a 'spring of the water of life' (21:6), and precious stones from Eden (21:19–20). Besides these more explicit connections to creation/ Eden, there are several more implicit references to creation/Eden through OT intertextuality. That is, there are several places in the OT that point back to creation in one way or another, and some of these texts lie in the background to Revelation 21 – 22. Quek's work, in particular, shows the way in which creation is invoked through references to Isaiah, Ezekiel and Exodus found in Revelation 21 – 22 (Quek 2004: 51–118). Quek successfully demonstrates that these multilayered references to creation/Eden are integrated with Revelation's temple language, with the result that 'John portrays the new Jerusalem as God's palace-temple, which encompasses the whole of the new creation. It is the eschatological fulfilment of the perfect world, which the historical temple, as microcosm, was supposed to represent. It is God dwelling with humanity in the new creation' (2004: 210). The assured hope that Revelation provides is that God's dwelling place is ultimately ours with him.

Conclusion

How are we to draw these various threads together? We have seen that, while the temple is generally regarded as superseding and replacing the tabernacle, both temple and tabernacle language is employed in the NT, usually with a deliberate distinction in place. We have seen that Christ replaces the temple as the location at which people may encounter the presence of God, and yet God's people themselves are described as the temple. We have seen that the earthly tabernacle meets its final fulfilment in the New Jerusalem (the dwelling place of God and the Lamb with their people) and as the restoration of creation, in which God dwells freely among his people once more, who, with perfect and unrestricted access, are able to draw near to God for all eternity.

Throughout these various descriptions, one element remains common. Central to the tabernacle concept is *the dwelling of God*. It is this one element that is able to explain, and bring together, the various ways in which tabernacle/temple language is employed in the NT. Jesus replaces the temple because, in him, God dwells among us. Those who trust in Christ are described as the temple of God because they are *in* Christ and Christ is in *them* by his Spirit. The New Jerusalem is the tabernacle of God because there God dwells freely with his people.

As such, the eschatological trajectory of the tabernacle theme in NT thought is as follows. The tabernacle/temple is replaced by one man. This is accomplished through the death and resurrection of Jesus. Then, others are added to him by faith, and are incorporated into the dwelling place of God. This takes place between Christ's resurrection and his return, as believers are united to him by faith and in the Spirit. Upon the arrival of the New Jerusalem, the dwelling of God ultimately expands to encompass the entire new creation.

This trajectory reveals unmistakable pastoral implications, as the holiness of the tabernacle/temple (as established in the OT) provides theological grounding for the holiness of God's people, the new temple. Furthermore, believers are assured of their genuine and free access to God through the One who has entered the heavenly tabernacle on their behalf. And ultimately this access will be 'face to face', as it were, when the dwelling of God will be with his people for all eternity in the holy palace-temple, the New Jerusalem.

As such, we could not choose more appropriate words with which to close than those of Revelation 21:1–4.

Then I saw a new heaven and a new earth, for the first heaven and the
first earth had passed away, and the sea was no more. And I saw the holy
city, new Jerusalem, coming down out of heaven from God, prepared as
a bride adorned for her husband. And I heard a loud voice from the
throne saying, 'Behold, the dwelling place of God is with man. He will
dwell with them, and they will be his people, and God himself will be
with them as their God. He will wipe away every tear from their eyes,
and death shall be no more, neither shall there be mourning, nor crying,
nor pain anymore, for the former things have passed away.'

Bibliography

Alexander, T. D. and S. Gathercole (eds.) (2004), *Heaven on Earth*, Carlisle:
    Paternoster.
Beale, G. K. (2004), *The Temple and the Church's Mission: A Biblical Theology of the
    Dwelling Place of God*, New Studies in Biblical Theology 17, Leicester:
    Apollos; Downers Grove: IVP.
Bonnington, M. (2004), 'New Temples in Corinth: Paul's Use of Temple
    Imagery in the Ethics of the Corinthian Correspondence', in Alexander
    and Gathercole, *Heaven on Earth*, 151–159.
Briggs, R. A. (1999), *Jewish Temple Imagery in the Book of Revelation*, Studies in
    Biblical Literature 10, New York: Peter Lang.
Clowney, E. P. (1987), 'The Biblical Theology of the Church', in D. A. Carson
    (ed.), *The Church in the Bible and the World*, Exeter: Paternoster, 13–87.
Cole, A. (1950), *The New Temple: A Study in the Origins of the Catechetical 'Form'
    of the Church in the New Testament*, London: Tyndale.
Coppens, J. C. (1973), 'The Spiritual Temple in the Pauline Letters and its
    Background', in E. A. Livingstone (ed.), *Studia Evangelica VI: Papers
    Presented to the Fourth International Congress on New Testament Studies Held at
    Oxford, 1969*, Berlin: Akadamie-Verlag, 53–66.
Dumbrell, W. J. (1994), *The Search for Order: Biblical Eschatology in Focus*, Grand
    Rapids: Baker.
Gaston, L. (1976), 'The Theology of the Temple', in F. Christ (ed.),
    Oikonomia: Heilsgeschichte als Thema der Theologie, Hamburg: Hebert Reich
    Evangelische Verlag, 32–41.
Koester, C. R. (1989), *The Dwelling of God: The Tabernacle in the Old Testament,
    Intertestamental Jewish Literature, and the New Testament*, Catholic Biblical

Quarterly Monograph Series 22, Washington: Catholic Biblical Association of America.

MacRae, G. W. (1978), 'Heavenly Temple and Eschatology in the Letter to the Hebrews', *Semeia* 12: 179–199.

Motyer, S. (2004), 'The Temple in Hebrews: Is it There?', in Alexander and Gathercole, *Heaven on Earth*, 177–189.

Palmer, J. (2004), 'Exodus and the Biblical Theology of the Tabernacle', in Alexander and Gathercole, *Heaven on Earth*, 11–22.

Peterson, D. (2004), 'The New Temple: Christology and Ecclesiology in Ephesians and 1 Peter', in Alexander and Gathercole, *Heaven on Earth*, 161–176.

Quek, T.-M. (2004), 'The New Jerusalem as God's Palace-Temple: An Exegetical Study of the Eden-Temple and Escalation Motifs in Revelation 21.1–22.5', MTh thesis, Regent College, Vancouver.

Rosner, B. S. (1991), 'Temple and Holiness in 1 Corinthians 5', *Tyndale Bulletin* 42: 137–145.

— (1998), 'Temple Prostitution in 1 Corinthians 6:12–20', *Novum Testamentum* 40: 336–351.

Salier, W. (2004), 'The Temple in the Gospel according to John', in Alexander and Gathercole, *Heaven on Earth*, 121–134.

Spatafora, A. (1997), *From the 'Temple of God' to God as the Temple: A Biblical Theological Study of the Temple in the Book of Revelation*, Rome: Gregorian University Press.

8. NAME ABOVE ALL NAMES: PREACHING EXODUS

Richard Gibson

Preaching from Exodus

Despite the best efforts of these chapters, it remains an act of great courage to place the book of Exodus on a preaching roster. There have been earnest encouragement and numerous valuable insights, but there has also been the reminder of persistent, perplexing difficulties, unresolved by reference to the original language and most thoughtful scholarship. We have also been reminded that as we stand to expound the message of Exodus we 'are standing on holy ground'. This is the great, foundational text of Israel's faith and ours. No preacher could be blamed for having a Moses moment: 'O Lord, please send someone else to do it' . . . 'I am slow of speech and of a slow tongue.' This response qualifies, not disqualifies, the preacher. I would not want someone preaching to me from Exodus who did not quake and tremble at the prospect. Yet the understandable temptation remains, to leave explanation of the name of God, the plagues, Yahweh's repentance, the law and the details of the tabernacle to those most qualified to handle the challenge: Sunday school teachers.

Only slightly more daunting is the challenge of giving people advice about how to preach from Exodus to a contemporary audience. By this stage of the book, it may feel like you have just flown in from a two-day holiday in Egypt via Israel with a stopover in Calvary, complete with some in-flight films provided by Greg Clarke, and in this concluding chapter you enter the taxi to be taken back to the suburb where you live so you can tell people all about the trip. It would be easy to do what taxi drivers do: take the longest possible route for the journey and bore you with issues you know are significant but do not have the energy to engage with after an exhausting journey.

There is no shortage of resources. In recent years, books tackling the hermeneutical issues raised by moving from OT to Christ have multiplied – with Greidanus, Goldsworthy, Clowney and Mathewson notable among the fruitful and profound (Greidanus 1999; Goldsworthy 2000; Clowney 2003; Mathewson 2002; Allen and Holbert 1995; Holmgren and Schaalman 1995). There is guidance on how to preach from narrative, legal texts, and the tabernacle accounts (Hart 1982; Poythress 1991). Others promise to explore a particular text only to drown the preacher's interest under a tide of critical issues. They end up the opposite of Moses' bush: consumed by the issues but hardly on fire with a message. One promisingly entitled article wearisomely surveyed published sermons of the preceding twenty years with suggestions of titles or ideas for expounding particular verses. In short, it would be easy to wander aimlessly through a wilderness of insights into preaching from Exodus, multiplying more observations, yet offering less and less help. The more conscientiously you approach this topic in terms of 'preaching *from* Exodus' the more diffuse and fruitless the result.

Preaching Exodus

So, in the interest of meandering with some purpose, this chapter reframes the task from 'preaching *from* Exodus', with its inevitable selectivity and diffusion, to simply 'preaching Exodus'. How should you conceive the task as you sit down to prepare? What are you doing when you stand up to preach? How do you evaluate whether you have done it when you lie down with a headache after attempting it? In other words, what is the essence of Exodus?

Expressed like this, some resistance is understandable. The quest for one integrating theme in Exodus is artificial and perhaps as elusive as the quest for the centre of Paul's theology. Yet on several occasions already in this school we have reached for the happiest way of encapsulating and integrating the book's message. Most commentators offer some kind of topic sentence, a working summary that helps us assemble the details and arrange them into some coherent narrative. In what follows, four such propositions are outlined and evaluated. In the light of their strengths and weaknesses, this chapter explores another possibility for articulating what it means to 'preach Exodus'.

The story of salvation

Our attention has already been drawn to the popularity of conceiving of Exodus as the archetypal story of salvation, deliverance or liberation. As Newsom reminds us, 'The story of the Exodus is *the* story of the Hebrew Scriptures . . . It is no accident that the story of the Exodus is the only story which the Torah instructs the people of Israel to retell. This story is central to their identity as God's people' (1987: 71). It does not take an encyclopedic knowledge of the OT to confirm this simple, but profound, claim. For this reason alone it is worth every preacher learning to tell and retell this story, to cultivate the kind of literacy required to make sense of the OT.

More significantly, for Christian readers, the Exodus becomes Jesus' story. Drawing upon virtually every existing interpretative means available to them, the New Testament writers used Exodus texts for interpreting *and* proclaiming God's act in Jesus. At the same time, Exodus texts are not only applied to Jesus; a continuity is seen between Israel and church as people of God.

Since the threads of the Exodus narratives have been sewn so thoroughly into the fabric of the NT,

> [t]he God of the exodus is *our* God, whose salvific activity we too have experienced. We are one with those Israelites who stood on the far shore

of the Red Sea and proclaimed the victory of their God. Their songs
have become our songs. (Fretheim 1991: 3)

Yet, for all this, there remain some limitations. The description
is most apt for the first fifteen chapters of the book and does not
readily and convincingly incorporate the subsequent material. Of
course, the subsequent chapters serve to clarify what Yahweh
saves his people for, but this is easily lost. As Greg Clarke and
Michael Raiter have demonstrated, this is the handle on Exodus
most conducive to the modern mind. Yet it is precisely the strip-
ping of the theological which this approach invites that leads to
popular and political misappropriations and distortions of the
original message.

It should also be noted that within the Christian canon, the
story of the exodus is not always related as a story of salvation.
Stephen in Acts 7 draws extensively on the narrative of Exodus,
but on his lips it becomes an exposition of Israel's perpetually
stiff neck and her liability to judgment. There, Stephen levels the
accusation 'You stiff-necked people, uncircumcised in heart and
ears, you are for ever opposing the Holy Spirit, just as your ancestors used to do' (Acts 7:51).[1] Exhibit A for the prosecution is
Exodus 32:

> Our ancestors were unwilling to obey him [Moses]; instead, they pushed
> him aside, and in their hearts they turned back to Egypt, saying to
> Aaron, 'Make gods for us who will lead the way for us; as for this Moses
> who led us out from the land of Egypt, we do not know what has
> happened to him.' At that time they made a calf, offered a sacrifice to the
> idol, and revelled in the works of their hands. But God turned away
> from them and handed them over to worship the host of heaven . . .
> (Acts 7:39–42)

Exodus as 'story of salvation' involves, or at least invites, an unfortunate reduction of the book's message.

---

1. All biblical quotations are taken from the NRSV unless indicated otherwise.

From slavery to worship

The second alternative could be summarized as 'freed to serve', and is captured pithily by Exodus 7:16: 'Let my people go, so that they may worship me.' According to Dumbrell:

> The general contours of the Book of Exodus are erected around this movement from slavery to the concluding picture of worship. The transition from slavery to worship is accomplished through a very great redemption, which is at the center of the book. Basic to all of Israel's later theology is the redemption of the exodus. (2002: 32)

Subsequently, Dumbrell adds the poetic but well-worn line 'By redemption, Israel passed into the service of the one whose service is perfect freedom' (2002: 37).

In the same vein, this trajectory is described by Fretheim by drawing attention to an alternative inclusio. Exodus narrates the journey 'from Israel's bondage to Pharaoh to its bonding to Yahweh. More particularly, the book moves from the enforced construction of buildings for Pharaoh to the glad and obedient offering of the building for the worship of God' (1991: 1). This handy summary has the advantage of embracing much more of the book, especially the legal material and tabernacle provisions. It also sends the preacher in a different direction for the NT's appropriation of Exodus and thus nearer to the contemporary hearer. Jesus' exchange with some Jews who believed in him in John 8 looms on the horizon:

> 'If you continue in my word, you are truly my disciples; and you will know the truth, and the truth will make you free.' They answered him, 'We are descendants of Abraham and have never been slaves to anyone. What do you mean by saying, "You will be made free"?' Jesus answered them, 'Very truly, I tell you, everyone who commits sin is a slave to sin. The slave does not have a permanent place in the household; the son has a place there for ever. So if the Son makes you free, you will be free indeed.' (John 8:31–36)

This recalls a question already raised by other contributors to this collection as to whether the goal of the exodus is best understood as sonship or service. While John 8 supports sonship (cf. Exod. 4:23), it is hard to imagine a better endorsement of service and commentary on the message of Exodus for people today than Romans 6:16–18:

> Do you not know that if you present yourselves to anyone as obedient slaves, you are slaves of the one whom you obey, either of sin, which leads to death, or of obedience, which leads to righteousness? But thanks be to God that you, having once been slaves of sin, have become obedient from the heart to the form of teaching to which you were entrusted, and that you, having been set free from sin, have become slaves of righteousness.

In Romans 12:1, Paul will transpose the same language 'present your bodies' into the sphere of worship: 'I appeal to you therefore, brothers and sisters, by the mercies of God, to present your bodies as a living sacrifice, holy and acceptable to God, which is your spiritual worship.'

It is hard to argue, then, with the appropriateness of 'Freed to serve' as a summary of the message of Exodus. However, there is a significant limitation worth noting. Like the first 'story of salvation' it remains too anthropocentric. As Gowan puts it, 'When Exodus is read with the question of the role of God in mind, it is seen to have another plot, running beneath the surface story of Israel's bondage, deliverance, and journey through the wilderness to Sinai' (1994: xvii).[2] 'Freed to serve' is not explicitly theological enough to do full justice to the refrain and burden of Exodus: 'By this you shall know that I am the LORD' (Exod. 7:17). More emphasis needs to be placed on the personal pronouns of Exodus 7:16: Let *my* people go that they may serve *me*. The possessiveness of the first pronoun warrants capturing, as does the directness of the object of the service expressed by the second.

---

2. Cf. Fretheim: 'at the heart of things, the Old Testament serves to bring people face-to-face with the Father of Jesus Christ, and in that encounter God speaks' (1991: 1).

God works sovereignly

In his book *The Message of the Old Testament*, Mark Dever makes an impressive effort not only to summarize Exodus but also to place God at centre stage. The book contains single sermons preached on the whole of each OT book. Rather disarmingly he comments, 'as much as Exodus is a story about Moses, when I read it again this week, I found that God is really the main character of the story' (2006: 89). Consequently, Dever crafts his 'thesis sentence' in different terms: 'God works sovereignly.' With it, he encompasses the message of the whole book of Exodus under three sections:

1. God works sovereignly (in Moses and Pharaoh).
2. God works sovereignly to save a special people (distinguishing them from all nations).
3. God works sovereignly to save a special people for his own glory.

With each section he points in the direction that preaching to a contemporary audience might lead. So, in chapters 1–18:

> Exodus challenges the common notion that God is passive. How many times have you heard God presented as a resource or power for improving your life, should you decide to use him? (2006: 88)
> . . . God is *not* passive. Circumstances do not determine God's plan; God's plan determines circumstances. (93)

Through the material recorded in the second section, chapters 19–31,

> Exodus challenges the common notion that God treats all people in the same way, or that God is a committed egalitarian. No, that is not the story in Exodus. God is certainly fair; he is the standard of justice. But God does mysteriously and graciously choose to extend mercy to some. (2006: 93)

Finally, in chapters 32–40,

> Exodus directly challenges the idea that God does everything for humanity's sake. Humans *are not* the ultimate purpose of creation. God's

own glory is! . . . The whole book, you could say, is about God
establishing his own fame! (2006: 100)

To substantiate his thesis sentence, and these expansions, Dever
hardly needs to go past the great refrain of Exodus 'you shall
know that I am the LORD'. This is the message Egypt has to learn,
with great reluctance, and at great personal cost: 'I will harden
Pharaoh's heart, and he will pursue them, so that I will gain glory
for myself over Pharaoh and all his army; and the Egyptians shall
know that I am the LORD' (cf. Exod. 7:17; 8:10, 22; 9:14, 29; 11:7;
14:8). This, too, is knowledge Israel must acquire through this
experience and cherish for generations. Yahweh is acting in order
'that you may tell your children and grandchildren how I have
made fools of the Egyptians and what signs I have done among
them – so that you may know that I am the LORD' (Exod. 10:2; cf.
29:46). This, then, is what Exodus is about and what it means to
preach Exodus today, according to Dever:

> It challenges our ideas of God as a passive, egalitarian servant, doesn't
> it? According to Exodus, God sovereignly saves a special people for his
> own glory. (2006: 104)

> He did then, and he still does today. That is what he is doing in the
> church. (103)

It is hard to argue with Dever about this thesis statement. You
cannot read Exodus without being confronted by the Lord who
makes law and demands obedience; the judge who punishes
Egyptian and Israelite alike; the unrivalled ruler of heaven. Having
raised God's arm aloft as the winner by knock out of the heavy-
weight title fight with Pharaoh, Moses and the Israelites declare that
the LORD is a warrior (Exod. 15:3). A little later we are assured, 'The
LORD will reign for ever and ever' (15:18). Yet, when I read the text
again, I couldn't help but feel that something had been lost, that
Dever's tidy and orthodox summary tames the wildness of Exodus
too much. Exodus is a disturbing book. In Exodus, Yahweh is a disturbing God. At crucial points, Exodus challenges commonly held
views of God's sovereignty and the way he exercises it.

Creation, sovereignty and suffering

This is the burden of Fretheim's fertile contributions to the study of Exodus. He insists that Exodus is richly informed by creation language. He is also convinced that Yahweh's sovereignty is at the heart of the book, and writes, 'God's sovereignty is evident in the divine initiative, the setting of the agenda, the will to deliver Israel, and the announced ability to accomplish this' (1991: 16). However, Fretheim's point is that sovereignty simply does not exhaust or do justice to the presentation of Yahweh in Exodus:

> Alongside this, however, are images not commonly associated with sovereignty. It is a divine sovereignty qualified by divine suffering, by a divine move of compassion, that enters deeply into the sufferings of the people. (1991: 16–17)

Implied by his comments is the claim that Dever's approach represents a significant reductionism. Fretheim (1991: 16–17) contends that sovereignty cannot be so defined and still be true to the texts; it needs some correction in view of other metaphors for God in Exodus. Moreover, it is not common for such studies to be mindful of the range of suffering images for God to be found in Exodus, that is, those metaphors that reflect divine entry into the sphere of the created such that God and God's ways with the world are genuinely affected thereby.

Again, Fretheim's objection is not to sovereignty as a leitmotif, but to an absolute, unqualified sovereignty. We can, as many have, choose to make sovereignty the controlling image and subjugate all others to it. To do so, according to Fretheim, is to attend selectively to some metaphors and ignore others. For him, Exodus not only declares *that* Yahweh is sovereign, but also *how* Yahweh exercises his sovereignty. One of the basic concerns of Exodus is:

> Who will finally be recognized as the sovereign one, Pharaoh or Yahweh? But an oft-forgotten parallel issue is: What is the appropriate nature of sovereignty? . . . Yahweh's sovereignty is qualified by suffering images, while Pharaoh's is not. It is Pharaoh who is the

unmoved mover . . . The God of Israel is a suffering sovereign.
(1991: 17)[3]

What Fretheim means by this is explained more fully in his exposition of chapter 3:7–12:

> God sees Israel's afflictions and 'knows' their sufferings. For God to
> 'know' the people's sufferings testifies to God's *experience* of this suffering,
> indeed God's *intimate* experience. God has so entered into their sufferings
> as to have experienced what they are having to endure. God does not
> remain safe and secure in some heavenly abode, untouched by the
> sorrows of the world. God is not portrayed here as a typical monarch
> dealing with the issues through subordinates or at some distance. God
> does not look at the suffering from the outside as through a window;
> God knows it from the inside . . . Yet, while God suffers with the people,
> God is not powerless in the face of it. (1989: 38)

Fretheim is not alone in speaking of the 'vulnerability' of
Yahweh (1989: 39). Passages in Exodus are often cited in support.
The remarkable exchange between Moses and Yahweh in Exodus
32:7–14 provides some of the most striking evidence for the claim.
There Yahweh is 'represented as a God who will change his plans
as a result of human intervention' (Gowan 1995: 93).[4] How do you
maintain the claim that 'God is *not* passive. Circumstances do not
determine God's plan' in the face of this incident? At crucial
points in the narrative, God is portrayed as passive and responsive
to other actors on the stage.

It is not my intention to open up, let alone explore in adequate
depth, the wider theological and philosophical issues inevitably
raised by speaking of a suffering God. It ought to be noted,

---

3. He further notes that 'God opens himself up to risk and vulnerability, for
   these persons could fail and God would have to begin again' (1991: 18).
4. Cf. Calvin: 'Hence we do plainly perceive the wonderful goodness of
   God, who not only hears the prayers of His people when they humbly call
   upon Him, but suffers them to be in a manner intercessors with Him'
   (1950: 3.341).

though, that these philosophical issues are raised just as much by Dever's treatment. His insistence that God is not passive echoes Greek philosophy and the scholastic *actus purus* more obviously than it does the Scriptures. What I do want to do is guard against a type of domestic deafness in reading Exodus: letting our tradition dull our ears to the confronting and disturbing in Exodus and so domesticate God in order to preach him.

Naming God

Rather than discuss such slippery and loaded terms as 'suffering' and 'vulnerability', the remainder of this chapter focuses on one disturbing feature of Exodus' characterization of Yahweh and offers a very different 'thesis statement', lifted from Exodus itself. This seems to me to be a compelling answer to the question of what it means to 'preach Exodus'. Yet be warned that the key characteristic of Yahweh I adopt is one that neither Dumbrell (2002) nor Dever (2006) mention, even in passing, when they discuss Exodus. I propose that preaching Exodus is essentially about naming God: confronting people with the character of God. As George Athas points out (in chapter 2 of this volume), 'to know someone's name is to know their personal details'. When God gives his name, we need to sit up and take note.

Understandably, the mention of God's name immediately conjures up Exodus 3 and the name 'Yahweh'. The giving of the name 'Yahweh' is a pivotal moment of self-revelation to which we have gravitated on several occasions already in these chapters. However, it is worth considering the significance of the giving of another name, God's second name, so to speak.

This name is found in Exodus 34, which provides one of the great moments of Yahweh's self-revelation. This is one of the classic 'read my lips' moments in all of Scripture. Brueggemann describes it as

> an exceedingly important, stylised, quite self-conscious characterization
> of Yahweh, a formulation so studied that it may be reckoned to be

something of a classic, normative statement to which Israel regularly
returned, meriting the label 'credo.' (1997: 216)

Verses 6–7 of Exodus 34 read:

The LORD passed before him, and proclaimed,

> 'The LORD, the LORD,
> a God merciful and gracious,
> slow to anger,
> and abounding in steadfast love and faithfulness,
> keeping steadfast love for the thousandth generation,
> forgiving iniquity and transgression and sin,
> yet by no means clearing the guilty,
> but visiting the iniquity of the parents upon the children
> and the children's children,
> to the third and the fourth generation.'

Brueggemann's claim for the subsequent significance of these
words is easily established by tracing the way they are invoked in
times of weal and woe for Israel (Num. 14:18; Neh. 9:17; Pss
103:8, 17; 145:8; Jer. 32:18–19; Nah. 1:3; cf. Deut. 5:9–10; 1 Kgs
3:6; Lam. 3:32; Dan. 9:4). In the light of its ubiquity, Fretheim dis-
cerns the creedal status of this description, but for him 'it may be
said to be a statement about God toward which the entire Exodus
narrative is driving' (1991: 17). The reason for this significance
within and beyond the book of Exodus lies in its answer to the
most urgent life and death question Israel has: What hope is there
for a nation that has spurned the covenant with flagrant, stiff-
necked rebellion? How can they have a future after receiving the
Decalogue, with its prohibition of idolatry, and then bowing down
before a golden calf? Yahweh's answer is bound up with the kind
of God he is. Space does not permit us to explore the significance
of each of the adjectives chosen to make himself known, but we
can say that

> the cumulative effect of all of these terms together, which bespeak
> Yahweh's intense solidarity with and commitment to those to whom

> Yahweh is bound . . . [is to assert that] Yahweh's life with Israel is
> marked by a fundamental, inalienable loyalty. Israel's life, at this pivotal
> point of risk in Exodus 34, is now guaranteed by the assertion on the
> very lips of Yahweh that Yahweh abides for Israel in complete fidelity,
> even among those who enact 'iniquity, transgression, and sin.'
> (Brueggemann 1997: 217)[5]

As Gowan puts it, 'Only the revelation that God is compassionate and gracious (34:6–7) enables the rest of Israel's story to
happen' (1994: xviii). From this moment on it 'constitutes a kind
of "canon" of the kind of God Israel's God is, in the light of
which God's ongoing involvement in its history is to be interpreted' (Fretheim 1991: 302). Yahweh gives himself to Israel in
such a way that she can rely upon his fidelity, tender-heartedness,
lovingkindness and patience. However, his people dare not presume
on his slowness to anger. He will not clear the guilty. Yahweh's
fidelity will never become Yahweh's domestication (Brueggemann
1997: 228).

Shame about the name

As God remakes the covenant, he makes it clear that its future is
founded on his faithfulness and compassion. And as he reissues
his requirements of Israel, Yahweh offers a single name in verse 14
for the kind of God he is: jealous. This is not a new description for
God. Israel should have known this already. It was made perfectly
clear in the course of the giving of the Decalogue, in support of
the prohibition of the worship of other gods: 'You shall not bow
down to them or worship them; for I the LORD your God am a
jealous God, punishing children for the iniquity of parents, to the
third and the fourth generation of those who reject me' (Exod.
20:5).

In 34:14, this quality is made more emphatic and unambiguous;
elevated from description to name: 'for you shall worship no other

---

5. See Ryken 2005: 1040–1043, for systematic reflection on each adjective.

god, because the LORD, whose name is Jealous, is a jealous God'. Block aptly observes that Jealous 'is not merely an attribute of God, it is an epithet' (1997: 14).

The context suggests that this one name offers a way of integrating the seven adjectives of verses 6 and 7. This is confirmed by the way the prophets so frequently trace God's compassion, mercy and anger to the intense jealousy of his love. Zechariah 8:2–3 connects anger to divine jealousy:

Thus says the LORD of hosts: I am jealous for Zion with great jealousy, and I am jealous for her with great wrath. Thus says the LORD: I will return to Zion, and will dwell in the midst of Jerusalem; Jerusalem shall be called the faithful city, and the mountain of the LORD of hosts shall be called the holy mountain.

The compassion implicit in this text is made explicit in Joel 2:18: 'Then the LORD became jealous for his land, and had pity on his people' (cf. Ps. 79:5; Zeph. 3:8; Nah. 1:2; Isa. 63:15).

To name God as Jealous is about as confronting as you can be to contemporary ears. If Exodus as story of liberation is Exodus at its most marketable, then the Jealous God must stand at the other end of the range. Ryken should probably be charged with understatement when he points out, 'If we were to put God's attributes up for a vote, jealousy wouldn't even make the top ten' (2005: 1054). If we delight to find more and more in the name Yahweh, we long to find less than jealous implies. We know all too well what jealousy means.

Understandably, Christian commentators have wanted to guard against any alignment of Yahweh with the Greek gods of envy, Phthonos and Nemesis. For Block, 'jealousy' is an inadequate and misleading rendering:

In common parlance jealousy tends to be associated either with envy and covetousness, the desire to own what someone else possesses, or exaggerated possessiveness over what one already owns, that is, an unwillingness to share it with others. In psychiatric terms, jealousy amounts to 'vindictiveness born of sexual frustration.'
(1997: 13)

Brueggemann is less inclined to blush:

> While the terms *jealous* and *jealousy* may be carefully nuanced, their
> meaning is the one we commonly connect to the English term *jealous*,
> for they refer to Yahweh's strong emotional response to any affront
> against Yahweh's prerogative, privilege, ascendancy, or sovereignty.
> (1997: 293)

On either reading, surely to insist on naming God as Jealous plays straight into the hands of critics of the biblical God, such as Dawkins and Hitchens. Greg Clarke (chapter 1 in this volume) has already drawn our attention to Dawkins's sneering mockery of God's 'jealous sulk' about Israel's breach of the covenant in Exodus 32. Frankly, it doesn't help much that the great hero and model of virtuous jealousy in the OT is Phinehas (Num. 25), the man who displayed his jealousy for Yahweh by running a spear through an Israelite man and Midianite woman. If ever Dawkins reaches Numbers it will not take much to caricature Phinehas as proto-terrorist and father of fundamentalism!

Of course the reason for this is that human jealousy is so often petty and corrosive of relationship, but not always. I shall never forget the fierce jealousy of one of my oldest and dearest friends when her marriage was threatened. Her husband had been having an affair with a younger woman for some years, and eventually conceived a child with her. Understandably, her friends, including Christian friends, urged her to leave him. In the midst of overwhelming grief and many, many tears, she explained with steely determination that she would not share her husband with anyone. She would not let him abandon her and their children for another partner. She was prepared to do whatever it took – patience, forgiveness, determination – to win him back. And she did. It was a remarkable spectacle to behold love

> strong as death,
>   passion fierce as the grave.
> Its flashes are flashes of fire,
>   a raging flame.
> (Song 8:6)

Instead of reading cynically, Block urges readers

> to hear in the word the legitimate, nay amazing, passion of God for one
> whom he loves. This love is not fueled by an exploitative need to
> dominate but by ardor for the well being of the object. (1997: 13)

As he further explains, the Impassioned one

> has committed himself to Israel, a devotion expressed in gracious
> redemption of the nation from bondage; and he rightfully expects
> grateful and exclusive loyalty in return. The intensity of his wrath at
> threats to this relationship is directly proportional to the depth of his
> love. It arises out of the profundity of his covenant love. Because he
> feels so deeply he must respond vigorously. His relationship with his
> people has been violated, and he must defend it. (1997: 14)

Preaching through Exodus

This, it seems to me, is what it means to 'preach Exodus' – to confront people with the jealous God who redeemed them; who expects their exclusive allegiance and fidelity; who wants them, mind, body and spirit; who demands their undivided attention; who will not brook any rivals for his affection; and who in his tender-hearted compassion and loving kindness is committed to doing what it takes to maintain that relationship, including provision for reconciliation and fellowship in the face of Israel's addiction to sin.

Exodus provides ample opportunity to confront people with this God, from the early chapters with their cosmic struggle over who will own Israel, to the grotesquely exploitative nature of Pharaoh's jealous possession of Israel contrasted with the divine jealousy that chooses, enters relationship, honours promises, takes initiative, protects, rescues and showers gifts, to the law with its uncompromising demand for an exclusive relationship, untriangulated by false and foreign gods: 'You shall not bow down to them or worship them; for I the LORD your God am a jealous God . . .' (Exod. 20:5). As Ortlund observes, 'When the love of Jealous is

offended, he burns. His love is not morally indifferent, pouring out
its benefits heedless of human response. He expects and requires
an ardent and faithful love in return' (R. Ortlund, cited in Ryken
2005: 1056). This extends to Yahweh's fierce anger at Israel's
breach of covenant; through to Moses' audacious appeal to
Yahweh's jealousy for his own name and reputation in Exodus
32:12–13:

> Why should the Egyptians say, 'It was with evil intent that he brought
> them out to kill them in the mountains, and to consume them from the
> face of the earth'? Turn from your fierce wrath; change your mind and
> do not bring disaster on your people. Remember Abraham, Isaac, and
> Israel, your servants, how you swore to them by your own self . . .

Finally, it comprehends the tabernacle's provision of a space for
fellowship and worship: Exodus confronts us with a jealous God
and what it means to cohabit with Yahweh's passion to have Israel
as his treasured possession.

In case this seems to be an unjustifiable lurch away from the
more programmatic description of Israel as God's Son in Exodus
4:22, to Israel as God's wife, let me remind you of what Yahweh
says immediately after naming himself Jealous in Exodus 34:

> You shall not make a covenant with the inhabitants of the land, for
> when they prostitute themselves to their gods and sacrifice to their gods,
> someone among them will invite you, and you will eat of the sacrifice.
> And you will take wives from among their daughters for your sons, and
> their daughters who prostitute themselves to their gods will make your
> sons also prostitute themselves to their gods. (Exod. 34:5–16)

This, then, is my proposed thesis statement for Exodus: 'the LORD,
whose name is Jealous, is a jealous God' (Exod. 34:14).

Ezekiel: preaching Exodus

Note, as the precedent for this proposal, the prophet Ezekiel. It is
hardly a startling claim to suggest that Ezekiel appropriated the

exodus narrative for preaching to his contemporary audience. Such is the foundational character of the exodus for all the Scriptures, that it is exceptional for a book not to invoke it. What is striking, however, is the extent to which Ezekiel draws on exodus traditions.[6] Of course, there are particular texts where this is most clear: Ezekiel 20 narrates the story of Israel in Egypt as a tale of rebellion. Early Jewish interpretation saw a connection between Exodus 19 – 20 and the chariot of Ezekiel 1 (see Teugels 1996: 595–602).

The reasons for perceiving Ezekiel as an example and model of what it means to 'preach Exodus' are more pervasive than a few isolated texts. First, much more than any other prophet, Ezekiel takes up the refrain of Exodus and litters his prophecies with it. More than sixty times the reason for an event is given as 'that you may know that I am the LORD'. Secondly, Ezekiel's oracles against the nations climax with an extended prophecy against Egypt. Mark Strom goes as far as to suggest that the literary structure of the final form of Ezekiel has deliberately been designed to conform to the pattern of Exodus:

> The sequence guides us from the people of God in bondage through the Lord's judgement of their oppressors into a renewed promised land. The structure is obviously the same as the original Exodus. (1989: 130)[7]

Unfortunately, Strom offers little to substantiate his claim, but even if it is disputed, chapters 40–48 undeniably leave us with a vision of God's sanctuary, the ideal temple at the centre of the world, where God dwells among his people. Just as in Exodus, 'the blueprint for the new temple emerges from heaven, as the pattern of the exodus tabernacle had' (1989: 130; cf. Ezek. 43:10–12; Exod. 25:9).

----

6. For a discussion of the dating of the composition of Exodus and Ezekiel and the implications for dependence either way, see Zimmerli 1979: 46–52; Lust 1996: 209–224; Patton 1996: 73–90. Cf. Hattori 1974: 413–424.

7. Strom argues that Revelation is patterned in the same way.

Finally, and more importantly for our purposes, Ezekiel consistently confronts Israel with the reality of God's jealousy. As Block points out:

> Ezekiel's performances arise out of perceived divine jealousy . . . [a jealousy that] expresses the underlying motif of his ministry, and one's interpretation of the word [*qin'â*] determines one's perception of the God whom it describes. (1997: 13)

In chapter 8, Ezekiel is ushered by one like a Son of Man to see for himself what Israel has done to provoke God's jealousy and bring upon herself the catastrophe that has befallen her. There at the entrance to God's sanctuary is the 'Image of jealousy which provokes jealousy', probably a statue of the Canaanite goddess Asherah, one of the foreign gods Israel was warned to destroy in Exodus 23:24. As Ezekiel burrows through a hole in the wall he sees the appalling sight of the elders of Israel in a dark room with images of creeping things, animals and Israel's idols. There are seventy elders, the same number as selected in Exodus 24 to ascend the mountain.

This is why Yahweh's glory will depart from the temple, and this is the reason Israel will face the fierce anger of God's judgment. She has not followed God's laws and so his jealousy has been activated:

> Thus says the Lord GOD:
>   This is Jerusalem; I have set her in the centre of the nations, with countries all around her. But she has rebelled against my ordinances and my statutes, becoming more wicked than the nations and the countries all around her, rejecting my ordinances and not following my statutes . . . My anger shall spend itself, and I will vent my fury on them and satisfy myself; and they shall know that I, the LORD, have spoken in my jealousy, when I spend my fury on them.
> (Ezek. 5:5–6, 13)

The full implications of God as the jealous, spurned lover are developed by Ezekiel in the most confronting images in chapters

16 and 23. It is not only feminist interpreters who find these images disturbing and semi-pornographic.[8]

> Thus says the Lord GOD, Because your lust was poured out and your nakedness uncovered in your whoring with your lovers, and because of all your abominable idols, and because of the blood of your children that you gave to them, therefore, I will gather all your lovers, with whom you took pleasure, all those you loved and all those you hated; I will gather them against you from all around, and will uncover your nakedness to them, so that they may see all your nakedness. I will judge you as women who commit adultery and shed blood are judged, and bring blood upon you in wrath and jealousy . . . So I will satisfy my fury on you, and my jealousy shall turn away from you; I will be calm, and will be angry no longer. (Ezek. 16:36–42)

The nations surrounding Israel should not take any comfort from Israel's predicament. Yahweh's jealousy for his relationship with Israel has real and terrifying implications for them too. In chapter 36, Edom is singled out for her exploitation of Israel's plight:

> thus says the Lord GOD: therefore I am speaking in my hot jealousy against the rest of the nations, and against all Edom, who, with wholehearted joy and utter contempt, took my land as their possession, because of its pasture, to plunder it. Therefore prophesy concerning the land of Israel, and say to the mountains and hills, to the watercourses and valleys, Thus says the Lord GOD: I am speaking in my jealous wrath, because you have suffered the insults of the nations; therefore thus says the Lord GOD: I swear that the nations that are all around you shall themselves suffer insults. (Ezek. 36:5–7)

---

8. Block says, 'the semipornographic style is a deliberate rhetorical device designed to produce a strong emotional response. For the translator whose aim is equivalent impact, the line between appropriate shock and offensive lack of taste is extremely fine' (1997: 467). Cf. van Dijk-Hemmes 1993: 167–176; Brenner 1996: 63–86.

It is precisely because Yahweh's name is Jealous that anger is not Yahweh's final verdict on Israel despite her stiff-necked sin. Just as in Exodus 34, in her darkest, most undeserving moment, there is hope in the character of the God who has bound himself to her. His passionate commitment to Israel means that he will not stand by while they degenerate back into the chaos of unbeing, because

> the jealousy of Yahweh can also provide a ground for Yahweh's
> passionate commitment to Israel. Thus Yahweh can be jealous 'for Israel'
> and therefore can be driven by strong feeling to intervene on behalf of
> Israel with the same passion and rage elsewhere turned against Israel.
> (Brueggemann 1997: 294)

So Ezekiel can prophesy hope for a future with Yahweh, protected and secure; a future premised alone on the jealousy of God:

> Therefore thus says the Lord GOD: Now I will restore the fortunes of
> Jacob, and have mercy on the whole house of Israel; and I will be jealous
> for my holy name. They shall forget their shame, and all the treachery
> they have practiced against me, when they live securely in their land with
> no one to make them afraid, when I have brought them back from the
> peoples and gathered them from their enemies' lands, and through them
> have displayed my holiness in the sight of many nations. (Ezek.
> 39:25–27)

Ultimately, God does not act for Israel's sake, and this, ironically, is what secures her future in the face of her continued addiction to sin. As if the pleas of Moses in Exodus 32 still ring in his ears, Yahweh recalls those days:

> And I said to them, Cast away the detestable things your eyes feast on,
> every one of you, and do not defile yourselves with the idols of Egypt;
> I am the LORD your God. But they rebelled against me and would not
> listen to me; not one of them cast away the detestable things their eyes
> feasted on, nor did they forsake the idols of Egypt. Then I thought I
> would pour out my wrath upon them and spend my anger against them
> in the midst of the land of Egypt. But I acted for the sake of my name,

that it should not be profaned in the sight of the nations among whom
they lived, in whose sight I made myself known to them in bringing
them out of the land of Egypt. So I led them out of the land of Egypt
and brought them into the wilderness. I gave them my statutes and
showed them my ordinances, by whose observance everyone shall live.
Moreover I gave them my sabbaths, as a sign between me and them, so
that they might know that I the LORD sanctify them. But the house of
Israel rebelled against me in the wilderness; they did not observe my
statutes but rejected my ordinances, by whose observance everyone shall
live; and my sabbaths they greatly profaned. Then I thought I would
pour out my wrath upon them in the wilderness, to make an end of
them. But I acted for the sake of my name, so that it should not be
profaned in the sight of the nations, in whose sight I had brought them
out. (Ezek. 20:7–14)

Brueggemann's comment on these and related texts conveys the
weight of the prophets' testimony to the character of God
revealed in Exodus 34:

The collage of texts concerning the glory, holiness, and jealousy of
Yahweh leave one astonished at the largeness and roughness of the claim
made for Yahweh, and the power and intensity with which that claim is
made. This is a God who will be taken seriously, who will be honoured
and obeyed, and who will not be mocked. (1997: 295)

Brueggemann does not only have Ezekiel's prophecies in mind,
but the comment could serve as an ideal summary of his preaching. At the same time, the paragraph could equally summarize the
message of Exodus from Yahweh's call of Moses to his showdown with Pharaoh, culminating in his overthrow of the horses
and riders of Egypt, to the uncompromising demands of the law,
to the renewal of the covenant, through to the portable place of
worship and the cloud that accompanied Israel. Ezekiel preached
Exodus. Ezekiel confronted his hearers with Yahweh, the God
whose name is Jealous.

Preaching and the jealousy of God

This chapter began with a confessed reluctance to offer advice
about how to preach from Exodus. You may have noticed how
assiduously this chapter has avoided doing anything like that. So it
is time to get into the taxi and head for the suburbs. The fundamental task of the Christian preacher of Exodus is to name God
truly. To do this, the Christian preacher needs to identify the
jealous God, whose name is Jealous, with the Lord Jesus.

> The move from covenant fidelity to costly pathos is a primary
> articulation of Yahweh in the Old Testament. The emergence of
> pathos is not everything to be said here about Yahweh, but it is a
> major and quite intentional affirmation . . . It is possible, in the horizon
> of Christian interpretation in the New Testament, to say that around
> the person of Jesus, Christian witness discerned that the pathos of
> Yahweh moved the next step to incarnation; that, is, God came to be
> personally and fully engaged in the centre of the life of the world . . .
> The move toward incarnation . . . is in some inchoate way already
> present in Yahweh's radical decision for covenantal solidarity with
> Israel and more radical decision toward pathos with Israel.
> (Brueggemann 1997: 302)

With respect to the jealousy of God, this is made clear from the
outset of John's Gospel. John 2 recounts Jesus' arrival at the
temple during the Passover. There he finds that the sanctuary
designed for reconciliation, fellowship, prayer and the blessing of
the nations has become a house of commerce. It is hard to imagine
him making the whip of cords, overturning tables, and driving the
traders and their animals out, without burning with righteous
anger. The disciples who witnessed this outburst saw a man consumed with jealousy for his Father's house (John 2:17; Ps. 69:9). As
you read on in the Gospels, again and again you are confronted by
Jesus:

> The LORD, the LORD,
> a God merciful and gracious,
> slow to anger,

and abounding in steadfast love and faithfulness,
keeping steadfast love . . .
forgiving iniquity and transgression and sin,
yet by no means clearing the guilty . . .
(Exod. 34:6–7)

Only one husband

One Christian preacher who knew the jealousy of God was the
apostle Paul, as is evident from 2 Corinthians 11:2–4:

> I feel a divine jealousy for you, for I promised you in marriage to one
> husband, to present you as a chaste virgin to Christ. But I am afraid that
> as the serpent deceived Eve by its cunning, your thoughts will be led
> astray from a sincere and pure devotion to Christ. For if someone comes
> and proclaims another Jesus than the one we proclaimed, or if you
> receive a different spirit from the one you received, or a different gospel
> from the one you accepted, you submit to it readily enough.

Paul does not necessarily have Exodus in mind as he writes this,
but he knows Jesus as the God of Exodus. In preaching the gospel
to the Corinthians in the first place, Paul conceives his role as a
matchmaker bringing two parties together in an exclusive relationship of commitment to each other. As the Corinthians embraced
his gospel, they pledged themselves to be married to Christ and
Christ alone. They never were or would be Paul's people: only
Christ's, and Paul was very clear about that as he pastored them. It
was Christ alone who had come for them, Christ alone who
wanted them enough to take on flesh, Christ alone who bound
himself to them, Christ alone who wore that grotesque wedding
band of thorns upon his head. It was Christ alone who redeemed
them from their slavery to the taskmasters that oppressed them
brutally – sin and Satan, masters willing to exploit them till they
dropped dead. It was Christ alone who wanted them enough to die
for them. It was Christ alone who in his tender-hearted compassion and lovingkindness secured their relationship with him from
the ravages of time, sin and death.

And Paul understood that the Corinthians were to be his pure
virgin. It was Christ alone who

> gave himself up for her, in order to make her holy by cleansing her with
> the washing of water by the word, so as to present the church to himself
> in splendour, without a spot or wrinkle or anything of the kind – yes, so
> that she may be holy and without blemish. (Eph. 5:25–27)

Paul knew this and knew that the Corinthians must know it. Jesus
deserves their exclusive loyalty and faithfulness. Jesus will not
suffer any rivals. Jesus will have their undivided attention. Jesus
wants them, body, soul and spirit. He wants their lives to be organ-
ized to reflect his holiness and purity: at home, at work, at church,
while they lie thinking to themselves as they go to sleep, when they
come out and when they come in. In Paul's contemporary context,
the threat came from false teaching, perversions of the gospel he
had betrothed them with, gospels that distort the law, that promise
prosperity, that urge asceticism, that settle for less than searching
obedience. Still today, the relationship between Christ and his
people is threatened by other gospels, gospels that allow less than
exclusive commitment to Christ.

Feeling divine jealousy

In pastoring and preaching to his contemporary audience, Paul felt
God's jealousy burn within him. Like Phinehas he knew what it
was like to run the sword of the Spirit through rebellious hearts.
Paul ached for people to remain faithful and true. He was anxious
when people were distracted or started to wander. He grieved over
their materialism, their self-centredness, their factionalism, their
sexual impurity, their willingness to dishonour the name of God
before the nations. Thus, says the apostle of Christ, 'besides other
things, I am under daily pressure because of my anxiety for all the
churches. Who is weak, and I am not weak? Who is made to
stumble, and I am not indignant?' (2 Cor. 11:28–29).

What sustained Paul in the midst of such pressure, anxiety and
indignation was that in the jealousy of God and Christ lay the

hope of all those who are weak, who stumble and struggle with their addiction to sin.

Perhaps, when all is said and done, this is the key to 'preaching Exodus' – to feel the very jealousy of God as we proclaim his name. Perhaps we should not dare to stand before others and bring them this word of the Lord until we ache and worry and grieve with the very jealousy of God. This is the pain and anxiety and grief that consumed Moses, Ezekiel, Jesus and Paul.

Exodus testifies to how much God wants Israel. As John Calvin writes:

> The Lord, who has wedded us to himself in truth, manifests the most burning jealousy wherever we, neglecting the purity of his holy marriage, become polluted with wicked lusts. But he especially feels this when we transfer to another . . . the worship of his divine majesty, which deserves to be utterly uncorrupted. In this way we not only violate the pledge given in marriage, but also defile the very marriage bed by bringing adulterers into it. (Cited in Ryken 2005: 1055)

Yahweh wanted Israel and would not settle for anything less.

Today, this very day, the Lord wants you and will not settle for anything less: 'God wants all our worship and all our praise. He wants us to give glory to him, and to him alone. Therefore all our idols must be broken; all our sacred stones must be smashed; all our goddess poles must be cut down' (Ryken 2005: 1057). This, it seems to me, is what it means to 'preach Exodus' to a contemporary congregation.

Bibliography

Allen, R. J., and J. C. Holbert (1995), *Holy Root, Holy Branches: Christian Preaching from the Old Testament*, Nashville: Abingdon.

Block, D. I. (1997), *The Book of Ezekiel: Chapters 1–24*, Grand Rapids: Eerdmans.

Brenner, A. (1996), 'Pornoprophetics Revisited: Some Additional Reflections', *Journal for the Study of the Old Testament* 70, 63–86.

Brueggemann, W. (1997), *Theology of the Old Testament: Testimony, Dispute, Advocacy*, Minneapolis: Fortress.

Calvin, J. (1950), *Commentaries on the Four Last Books of Moses Arranged in the Form of a Harmony*, Grand Rapids: Eerdmans, 1950.

Clowney, E. P. (2003), *Preaching Christ in All of Scripture*, Wheaton: Crossway.

Dever, M. (2006), *The Message of the Old Testament: Promises Made*, Wheaton: Crossway.

Dijk-Hemmes, F. van (1993), 'The Metaphorization of Women in Prophetic Speech: An Analysis of Ezekiel 23', in A. Brenner and F. van Dijk-Hemmes (eds.), *On Gendering Texts: Female and Male Voices in the Hebrew Bible*, Leiden: Brill, 167–176.

Dumbrell, W. J. (2002), *The Faith of Israel: A Theological Survey of the Old Testament*, 2nd ed., Grand Rapids: Baker Academic.

Fretheim, T. E. (1989), 'Suffering God and Sovereign God in Exodus: A Collision of Images', *Horizons in Biblical Theology* 11: 31–56.

— (1991), *Exodus*, Interpretation, Louisville: John Knox.

Goldsworthy, G. (2000), *Preaching the Whole Bible as Christian Scripture*, Leicester: IVP.

Gowan, D. E. (1994), *Theology in Exodus: Biblical Theology in the Form of a Commentary*, Louisville: Westminster John Knox.

— (1995), 'Changing God's Mind', in Holmgren and Schaalman, *Preaching Biblical Texts*, 90–104.

Greidanus, S. (1999), *Preaching Christ from the Old Testament: A Contemporary Hermeneutical Method*, Grand Rapids: Eerdmans.

Hart, I. (1982), 'Preaching on the Account of the Tabernacle', *Evangelical Quarterly* 54: 111–116.

Hattori, Y. (1974), 'Divine Dilemma in Ezekiel's View of the Exodus: An Exegetical Study of Ezekiel 20:5–29', in J. H. Skilton (ed.), *The Law and the Prophets: Old Testament Studies Prepared in Honor of Oswald Thompson Allis*, Nutley: Presbyterian & Reformed, 413–424.

Holmgren, F. C. and H. E. Schaalman (eds.) (1995), *Preaching Biblical Texts: Expositions by Jewish and Christian Scholars*, Grand Rapids: Eerdmans.

Lust, J. (1996), 'Exodus 6,2–8 and Ezekiel', in M. Vervenne (ed.), *Studies in the Book of Exodus: Redaction-Reception-Interpretation*, Leuven: Leuven University Press, 209–224.

Mathewson, S. D. (2002), *The Art of Preaching Old Testament Narrative*, Grand Rapids: Baker Academic.

Newsom, C. A. (1987), 'Retelling the Story of the Exodus: Homiletical Resources for the Season after Pentecost', *Quarterly Review* 7.2: 71–100.

Patton, C. (1996), '"I Myself Gave them Laws that were not Good": Ezekiel

20 and the Exodus Traditions', *Journal for the Study of the Old Testament* 69, 73–90.

Poythress, V. (1991), *The Shadow of Christ in the Law*, Brentwood: Wolgemuth & Hyatt.

Ryken, P. G. (2005), *Exodus: Saved for God's Glory*, Preaching the Word, Wheaton: Crossway.

Strom, M. (1989), *Days Are Coming: Exploring Biblical Patterns*, Sydney: Hodder & Stoughton.

Teugels, L. (1996), 'Did Moses See the Chariot? The Link Between Exod 19–20 and Ezek 1 in Early Jewish Interpretation', in Vervenne, *Studies in the Book of Exodus*, 595–602.

Zimmerli, W. (1979), *Ezekiel 1*, Hermeneia, Philadelphia: Fortress.

INDEX OF AUTHORS

INDEX OF SCRIPTURE REFERENCES

**INTERTESTA-
MENTAL
LITERATURE**